THE CONTEMPORARY
BRITISH HISTORY PLAY

Recent Titles in
Contributions in Drama and Theatre Studies

Assessing the Achievement of J. M. Synge
Alexander G. Gonzalez, editor

Maria Irene Fornes and Her Critics
Assunta Bartolomucci Kent

Jekyll and Hyde Adapted: Dramatizations of Cultural Anxiety
Brian A. Rose

The Dramatic Art of David Storey: The Journey of a Playwright
Herbert Liebman

American Labor on Stage: Dramatic Interpretations of the Steel and Textile
Industries in the 1930s
Susan Duffy

David Hare: Moral and Historical Perspectives
Finlay Donesky

Comedy in the Weimar Republic: A Chronicle of Incongruous Laughter
William Grange

Sam Shepard and the American Theatre
Leslie A. Wade

Harold Pinter and the New British Theatre
D. Keith Peacock

Ibsen and Early Modernist Theatre, 1890–1900
Kirsten Shepherd-Barr

The Theatre Team: Playwright, Producer, Director, Designers, and Actors
Jeane Luere and Sidney Berger, editors

Homosexualities in the English Theatre
John Franceschina

THE
CONTEMPORARY BRITISH HISTORY PLAY

RICHARD H. PALMER

Contributions in Drama and Theatre Studies, Number 81

Greenwood Press
Westport, Connecticut • London

PR
739
.H5
P35
1998

Library of Congress Cataloging-in-Publication Data

Palmer, Richard H.
    The contemporary British history play / Richard H. Palmer.
       p. cm.—(Contributions in drama and theatre studies, ISSN
0163–3821 ; no. 81)
    Includes bibliographical references (p.   ) and index.
    ISBN 0–313–30497–1 (alk. paper)
    1. Historical drama, English—History and criticism. 2. English
drama—20th century—History and criticism. 3. Literature and
history—Great Britain—History—20th century. I. Title.
II. Series.
    PR739.H5P35 1998
    822′.0514049091—dc21   97–38985

British Library Cataloguing in Publication Data is available.

Copyright © 1998 by Richard H. Palmer

Library of Congress Catalog Card Number: 97–38985
ISBN: 0–313–30497–1
ISSN: 0163–3821

First published in 1998

Greenwood Press, 88 Post Road West, Westport, CT 06881
An imprint of Greenwood Publishing Group, Inc.

Printed in the United States of America

The paper used in this book complies with the
Permanent Paper Standard issued by the National
Information Standards Organization (Z39.48–1984).

10 9 8 7 6 5 4 3 2 1

37837521

Who will write the history of the rewriters of history?
Howard Brenton, *H.I.D. (Hess is Dead)*

Contents

Acknowledgments

The College of William and Mary granted a research leave that enabled me to do the initial investigation for this study. I am also indebted to William and Mary's Swem Library, particularly to the persistence of the Interlibrary Loan staff and of Stephen Clark. The Victoria and Albert Museum's Theatre Collection housed at the Theatre Museum near Covent Garden provided its valuable archive of clippings and programs. My colleague Susan Chast attempted to keep me on course in the chapter on feminist history, and Louis E. Catron, as always, furnished a steady source of encouragement. My wife, Rebecca, in addition to proofreading services, supplied her usual forbearance in the face of the fact that we are slaves to different keyboards, she to the piano and I to the computer. I am particularly grateful to the British theatre for providing, during our thirty-five years of regular visits, a consistent array of stimulating and often provocative productions, almost always well-done, and at a price, particularly during the early years, that made it possible to see nine plays a week and still eat!

1

Introduction

> graves at my command,
> Have wak'd their sleepers; op', and let them forth
> By my so potent art.
>
> *The Tempest*, V, i, 48–50

Prospero, by tradition a mouthpiece for Shakespeare's reflections on his own art, voices a very modern realization that the past serves present demands. Just as Shakespeare was indebted to his historical sources, Plutarch, Halle, and Holinshed, so his attitude about history reflected theirs. In one of the dedications to Holinshed's *Chronicles*, John Hooker stated very clearly the widely held Elizabethan belief that the value of history rested in its contemporary application: "No realme, no nation, no state, nor commonwealth throughout all Europe, can yeeld more nor so manie profitable lawes, directions, rules, examples and discourses, either in matters of religion, or of civill government, or of martiall affairs, than doo the histories of this little Isle of Britaine or England."[1]

Putting aside theatre's intrinsic urge to seduce its spectators with the illusion of truth, history on stage has remained committed to the idea of the past as parable, even after nineteenth-century historians conceived of history as objective fact with no necessary message, and the theatre bent itself to the positivists' call for realism. In the later decades of the twentieth century, historical drama changed again in response to new attitudes about history. Many historians now question both the ability and the need of history to maintain objectivity, and history has been pressed into the service of a variety of political and intellectual agendas. A more controvertible approach to history itself once again conforms to the traditional polemics of historical drama. History, however, has not merely regressed to its prepositivist forms. The viewpoints of the New Historians are far more varied, and modern history plays have adapted similarly varied strategies for reflecting multiple ideas about history.

The British theatre, where historical drama maintains its popularity, provides a particularly good place to examine the relationship between history plays and changing concepts of history. Although television, film, and novels satisfy much of the public's taste for fictionalized history in the United Kingdom, staged forms continue to thrive. Three or four new scripts, based on historical material and written by established playwrights, appear most seasons, and revivals of history plays, both British and foreign, remain a regular component of the seasons of nonprofit theatres. A London theatregoer almost always has a choice of history plays, which constitute 10 to 15 percent of the offerings in a typical season. Most major playwrights have written at least one history play, and many, including John Arden, Peter Barnes, Edward Bond, Robert Bolt, Howard Brenton, Caryl Churchill, Pam Gems, John Osborn, Terence Rattigan, and Peter Shaffer, have written more than one.

In contrast, history plays by Americans appear much less frequently in professional theatre, being relegated largely to television, film, or outdoor summer theatres. Outdoor historical drama in the United States has few counterparts in England, but Britain has its share of community pageants, a form that originated in England in the early twentieth century and inspired American pageantry that developed into the outdoor theatre movement.[2] History plays professionally produced in America frequently originate in England, and American history is dramatized in the United States less than British history on the English stage.[3] Even popular historical plays by American playwrights like William Goldman's *Lion in Winter* (1966), Bernard Pomerance's *The Elephant Man* (1977), and Ted Tally's *Terra Nova* (1977) are based on English history and emulate the style of English historical drama. History plays by American playwrights, including *The Elephant Man* and Richard Nelson's *Columbus and the Discovery of Japan* (1992), were initially staged in Britain with its more receptive audience for historical drama.

The long lineage of the British history play dates to John Bale's *Kynge Johan* in the first half of the sixteenth century,[4] and includes Shakespeare's great chronicles from *Henry VI* in 1591 to *Henry VIII* in 1613, plays that exerted a large influence on subsequent historical drama. In the seventeenth century historical subjects still appeared on stage, usually as tragedies, but the process of accentuating the personal aspects of historical figures, frequently to develop conflicts between love and honor or duty, began. Historical drama gained new prominence with romantic writers in the nineteenth century, particularly on the Continent, and English poets, including Wordsworth, Coleridge, Southey, Byron, Tennyson, and Browning, all attempted history plays after the German models of Kotzebue and Schiller. In spite of occasional dutiful performances of these plays, the historical romance remained the popular form on the late nineteenth-century English stage, done at its best by Tom Taylor.

Twentieth-century British history plays before the 1950s reflect two prevalent traditions: didacticism and romanticism. The principal influence of the first was George Bernard Shaw, who successfully bent history to serve his social philosophy in plays like *Man of Destiny* and *Caesar and Cleopatra*.[5] Shaw had few direct British imitators, but the French playwrights Jean Anouilh and Jean Giraudoux reflect his influence with history plays popular in Britain. Christopher Fry's translations, beginning with Anouilh's *The Lark* and Giraudoux's *Tiger at the Gates*, both in 1955, were particularly successful. The romantic histories carry on a tradition begun in the nineteenth century and were written according to a few widely accepted formulas, best exemplified by Elizabeth Mackintosh, who wrote under the pen name George Daviot, and by James Forsyth. Historical characters who speak in blank verse or "elevated" prose become entangled in ill-fated love affairs. The plays, with multiple scenes and moderate-sized casts, retained some pageantry, but rather than being epic in scope, they focus on relatively short periods, depicted with a degree of realism, during which the central dramatic conflict arises and resolves itself.

Some writers argue that in the twentieth century, a focus on scientific progress and the rise of modernism produced a waning interest in historical studies. Hayden White placed the beginnings of this denigration of history in the decade preceding World War I, when "hostility towards the historical consciousness and the historian gained wide currency among intellectuals in every country of Western Europe."[6] In *The Death of the Past*, J. H. Plumb argues that a technological society oriented toward change rather than conservation finds "no sanction in the past and no roots in it."[7] David Leon Higdon, in *Shadows of the Past in Contemporary British Fiction*, points out that "the overthrow of tradition and the expulsion of history became key ideas in modernist art," but that discontent with the present and future, that surfaced in the 1950s, reawakened an interest in the past.[8]

Particularly during the last forty years, changing theatre conventions and challenges to traditional approaches to history itself appear to have revitalized the history play. New ideas undermined both theatrical and historical precedent, opening the way for the best British dramatists to explore new approaches to historical drama, a process that we will examine.

The year 1956 marks the beginning of the so-called New Wave of British theatre, a revival launched by the production that year of John Osborne's *Look Back in Anger*. In 1956 Bertolt Brecht's Berliner Ensemble also visited London, performing *The Caucasian Chalk Circle* and *Mother Courage*, plays demonstrating Brecht's distinct approach to historical drama. Where Osborne's play initiated a new wave of social realism, Brecht's plays introduced new theatricalism and a novel way of viewing history.

The abolishment of censorship in 1968 provided a further opportunity to dramatize historical material formerly banned or in a manner previously taboo, a trend studied in D. Keith Peacock's *Radical Stages: Alternative History in Modern British Drama*.[9]

The purpose of this book is to examine how these new attitudes about history and staging innovations have influenced British history plays written since 1956 and to discover how changes in the form and content of the modern British history play relate to changing concepts of history itself.

PLAYWRIGHTS' JUSTIFICATIONS FOR WRITING HISTORY PLAYS

As a principal reason for turning to historical subjects, playwrights stated that setting a play in a historical period distances the material from the demands of modern realism. Robert Bolt in a preface to *A Man for All Seasons* said that a historical setting enables him to treat characters "in a properly heroic, properly theatrical manner," as modern values are basically antiheroic.[10] In an interview in *Plays and Players*, Bolt said, "If people are wearing cloaks and funny hats and don't travel on 29 buses as it were, you don't really know the minutiae of their daily lives, you are helped to escape from this tremendous undertow of representation."[11] Simon Gray observed that a play set in the past "has about it some of the aspects of the sublime."[12]

Other writers saw the history play as an antidote to the narrow domestic scope of much realistic drama. For Edward Bond, a historical perspective gives his work the social context that he demands as a Marxist writer: "The bourgeois theatre set most of its scenes in small domestic rooms, with an occasional picnic or a visit to the law courts. . . . But we need to set our scenes in public places, where history is formed, classes clash and whole societies move. Otherwise we're not writing about the events that most affect us and shape our future."[13] In the preface to *The Woman*, Bond observed that Chekhov's characters "exist between the important events of history, and so they have very little else apart from their emotional life. *We* must be caught up in the events of history. But we must also be in control. We must analyze these events, not merely reproduce them."[14]

David Hare, also from a Marxist perspective, sees history as offering assurances that social change can occur:

if you write about now, just today and nothing else, then you seem to be confronting only a stasis; but if you begin to describe the movement of history, if you write plays that cover passages of time, then you begin to find a sense of movement, of social change, if you like; and the facile hopelessness that comes from confronting the day and only the day, the room and only the room, begins to disappear and in its place the writer can offer a record of movement and change.[15]

Robert Bolt in his preface to *Vivat! Vivat Regina!* stressed the extent to which historical material stimulates audience credence:

The audience brings a special credulity to a history play. They credit the events they see enacted with a degree of actuality not claimed for events—like Shylock's bargain—which are purely theatrical. We are additionally moved when an actor plays out the noble death of an historical character by the knowledge that some such person did make some such death. And the playwright exploits this. Because everybody in the audience knows that Joan of Arc really was executed the playwright can take her death with an authority and an appearance of inevitability which he would otherwise have to work for. He can only honour this double debt to his characters and to his audience by sticking to facts.[16]

Peter Barnes also comments on the sense of probability that historical trappings lend to a play: "Nothing a writer can imagine is as surrealistic as the reality. Everything has happened. The difficulty is finding the record of it. Of course, historical truth is no guarantee of dramatic truth. But it makes for a certain confidence between author and audience; a reassuring feeling of firm ground under the feet."[17]

DEFINITION

The term *history play* is imprecise, and generic boundaries are not easy to establish. The division of the First Folio edition of Shakespeare's plays in 1623 into three categories—comedies, tragedies, and histories—points to the possibility, even at this early date, that histories were considered to be distinct from comedy and tragedy.[18] In the early seventeenth century, this distinction occurred in the context of structural assumptions that tragedies end unhappily, comedies happily, and histories, presumably, end without similar emotional overtones. In later structuralist language, tragedy was dominated by a falling action, comedy by a rising action, and the history play by a structure delineated only by the passage of time. William Dinsmore Briggs, in 1914, defined the chronicle history as a play that treated historical materials "in a way to bring out their accidental (particularly chronological) relations, recognizing as a rule no other principle of connection than that of personality, and having the general character of a survey of a more or less arbitrarily limited period."[19]

Some writers attempt to differentiate between history in drama and historical drama as a genre by describing the latter as a "chronicle." Morton White, in *Foundations of Historical Knowledge*, distinguishes in historical studies, not drama, between the chronicle, a "conjunction of statements," and history, which is "predominantly . . . integrated from a causal point of view."[20] E.M.W. Tillyard observed that the early English chronicle plays tended to "exploit the mere accident of successive events,"[21] but he did not make this a basis for defining the chronicle as a separate genre. Irving Ribner in *The English History Play in the Age of Shakespeare* rejected any meaningful distinction between a chronicle and a history play.[22]

The inclusion of *Richard II* and *Richard III* among the history plays by the editors of Shakespeare's folio edition indicates the difficulty they had distinguishing between tragedy and the history play. In the twentieth century, E.M.W. Tillyard, Alfred B. Harbage, and Lily Bess Campbell differentiated the predominantly political sphere of the history play from the personal perspective of tragedy.[23] Irving Ribner rejected any exclusion of tragedy from the category of history plays, but he placed "biographical" drama in a separate classification because it focuses on private lives rather than the public events that he considered to be the appropriate domain of the history play.[24] Today's New Historians would condemn this political bias as an overly narrow approach to history.

Suzanne Langer proposed that the difference between tragedy and the history play lay in the degree of concentration. Tragedy presents the growth, maturity, and decline of an individual who "spends himself in the course of the one dramatic action."[25] The history play, owing more to the tradition of epic poetry, lacks this degree of focus.

From its beginnings in ancient Greece, Western theatre has portrayed historical events, but this dramatization of the past has not in itself been a sufficient basis for classifying a play as a historical drama. As early as the fourth century B.C. Aristotle was struggling with the theoretical relationship between history and tragedy. He contended that tragedies based on history increase the audience's perception of the probability of the action and consequently heighten its emotional impact, but the dramatic poet is not bound to recount "what has happened," but has an obligation to show matters as "they ought to be."[26]

Aristotle's perception of history as an area of accomplished fact anticipates the positivist view of history as objective truth. This notion of the independent validity of historical data underpins the naive definition of historical drama offered by Niloufer Harben in *Twentieth-Century English History Plays from Shaw to Bond.* For Harben, the litmus test for a history play is that it "evinces a serious concern for historical truth or historical issues. . . . This would exclude plays whose concern with history is sketchy and peripheral, plays which are romantic and sentimental in their approach to history, which reveal an ignorance of or indifference to the facts."[27] Inexplicably, Edward Bond's spoof of history in *Early Morning* meets Harben's test but Peter Shaffer's *Royal Hunt of the Sun* does not.

In an era when historical studies have called into question the "shaker and mover" tradition of focusing on major players in historical events, the question of whether a history play can contain "fictional" characters and events becomes moot. Social history, for example, deals with individuals and groups who were not in the spotlight and who left no records of their particular lives. A playwright who undertakes this subject must invent details to a degree reserved only for minor supporting characters in traditional biographical histories. New ideas about the appropriate subject matter for historical study require a redefinition of the distinction between fact and fiction. David Edgar coined the term *faction* to describe the fictional reconstruction of events based on a factual context.[28]

FACTUALISM

If one takes R. G. Collingwood's definition of history as the reenactment of past events,[29] history emulates theatre. For Herbert Lindenberger the term *historical drama* implies a tension between fact and fiction: "the first word qualifying the fictiveness of the second, the second questioning the reality of the first."[30] Fact and fiction are contrasts that traditional theatre obscures. Most theatre presents itself to varying degrees as "true," "a lie come true." Acting is partly deception, the art of convincing the audience that an actor *is* the character. Even with Brecht's third-person acting style that self-consciously acknowledges the artifice of theatre, the audience still accepts the characterization as somehow true within the context of the story being dramatized. Most drama says, "This could have happened" or "This might have happened," but historical drama usually insinuates further, "This did indeed happen." A play that presumes to reenact a historical event makes an appeal for belief that goes beyond the normal request for a suspension of disbelief. When Ben Jonson cited his sources in the preface to his edition of *Sejanus,* he was asserting external verifiability, not simply dramatic credibility.[31]

Historical data, by itself, is notoriously incomplete in ways that frustrate the curiosity of audience members and fulsome in ways that bore them. The solution for playwrights has been to rearrange, interpolate, and invent, expanding upon what is presumably known as far as the limit of violating accepted fact or losing credibility. John Dryden explained in the eighteenth century, "Where the event of a great action is left doubtful, there the Poet is left Master."[32] The contemporary playwright Ann Jellicoe states, "The playwright must present the facts as s/he sees them in a certain relationship and must imagine what happens in the empty spaces."[33] In practice, playwrights can be free and easy with the "facts" even when events are not doubtful.

Drama requires detail, conciseness, and an arrangement of events that structure the response of the audience. As Jellicoe emphasizes, a history play is "history shaped by art to tell a story, make a point, reveal a truth." She advocates a degree of traditional dramatic structure: "History may be all the facts as we know them; art is a selection and organization of facts so as to present a sequence of images, having a relationship with each other which leads to a climax or resolution."[34]

Jellicoe, in *Community Plays: How to Put Them On*, discusses how to use documentary resources and research committees to develop a history play, but she insists on the unattainabilty of historic accuracy and the importance of recognizing artistic invention: "People may have to be educated that there cannot be total historical accuracy, that it doesn't exist, and if it did exist it would still have to be reshaped to make a play."[35]

The historical accuracy of drama has always been problematic, but the factual basis of history has been little better, as revisionist historians in the latter half of the twentieth century have been quick to note. If Shakespeare distorted truth to flatter the Tudor ruling powers, he only reflected the biases of Edward Hall and Raphael Holinshed, the historians whose work he used as sources. Although historians have come a long way from the amalgam of rumor, legend, and authorized parable that passed for history until the eighteenth century, even the work of positivist historians, who made a fetish of objectivity, contains some inevitable bias. At the very minimum, the selection of what data to recount reflects the subjective judgment of the relative importance of the variety of material available to the historian.

TYPES OF DRAMA USING HISTORY

Plays utilizing historical material fall into the following categories ranged along a continuum from plays with largely fictional characters in a period setting to the purported documentary reenactment of an actual event:

1. Characters and situation are largely fictional, but the style of the play mimics that of a play from an earlier period. The medium is more historical than the content in such plays as Edward Bond's *Restoration* or Timberlake Wertenbaker's *The Grace of Mary Traverse*.

2. Plays based on legendary sources, that may or may not have historical foundation, contain characters known to the audience, who possess some degree of historic validity for the audience. John Arden and Margaretta D'Arcy's dramatization of Merlin and King Arthur, *The Island of the Mighty*, and Edward Bond's *Lear* fall into this group.

3. Even with fictional characters, some plays have their setting, characterization, and action determined by a historical period. Herbert Lindenberger, citing Brecht's *Mother Courage*, calls this "the unhistorical history play."[36] The period trappings add a degree of historic legitimacy but less than the depiction of "actual" persons. The audience has no independent expectations regarding specific characters. A large number of "period plays" fall into this category.

4. Fictional characters react to a background of actual historical events in plays such as Stephen Lowe's *Touched* or Caryl Churchill's *Light Shining in Buckinghamshire*. This recreates historical events known to the audience without focusing on major historical personalities. Playwrights who depict "bottom up" history often use this approach.

5. Plays that depict specific historical characters and situations, but in a recognizably exaggerated fashion, include travesties of history such as Arden and D'Arcy's *The Hero Rises Up* or Bond's *Early Morning*.

6. In many plays historical figures interact with fictional characters, sometimes in real, sometimes in imaginary circumstances. Historical romances fall largely into this group.

7. Recognizable figures from the past appear principally in private and therefore largely imaginative circumstances. This category includes most biographical drama.

8. A play may depict, as accurately as possible, the behavior of historical figures in reported events. The extreme form of this is the historical "documentary play" or "docudrama." Film and television have largely preempted realistic documentaries, but a more presentational version has developed in the theatre; it includes plays such as the documentaries produced by Peter Cheeseman at Stoke-on-Trent.

The narrowest definitions confine the history play to only the final categories, but a less restrictive approach reveals more about the varied strategies for using history in drama. This wider purview will be used in this study. Rather than confining ourselves to an ill-defined genre, we will examine the dramatic uses of history in whatever guise.

A tendency to equate history plays with so-called costume drama exists. Incidents remote in time call up different audience expectations than current events, but no specific length of time must pass to qualify an event as historical. Michael Hasting's *Lee Harvey Oswald* was staged in 1966, three years after the depicted events occurred. In the nineteenth century, before radio, film, and television coverage, important military or public events were reenacted on the stage within days of their occurrence and would have been properly considered history plays.

MODERNITY

Past and present are also imprecise distinctions in the theatre. Most theatre that is not improvisational presents itself as accomplished fact, an event, the end of which has already been determined even as the audience watches the beginning. But, contradictorily, time in the theatre is usually present time. Even past events are replayed as if they are occurring in the presence of the audience. As Friedrich Schiller observed, "All dramatic forms turn the past into the present."[37]

The misperception exists that seeing history from the perspective of the present is a uniquely modern practice. Niloufer Harben declares, "A pronounced feature of the twentieth-century English history play is the overt treatment of the past in terms of the present." He mistakenly asserts that this approach originates with George Bernard Shaw.[38] Ruby Cohn echoes this error with the statement that "the systematic exploitation of history for modern instruction awaited the twentieth century."[39] Both ignore a long tradition of interpreting the past in terms of the present. Medieval historians searched the past for clues to the future,[40] and the Elizabethans justified the study of history by its relevance to their present needs.[41]

This present-minded reading of the past was labeled "Whig History" in 1931 by Herbert Butterfield, who argued that the true job of the historian is to discover the past's unlikeness to the present.[42] The strategy of contemporary historians is more to acknowledge the inescapable stamp of the present on the past.

THE VIEW OF HISTORY IN HISTORICAL DRAMA

Assumptions regarding history prevalent at the time that it is written have always shaped historical drama. The Elizabethan history plays consistently organized events to emphasize political, social, or religious lessons, assuming that past events paralleled and could serve as a guide to present behavior. However, we can already see in Shakespeare's histories an awareness of the extent to which private behavior influences public events. In England in the late seventeenth century, heroic treatment dominated dramatized history and focus shifted from political maneuvering to personal love/honor conflicts. This romantic trend continued in the early eighteenth century as Nicholas Rowe, with plays like *The Tragedy of Jane Shore* and *Lady Jane Grey*, popularized a version of the history play in which the love intrigues of characters caught in the grip of passion shape politics.[43] This change reflected the Renaissance return to the humanistic history of the ancients but with the important difference that humans were seen in the Christian tradition as creatures of passion and impulse rather than of intellect. While abandoning the medieval idea that history repeats itself, neoclassical historians held that in the midst of incidental change, human nature remains eternally immutable. As R. G. Collingwood observed, in the Renaissance, "History thus became the history of human passions, regarded as necessary manifestations of human nature."[44] This idea of unchanging human nature persists into some post–World War II drama as we can see in Christopher Fry's explanation for the repeated use of historical material in his plays: "There's something to be gained by being somewhat at one remove from to-day—you get a chance to look at what you might call the permanent condition of man—and I can never really see more than minor distinctions between the past and the present, differences in kind rather than being."[45] Fry speaks for an older uniformitarian view of history that was much in dispute by the time he wrote this in 1961.

Changes in nineteenth-century notions of history had little influence at the time on the British theatre, frozen by its dependence on a mass audience that was not immediately sensitive to intellectual changes, but in France and Germany, Shakespeare's plays became rallying points for romanticism. The romantic view of history, like the medieval, was that historical events were manifestations of a higher power. History progressed through conflict to a level closer to this transcendent ideal. Strife such as that between royal prerogative and individual freedom or between society and nature were thus seen as means for furthering a dialectic process. The study of the past revealed not so much parallels to the present as the present nascent.

The antiquarianism stimulated by romanticism did spark an interest in greater accuracy in period staging in England, a fashion further encouraged in the late nineteenth century by the rise of positivism, a philosophical system that rejected the spiritual concerns of romanticism and focused on observable experience and measurable phenomena. Among historians this led to greater emphasis on data gathering and the verifiability of information. In the theatre the ultimate expression of positivism was naturalism, but this had little effect on the history play because of the difficulty and prohibitive cost of extreme historical realism. Historical naturalism had a greater impact on film, which was better able technically to replicate historical details in setting.[46] Accurate period costumes were more affordable and consistent with the attempt to focus on realistic characterization, and were consequently a more frequent feature of nineteenth- and twentieth-century historical drama, but in general, the history play remained a refuge from naturalism.

One manifestation of positivism that did influence historical drama was the documentary drama, the incorporation of verbatim historical documents into a production. Pioneered in the 1930s by the American Federal Theatre Project–sponsored Living Newspapers, this technique was incorporated into a variety of British historical drama, often plays with a political agenda at odds with the objectivity presumably implied by the use of documentary material.

Twentieth-century history plays continue to mirror vogues in historical method, but no one methodology dominates; so we encounter approaches to historical drama as numerous as approaches to history itself. The proliferation of historiographical studies reflects this fragmentation of methodology. Historians before the twentieth century, without an environment of conflicting methodologies, were not notably self-reflective, but particularly since World War II, studies of the philosophy of history and historiography have proliferated, a response to the variety of historical approaches and an acknowledgment that the hand of the historian marks the past.

Two major twentieth-century challenges to traditional history precipitated a number of other distinct reactions. The Marxist historians, beginning in the Soviet Union before World War II and in Britain after the war, provided the first new approach to history, shaped foremost by a clearly articulated political philosophy. The second major effort to revise the methods of historic inquiry occurred after World War II, when a group of French historians known as the *Annalistes* shifted their attention away from traditional focus on war and politics in order to deal with economic, social, cultural, or demographic processes. These recent trends in historiography are often lumped under the term *New History*, to differentiate them from traditional, or by implication, "Old" History.

OLD HISTORY

At least as defined by the New Historians, Old History consists principally of a narrative, chronologically organized and presented as objective fact, of political and military events, whose importance is determined by the dominant hegemony, and of the men who shape these events, all seen from a Eurocentric viewpoint. This approach raises objections on every level. The New Historians reject the possibility of objectivity, distrust the effectiveness of narrative as a device for analyzing history, stress the relative unimportance of chronology in understanding history, discredit the significance of political and military activities to the majority of people, question the power of individuals to shape events, repudiate the emphasis given in past histories to largely masculine activities, and repudiate the bias of an exclusively European viewpoint.

Biographical History

Traditional history tended to organize itself around events—wars, reigns, nation building activities, and political movements—but embedded within was the assumption, intensified by the nineteenth-century romantic interest in the individual, that personality shapes historic events. Most Old History therefore emphasizes the role of political or military leaders, often expressed as biographical history. Even when historians looked at groups of people, they approached the problem by concentrating on an outstanding representative of the group. When historians first began to write cultural history in the late nineteenth century, they assumed that prominent artists were the principal shapers of taste and forces for aesthetic change. History, particularly in the theatre—with its circumscribed time frame, staging limitations, and emphasis on the actor—still appears most frequently in the guise of biography.

THE NEW HISTORY

Earlier historians guarded against distortion in their work by rejecting claims for contemporary social relevance, an effort seen by the New Historians as essentially a conservative rejection of anything that calls into question dominant mythologies or current institutions. The New Historians say that because total objectivity remains unattainable, history may as well be written from a clearly stated position, political or otherwise. Carried to an extreme, this acceptance of the inescapability of the historian's perspective becomes *engagé* history, advocacy rather than analysis. A variety of often conflicting polemic histories on any subject can result.

The terms that follow describe specific approaches taken by New Historians, but many of the categories overlap, for example, in a Marxist and a feminist sociohistory such as Juliet Mitchell's *Woman's Estate*. Some methodologies lend themselves less readily to dramatization than others. Quantification, for instance, was important both to traditional positivist historians and to more recent econometric and Cliometric historians. Econometric history operates on the assumption that measurable economic factors control individual behavior. Cliometrics assumes that human behavior is best understood as a system of relationships in which variables can be quantified so that when the value of any one changes, the effect on the system as a whole can be calculated. Other than providing supporting statistics for docudrama, this kind of numerical analysis seems ill suited for dramatization.

Psychohistory

Psychohistory retains the traditional emphasis on prime movers but shifts the focus to psychiatric rather than political or social causes. The histories are usually committed to a specific school of psychoanalysis. Psychobiography concerns itself with an individual, psychohistory with collective entities: groups, classes, societies. Biographical history operates on the assumption that individuals shape events, but it differs from psychohistory, which searches for underlying motives and intentions. For instance Erik Erikson's *Young Man Luther*, which exerted a strong influence on John Osborne's *Luther*,[47] approaches the Reformation largely in terms of Luther's anal compulsiveness. Herbert Lindenberger sees this psychological inquisitiveness as a continuation of "the domination of private (as against public) experience within all forms of literature during the last two centuries."[48]

Oppositional History

New History was fundamentally revisionist, rejecting the prevailing historiography of the establishment, often by directly contradicting the values of official histories. One strategy for accomplishing this was to develop the point of view of any group or individual outside that establishment, thus "oppositional history" or "alternative history." Included here are colonial histories and so-called losers' histories that study defeated people, prisoners, criminals, outcasts, or individuals of ethnic or religious minorities. British history plays deal less with racial minorities than American dramas.

Marxist History

Marxist history was the earliest and has been the most sustained alternative to traditional history. While subscribing to various theories of history, the Marxists share a focus on class struggle, an economic bias, and a presumption of progress in their analysis of events. Early Marxist history espoused historical determinism, offering, as Keith Peacock observes, "little scope either for the portrayal of the influence of individuals upon the historical process or for dramatic tension and character development."[49] Later Marxists emphasized that choices made by individuals or groups advance or retard the historical process, an assumption shared by Brecht. Although Marxist histories often focus on the working classes, the Marxist historians Elizabeth and Eugene Fox-Genovese have objected to social historians who dwell on the daily lives of people instead of class struggle, who romanticize ordinary life, denying the theory of immiseration that provides the Marxist impulse for revolution.[50]

Several major writers of historical drama have been avowed Marxists, such as Edward Bond and Howard Brenton, and others have written under the influence of Marxist histories. Caryl Churchill's *Light Shining in Buckinghamshire*, for instance, seems strongly influenced by Christopher Hill's *The World Turned Upside Down: Radical Ideas During the English Revolution*.[51]

Social History

Social History focuses on the minutiae of everyday life, using quantifiable measures of external behavior such as riots, voting patterns, and census comparisons.[52] Where traditional historians study what they define as *important* people, events, and movements—"history from above," or "elitist history"—the New Historians concentrate more on "history from below" or "populist history." In historical studies as well as history plays, this results in what the traditionalist might describe as "out of focus history," with political or martial events in the background and "fringe" players in the foreground. This more democratic approach incorporates *mentalité history*, a term coined by the *Annalistes* to describe the study of popular beliefs, customs, modes of behavior, and attitudes, modeled on humanistic anthropology.

Local History

Local history was written in the nineteenth century, but among the New Historians, an emphasis on the distinctiveness of a locality repudiates the stress on nationalism in most traditional histories. Natalie Davis's *The Return of Martin Guerre*, which was made into a 1982 film and a 1996 musical by Claude-Michel Schönberg and Alain Boubil, ignores the developments of the court of François I and depicts the social attitudes of peasants in sixteenth-century France by reconstructing the life in a single French village. Local histories tend to be sociohistories. Dramatization of local history in England goes back to the community pageants early in the twentieth century, but community themes resurged in the 1970s as plays such as David Edgar's *Entertaining Strangers* or Keith Dewhurst's *Lark Rise* and *Candleford* reached the stage of the National Theatre.

Feminist History

Feminist history concentrates on women who were shakers and movers, largely neglected by earlier historians; on the impact of historical events on women; and on women's involvement in domestic activities that were of little concern to traditional historians. This fits into a broader development of oppositional history.

Deconstructionist History

Deconstructionist history attacks the narrative matrix that relates a chronological sequence of connected events that tell a story over a significant period. For example, Theodore Zeldin advocates using *pointillisme*, "breaking down the phenomena of history into the smallest, most elementary units—the individual actors in history—and then connecting those units by means of 'juxtapositions' rather than causes. The reader would then be free to make 'what links he thinks fit for himself,' "[53] a methodology that accurately describes Caryl Churchill's *Top Girls*. According to Phillippe Carrard, the *Annalistes'* argument against narrative was a political gesture intended to highlight the rejection of traditional historiography, but as they became more established the New Historians began to revert to many older methods, including chronological arrangements.[54]

Postmodern History

Postmodern history utilizes deconstructionist methods. Jean François Lyotard described the postmodern condition in historical studies as "incredulity toward metanarratives."[55] Giovanni Levi proposed a more narrowly focused "microhistory," which reduces the scale of observation and intensifies the study of documentary material, as a solution to this problem. Microhistory "tries not to sacrifice knowledge of individual elements to wider generalization, and in fact it accentuates individual lives and events."[56] A disregard for periodicity or for the chronological organization of traditional history also characterizes postmodernist history.

Drama does not alone reflect the influence of New History. In her study *Traces of Another Time: History and Politics in Postwar British Fiction*, Margaret Scanlan observes that British historical novels after World War II "become a field of exploration, a space in which shared epistemological concerns of literary modernism and contemporary historiography meet." For example:

We find a rebirth and development of the skeptical and critical historical novel that Thackeray wrote. Such fiction looks back to a public past, most often in the world wars or to conflicts in countries like India and Ireland once under English rule. The particular moments chosen are mostly inglorious and violent; the novels are more likely to evoke defeats than victories, stupidity and arrogance than heroism.[57]

Similar trends exist in the treatment of history in film and on television.

The following chapters explore in detail the way in which the form and content of British history plays exhibit specific historiographic approaches. These views of history do not have to be the exclusive domain of the professional historian. Historians are influenced by and, in turn, influence popular ideas about the past. We can assume that some of the issues raised by New Historians have entered public debate when the *Daily Telegraph* critic John Coldstream, in a review of Brian Friel's 1988 play *Making History*, quotes the historian E. H. Carr's best-seller, *What Is History?*

E. H. Carr stated that the realm of historical truth lies somewhere between "the north pole of valueless facts and the south pole of value judgments still struggling to transform themselves into facts."

The historian, he declared, is balanced between fact and interpretation, between fact and value. He cannot separate them. Furthermore, history in its essence is change, movement, progress. It can be written "only by those who find and accept a sense of direction in history itself."[58]

Historical methodology also reflects social and political values and serves either to reinforce or to challenge those values. Few writers of historical drama are, like Robert Bolt and Alan Bennett, trained historians; most derive their materials from secondary sources. A specific source may follow a particular historical methodology, but playwrights more often read a range of books on their subjects, and the dramatic product reflects an attitude about history that the writer shares with his or her audience—or intentionally challenges an attitude that the writer assumes the audience possesses.

NOTES

1. In Raphael Holinshed, *Chronicles of England, Scotland, and Ireland* [1577, 1587], Vol. 6 (London: J. Johnson, 1807–8).

2. See Caroline Hill Davis, comp., *Pageants in Great Britain and the United States, A List of References* (New York: New York Public Library, 1916).

3. A notable exception is Arthur Miller's *The Crucible*.

4. Probably first performed in 1539.

5. See Niloufer Harben, *Twentieth-Century English History Plays from Shaw to Bond* (Totowa, NJ: Barnes & Noble, 1988).

6. "The Burden of History," *Tropics of Discourse* (Baltimore: Johns Hopkins University, 1978), p. 31.

7. J. H. Plumb, *The Death of the Past* (Boston: Houghton Mifflin, 1970), p. 14.

8. David Leon Higdon, *Shadows of the Past in Contemporary British Fiction* (Athens: University of Georgia, 1985), p. 5.

9. Keith D. Peacock, *Radical Stages: Alternative History in Modern British Drama* (Westport, CT: Greenwood Press, 1991).

10. Robert Bolt, *A Man for All Seasons* [1960] (New York: Vintage, 1990), p. xvii.

11. *Plays and Players*, Dec., 1963.

12. Simon Gray, *Plays: One* (London: Methuen, 1986), p. xi.

13. "Us, Our Drama and the National Theatre," *Plays and Players* 26, no. 1 (Oct. 1978), p. 8.

14. *The Woman* (London: Eyre Methuen, 1979), pp. 126–27.

15. David Hare, "A Lecture Given at King's College, Cambridge," in *Licking Hitler* (London: Faber & Faber, 1978), p. 66.

16. Robert Bolt, *Vivat! Vivat Regina!* (London: Heinemann, 1971), p. vii.

17. Preface to "Leonardo's Last Supper," in *Collected Plays* (Portsmouth, NH: Heinemann, 1981), p. 122.

18. Irving Ribner, *The English History Play in the Age of Shakespeare*, rev. ed. (New York: Barnes & Noble, 1965), p. 26, argues that the Elizabethans made no such distinction and that the folio editors only intended to indicate by their separation which plays dealt with the English kings.

19. *Marlowe's Edward II* (London: 1914), pp. xxi–xxii, quoted by Ribner, *The English History Play*, pp. 6–7.

20. Morton White, *Foundations of Historical Knowledge* (New York: Harper & Row, 1965), pp. 222–25.

21. E.M.W. Tillyard, *Shakespeare's History Plays* (New York: Macmillan, 1946), p. 99.

22. Ribner, *The English History Play*, pp. 5–6.

23. Tillyard, *History Plays*, p. 321; Alfred B. Harbage, *As They Liked It* (New York: Macmillan, 1947), p. 124; Lily Bess Campbell, *Shakespeare's "Histories": Mirrors of Elizabethan Policy.* (San Marino, CA: Huntington Library, 1947), p. 17.

24. Ribner, *The English History Play*, p. 194.

25. Suzanne Langer, *Feeling and Form* (New York: Charles Scribner's Sons, 1953), p. 357.

26. *The Poetics*, IX.

27. Harben, *Twentieth-Century English History Plays*, pp. 18–19.

28. Peacock, *Radical Stages*, p. 169.

29. R. G. Collingwood, *The Idea of History* [1946], rev. ed. (Oxford: Clarendon, 1993), p. 282.

30. Herbert Lindenberger, *Historical Drama: The Relation of Literature and Reality* (Chicago: University of Chicago, 1975), p. x.

31. Ben Jonson, *Sejanus,* in *Three Plays* (New York: Hill & Wang, 1961), p. 108.

32. "Preface" to *Don Sebastian,* in *Four Tragedies,* ed. L. A. Beaurline and Fredson T. Bowers (Chicago: University of Chicago, l967), p. 287.

33. Ann Jellicoe, *Community Plays: How to Put Them On* (London: Methuen, 1987), p. 144.

34. Ibid.

35. Ibid.

36. Lindenberger, *Historical Drama,* p. 25.

37. "Ueber die tragische Kunst," in *Werke* (Weimar: H. Böhlaus Nachß, 1943), vol. 20, p. 165.

38. Harben, *Twentieth-Century English History Plays,* p. 6.

39. Ruby Cohn, *Retreats from Realism in Recent English Drama* (Cambridge: Cambridge University, 1991), p. 161.

40. Collingwood, *The Idea of History,* p.55.

41. Tillyard, *History Plays,* pp. 54–59 and Ribner, *The English History Play,* p. 24.

42. Herbert Butterfield, *The Whig Interpretation of History* [1931] (New York: W. W. Norton, 1965).

43. Matthew H. Wikander, *The Play of Truth & State: Historical Drama from Shakespeare to Brecht* (Baltimore: Johns Hopkins University, 1986), p. 89.

44. Collingwood, *The Idea of History,* p. 57.

45. Christopher Fry, "Talking of Henry," *The Twentieth Century* 169 (Feb. 1961): 189.

46. See A. N. Vardac, *Stage to Screen: Theatrical Method from Garrick to Griffith* (Cambridge, MA: Harvard University, 1949).

47. Erik Erikson, *Young Man Luther* (New York: 1958).

48. Lindenberger, *Historical Drama,* p. 122.

49. Peacock, *Radical Stages,* p. 14.

50. Elizabeth Fox-Genovese and Eugene D. Genovese, "The Political Crisis of Social History," *Journal of Social History* (Winter 1976): 213–15.

51. Christopher Hill, *The World Turned Upside Down: Radical Ideas During the English Revolution* (New York: Viking, 1972).

52. This approach was anticipated in England by J. R. Green's *History of the English People* (1877–80).

53. Theodore Zeldin, "Social History and Total History," *Journal of Social History* (Winter 1976): 242–43.

54. Philippe Carrard, *Poetics of the New History: French Historical Discourse from Braudel to Chartier* (Baltimore: Johns Hopkins University, 1992), p. 72.

55. Jean François Lyotard. *The Postmodern Condition,* trans. Geoff Bennington and Brian Massumi (Manchester: Manchester University, 1984), p. xxiv.

56. Giovanni Levi, "On Microhistory," in *New Perspectives on Historical Writing,* ed. Peter Burke (University Park: Pennsylvania State University, 1993), p. 109.

57. Margaret Scanlan, *Traces of Another Time: History and Politics in Postwar British Fiction* (Princeton, N.J.: Princeton University, 1990), pp. 6–7.

58. *Daily Telegraph*, Sept. 17, 1988, quoting E. H. Carr, *What Is History?* [1961] (New York: Alfred A. Knopf, 1962).

2

Biographical History Plays

The biographical history play survives in the contemporary British theatre as a remnant of Old History, but even here changes result from the pressures of new historical approaches. The interest that all drama holds is essentially human; abstraction never gained a foothold in theatre outside the didacticism of the medieval church. From the sixteenth century, the principal course of historical drama was biographical, with an underlying assumption that a few important individuals shape major events. This central figure often provided the only source of unity in the episodic chronicle plays. In the tentative first experiment with the form of historical drama, John Bayle in *Kynge Johan* deemphasized individual characterization for the sake of political and moral allegory, but the true developers of the chronicle play, Shakespeare in the Henry VI cycle and Marlowe with *Edward II*, while retaining some emblematic significance for their protagonists, began to show how the strengths and, particularly in these cases, the weakness of individual rulers influenced political events. Although the debate as to whether the "man" makes the moment or the moment the "man" begins to surface only in the nineteenth century, the interplay of public and private imperatives certainly concerns Shakespeare in the Henry IV–V trilogy, justifying his dramatization of Hal's interaction with Falstaff and his gang and leading to Henry V's realization of the tension between the role playing of kingship and the humanity of the player. Hal's youthful capers are never truly "private." His "mucking" contributes to his education for kingship and sets up his rejection of the world of vice and self-interest represented by Falstaff and his gang, a gesture with all the emblematic overtones of the earlier historical moralities.

The emphasis on a principal figure in historical drama does not mandate a heroic protagonist. Early writers were as much intrigued by failure as by success and dramatized the hapless reigns of King John, Edward II, Richard II, Henry VI, and Richard III. The protagonists in biographical histories are typically the "shakers and movers," usually important political figures or occasionally individuals significant in some other field. Contrast this with a play like Caryl Churchill's *Light Shining in Buckinghamshire*, where different actors play the same character to deemphasize the importance of individuals to the historic event. On the one hand, we have biographical drama centered on a historical character. On the other, a play focuses principally on historical events seen apart from the influence of specific characters.

The minor players in history plays exist largely to bring the principals into relief. Playwrights are more likely to fictionalize characters distant from the center of power, partly because these characters usually leave little record of their brush with history and thereby give the author more room for invention.

The ingredients of mainstream historical drama emerged early on: important historical figures whose actions, both private and public, have political consequences and convey an overriding message to the watchers of the drama. The Elizabethans assumed the intertwining of personal and public strands. In the seventeenth century, the private began its ascent over the political and the message was more likely to have ethical or social than political overtones. The love-honor conflicts that came to dominate English dramatizations of history by the late seventeenth century showed the ascendancy of personal over political concerns. Herbert Lindenberger, in *Historical Drama: The Relation of Literature and Reality*, notes the domination of private over public experience in all forms of literature during the last two centuries, with an accompanying increase in psychological inquisitiveness.[1]

In Germany, particularly with the plays of Friedrich von Schiller, political consciousness reemerged in historical drama, a change that British writers began to follow only with George Bernard Shaw in the early twentieth century. However, Schiller, from a romantic context, and Shaw from the viewpoint of social Fabianism, still saw the individual as the principal agent of social and political change and retained a biographical thrust in their history plays.

Traditional historiographers attempted to differentiate biography from history. "Nothing causes more error and unfairness in man's view of history than the interest which is inspired by individual characters," wrote the famous Cambridge historian Lord Acton in 1863.[2] The modern historian Cicely Veronica Wedgwood voiced a contrary position: "The behavior of men as individuals is more interesting to me than their behavior as groups or classes. History can be written with this bias as well as another; it is neither more, nor less, misleading."[3] The difference implied is that biographies concentrate on an individual or, in rare cases, a group of individuals related in a significant way—prosopography—whereas history emphasizes events or institutions, with individuals seen only as contributors. The course of a life, narratively depicted, tends to organize biographies, but histories use political, geographic, military, or periodic schemes of demarcation. Biographies usually place more emphasis on the individual's personal as opposed to public life, but recent thought, particularly among feminist and social historians, calls into question the distinction between the private and the public, arguing that the history of private life, whether of a group or of an individual, may have significance equal to or greater than that of public events. Contemporary biographical drama ranges from plays that principally develop the public life of their protagonists, like Arden's *Left-Handed Liberty*, to plays like Nicholas Wright's *Mrs Klein*, which largely ignore the events that make their protagonists famous and concentrate instead on aspects of their personal life.

The largest group of historical dramas after 1956 continues in the biographical mainstream of British historical drama, but these plays increasingly reflect changing attitudes about history that call into question the efficacy of the biographical approach. The biographical histories fall into four groups: traditional shaker and mover plays, psychohistories that apply the methods of Freudian analysis to historical figures, domestic history that shows the interest of twentieth-century historical studies in the private life even of public figures, and alternative histories that reflect the refocusing of New History on the victims rather than the agents of historical change. We will discuss the last group in later chapters.

TRADITIONAL "SHAKER AND MOVER" BIOGRAPHIES

One persistent strain from pre–World War II theatre was the history play in verse, which consistently used a biographical approach. T. S. Eliot's *Murder in the Cathedral*, first performed in 1935, provided a model, as did of course Shakespeare's works. Verse drama proved to be a disappearing genre, having all but vanished by the 1980s, but up to that point Christopher Fry in England and Archibald MacLeish in the United States continued experiments begun by Eliot and Maxwell Anderson, using verse both for plays with contemporary settings and more often for historical drama. Subject matter from history reduced expectations for realism and made the audience more accepting of verse. A dozen of these verse historical plays were written between 1956 and 1970, but only two, Christopher Fry's *Curtmantle* (1962) and Charles Wood's *'H'* (1970), were produced in the regular commercial, albeit subsidized, theatre. James Forsyth's romances *Héloïse* (1951) and *The Other Heart* (1952) were the last verse histories by a British playwright staged in West End theatres.[4] Most of these verse plays were published without indications of any production: Harry Waine's *Oliver Cromwell* (1958) and its sequel *The Lord Protector* (1963); Ronald Duncan's *Abelard & Héloïse* (1961); Brian Pearce's *Conchubar* (1963), *Paola and Francesca* (1965), and *The Eagle and the Swan* (1966), which deals with King Harold; and Morris West's *The Heretic* (1970), a martyr play about the late sixteenth-century heretical philosopher Giordano Bruno. Robert Kemp's *Master John Knox* (1960) was commissioned by the Church of Scotland to commemorate the four hundredth anniversary of the Reformation; Christopher Fry's *Curtmantle* (1961) premiered at the Stadsschouwburg Theatre, Tilburg, Holland; and Robert Gittings's *Conflict at Canterbury* (1970) was written for *Son et lumière* performances during the Festival at Canterbury Cathedral in 1970. Gittings also did the *Son et lumière This Tower My Prison* (1961) and another for St. Paul's Cathedral.[5]

These verse histories owe more to Shakespeare than to any modern theatrical or historical trends. Robert Kemp's *Master John Knox* is probably among the better of the type. Kemp, a Scots journalist and writer, had published earlier verse histories, including *The Saxon Saint* (1950) and *The King of Scots* (1951).[6] *Master John Knox* employs Elizabethan staging conventions, including a balcony "above" and soliloquies. The characters use a Scots dialect and the unobtrusive blank verse varies periodically with two- or three-stress lines. The play has twenty-six scenes with thirty roles, not counting extras. Kemp effectively uses a small band of soldiers to provide transitions between scenes and some feeling of continuity. The play deals almost exclusively with Knox's public life: the first half with the conflict between Reformers and the queen mother; the second half with Knox's reactions to Mary Queen of Scots. That James Stewart seems as much the protagonist as Knox creates something of a focus problem. Sketchy character development relies on stereotypes. Although Kemp crowds a bit too much action into the final scenes, he knows how to build tension and conflict.

Christopher Fry, with T. S. Eliot, was the most important writer of verse drama in England after World War II. His extravagant, highly energetic, and richly figurative language was unique and made his plays very popular in the postwar years, but he ignored the new trends of realism, absurdism, and the epic that entered the theatre in the late fifties, and his popularity consequently suffered. Fry had worked with historical materials as early as 1938 with *The Boy with a Cart: Cuthman, Saint of Sussex* and used period settings for *A Phoenix Too Frequent* (1946), *The Lady's Not for Burning* (1948), and *The Dark Is Light Enough* (1954). He also adapted historical plays of Anouilh, *The Lark* (1955), and of Giraudoux, *Tiger at the Gates* (1955) and *Judith* (1962). *Curtmantle*, which was performed in Edinburgh and by the Royal Shakespeare Company in London in 1962 after its 1961 Dutch premiere, deals with the clash between Thomas à Becket and Henry II from Henry's point of view. Staging is handled in a Shakespearean fashion without scenery. Fry's stage directions reveal his consideration for theatrical transitions between scenes and a heavy reliance on lighting to indicate the passage of time. Fry takes considerable liberty with the clock and compresses events into a generalized theatrical time frame. Act I covers the period from 1158 to 1163; act II, 1163–70; act III, 1174–89. The staging is very theatrical and Fry uses a number of narrative devices. Eleanor functions as a choral figure, but less as an objective observer than as an apologist for Henry. William Marshal acts as occasional narrator, and groups of characters identified as "The Bishops" or "The Talk" in a few instances serve a more conventional choral function of representing the voice of the "community of observers." At the center of the play Fry places an almost formal twenty-minute debate between Henry and Becket, relieved only by the inventiveness of Fry's verse.[7] The language of the play, which alternates between prose and blank verse, reveals less of Fry's poetic prowess than other works. Although the play provides more in-depth character study than any other Fry play, its principal concern is thematic, a search for a synthesis between secular and religious law.

The real challenge to the biographical bias of historical drama in Britain came from a Bertolt Brecht play, and ironically, from one of his most biographical dramas, *Galileo*, the English version of which was produced by Bernard Miles at the Mermaid Theatre on June 16, 1960. While Brecht focused on a prominent historical figure, he invited us to see how social forces shaped that individual's actions. At the same time, Brecht disavowed social determinism because he wished to reinforce the possibility for modern social change by showing past events shaped by human choices that made otherwise would have produced different results. Brecht, therefore, while rejecting the idea that social forces beyond their control victimize his characters, invited a degree of social scrutiny quite beyond that contained in any history plays that had gone before.

One of the first English history plays to invoke the influence of Brecht, and in many respects the major impetus to postwar historical drama, was Robert Bolt's *A Man for All Seasons*, first produced in a radio version in 1954, televised in 1957, and staged in July of 1960 at London's Globe Theatre with Paul Scofield playing Sir Thomas More a role repeated in a successful 1966 film version. Bolt's use of a narrator who plays multiple characters but also addresses the audience "out of character," an episodic plot structure, a protagonist victimized for his intellectual beliefs, and the proximity with the Berliner

Ensemble production of *Galileo* in London invited comparisons between *Galileo* and *A Man for All Seasons*.

Bolt's play dramatizes More's fall from the chancellorship of England and eventual execution for refusing to take the oath acknowledging the annulment of Henry VIII's marriage to his first wife, Catherine. Although the play dramatizes major political figures including Henry, Cardinal Wolsey, Thomas Cromwell, and the Duke of Norfolk, it emphasizes More's personal tragedy, the impact of his decision on his family and on himself. Bolt thus avoids the frequent pitfall in which a martyr's other-worldliness and the rewards of martyrdom undermine any grief resulting from the martyr's death. As the play's title implies, More was very much a man of his world, who embraced life and struggled to avoid execution. If anything, deprived of a clear external affirmation for the value of More's death, the play leans heavily in the direction of pathos. With a cynical view of the political system that More serves and a begrudging acknowledgment at best of the rewards that Catholicism reserves for its martyrs, Bolt comes close to creating the feeling that More's self-sacrifice is a wasted gesture.

More's decisions are motivated by a sense of self that reflects Bolt's modern existentialism to a greater extent than More's humanistic Catholicism. When defending the apostolic succession of the pope, Bolt's More explains to his friend Norfolk, "What matters to me is not whether it's true or not but that I believe it to be true, or rather, not that I *believe* it, but that *I* believe it."[8]

In spite of its success, *A Man for All Seasons* met a good deal of negative critical response, driven partly by Bolt's older biographic bias rather than a modern socially conscious approach. Kenneth Tynan, one of the principal apologists for Brecht in England, set the terms for the attack in an *Observer* review when he contrasted Brecht's public and materialistic interpretation of history in *Galileo* with Bolt's private and individualistic view in *A Man for All Seasons*: "Compare them, and it soon becomes obvious that Mr. Bolt's method is more constricting. Since there can be no battle of ideologies, he must reduce everything to personal terms; the gigantic upheavals of the Reformation dwindle into a temperamental squabble between a nice lawyer who dislikes divorce and a lusty monarch who wants an heir."[9]

In the next issue of *The Observer*, Bolt responded to Tynan's review: "I am grateful for the comparison he drew between *A Man for All Seasons* and *Galileo*—indeed I impudently challenged it by misquoting Brecht's most celebrated line at the climax of my own play." Bolt argued that in spite of its political context, the appeal of *Galileo* lay essentially in the characterization, that "the personal is not 'merely' personal," and that "both plays are about uncommon individuals but both are also about organized society."[10]

In response, Tynan broadened the debate, contending that Bolt's arguments

seem to me to be founded on premises that expose, quite poignantly, the limitations of our Western approach to historical drama.

Mr. Bolt surveys his chosen slice of the Tudor era with the right end of the telescope firmly clapped to his eye: what he sees is Sir Thomas More, in dominant close-up, with everything else out of focus. A hint, now and then, is lightly dropped that More's obduracy was not only a crafty individual challenge to Tudor law but a social and political threat to the whole process of the English Reformation. Once dropped, however, these hints are rapidly swept under the carpet and forgotten. Mr. Bolt is primarily absorbed in the state of More's conscience, not in the state of More's England or More's Europe.

Brecht, on the other hand, though he gives us an intimate study of Galileo's conscience, takes pains to relate it at every turn to Galileo's world and to the universe at large. . . . Brecht's play deals with Galileo *and* the postponed dawn of the age of reason. Mr. Bolt's play deals with More, *tout court*.[11]

Tynan correctly saw that Bolt's emphasis on the personal dimension of historical players lacks Brecht's overt social intention. For Brecht, the situation is more important than the individual within it; the character functions to expose the situation. Bolt focuses on character; the event exists to place the character in relief. However, Bolt, not Brecht, is in the mainstream of English historical drama.

In his preface to the play, written in September of 1960, Bolt restates his argument for a humanistic approach: "When an economy collides with a religion it is living men who collide, nothing else (they collide with one another and within themselves)." In an obvious cut at Marxist critics, Bolt complains, "Theoreticians seem more and more to work the other way round, to derive the worker *from* his economy, the thinker *from* his culture."[12]

Brecht's characterization of Galileo was also an antiheroic debunking of the mythical hero of science, whereas for Bolt, one of the appeals of historical drama is the opportunity it presents for heroism. In the preface to *A Man for All Seasons*, he says that a historical setting enables him to treat characters "in a properly heroic, properly theatrical manner."[13] This appeal is at least partly stylistic. Bolt in a 1963 interview in *Plays and Players* stated, "I wrote an historical play—largely, I think, as a sort of Dutch courage, because if people are wearing cloaks and funny hats and don't travel on 29 buses as it were, you don't really know the minutiae of their daily lives, you are helped to escape from this tremendous undertow of representation."[14]

Other critics believed that Bolt used the trappings of historical drama in place of well-developed characterization. A. Alvarez, in *New Statesman*, wrote,

"Period costume is a substitute for depth of analysis. Provided you dress the actors up, you can get away with types instead of people. In a costume play you can tell a man's morals by the cut of his gown. Why, for example, were we never given the reason for Cromwell's savage hounding of More?"[15] Philip Hope-Wallace wrote in *The Guardian*, "The piece, so well imagined and neatly contrived, remains a decent, modern example of the historical costume play and never moves even momentarily into the greater field of tragedy."[16]

Tynan's view that Bolt was out of touch with social reality persists in subsequent criticism. Richard Cave, for example, writes in 1988, "The *metaphors* of Bolt's plays tend to be, if not reductive, at least restrictive interpretations of history as the expression of powerful quixotic personalities; they are not metaphors that, resonating with possibilities of interpretation, creatively disturb an audience's imagination."[17]

Bolt persisted in his personalized view of history. In 1970 his dramatization of the conflict between Elizabeth I and Mary Queen of Scots, *Vivat! Vivat Regina!*, appeared at Chichester and the Piccadilly Theatre. Cave writes:

This is a *simple* form because there is no attempt to reach beyond the study of a passionate and a cerebral personality in conflict together; the historical evidence is selected and shaped to elucidate this pattern of opposites; but the effect in performance is rather to suggest that Elizabeth's brilliant policy-making was, in Freudian terms, compensation for a repressed sexual identity and that Mary is little more than a wilful exhibitionist.[18]

We will discuss this play in more detail in the context of feminist history, but it avoids any serious engagement with the political or social framework of its own sixteenth-century setting. To the dismay of critics and playwrights who espouse a social or political function for theatre, Bolt's plays also sidestep contemporary political relevance.

Bolt's *State of Revolution*, a dramatization of the major figures of the Russian revolution, which premiered at the National Theatre's Lyttleton in 1977, goes to the heart of the issue of the conflict between personality and social forces as shapers of history. Bolt establishes the theme early in the play when his narrator, Anatole Vassilyevich Lunacharsky, states, "The personal of course is marginal. The historically determined movement of the masses is alone decisive."[19] Lenin declares, "Big events aren't formed by people, people are formed by big events" (39), and when his wife says, "A month ago you said that the revolution was not to be looked for," Lenin retorts "I didn't look for it. —I found it" (50–51). Later, when Trotsky agrees to lead the Red army, Stalin comments, "We seem to have found our Bonaparte," precipitating a salvo from Trotsky that Stalin exhibits an alarming ignorance of the Marxist view of history: "The 'Man of the Moment' is not a 'great man', he is merely the man that the moment needs" (65). The play itself, however, demonstrates the contrary position. For example, Bolt uses a strong staging image of Lenin's famous arrival from exile to show his impact on the chaos created by bickering factions during the early stages of the revolution: "The din is interrupted by the blast of a locomotive whistle. They freeze. The light begins to darken. Lenin enters in travelling clothes and carrying a bunch of red flowers" (45). Lenin's habit of taking ruthlessly extreme positions, which Bolt has demonstrated early in the play through the almost casual discussions of the exiled revolutionaries, now gives the disjointed revolution a sense of direction. In the final lines of the play, Lunacharsky, who grieves the loss of humanistic ideals in the revolution, ironically comments on the tension between personal and social forces of history: "You see, I cannot guess what cosmic irresponsibility may lurk beneath my sometime wish for gaslight in the library, my mother making music and my father speaking French" (108).

The biographical sketches of the major characters that Bolt prefaced to the published version of the play indicate his focus on characterization, but the main critical objections to *State of Revolution* were not that Bolt missed the political issues, but that he failed to create convincing characterizations. For example, F. Marcus, reviewing for the *Sunday Telegraph*, wrote, "Robert Bolt's new play about Lenin turns out disappointingly as a stodgy history lesson. The characters refuse to come to life and the theme—the attainment, exercise and delegation of power—remains abstract."[20] D. Z. Mairowitz, writing for *Plays and Players*, complained, "All of the Bolsheviks are seen as if with historical hindsight, as they *became*, as they stand for us *now* in frozen images, but not as they certainly must have been—passions and hatreds worn on their sleeves— while fighting to keep the Revolution alive." Mairowitz accused Bolt of "turning his *dramatis personae* into a collection of attitudes rather than fully-drawn characters with voices and lives and unpredictabilities of their own. They end up speaking abstractly and impersonally as if in the throes of perpetual debate."[21]

The abrogation of personal goals to the needs of the state, which was also a theme in *A Man for All Seasons* and *Vivat! Vivat Regina*, takes a slightly different direction here. Bolt does little to develop the personal lives of his characters beyond their involvement in the revolution. When we see the characters "at home," they largely spend their time debating ideological issues. The maw of Communist power consumes not family and lovers here but humanistic ideals, defended principally by Lunacharsky and by the poet Gorky. Holding lists of people imprisoned or executed by the Cheka, the Soviet secret police, Gorky turns on Lenin: "You promised us new life, release, refinements, unimaginable forms. And all you have released is atavistic envy. There is no novelty whatever in your revolution, Vladya; no love, nor life, nor hope, nor even curiosity. It is merely ferocious" (88). Bolt's sympathies are principally with the humanists, not the Marxists. He has little interest in issues of economic oppression and class struggle as seen by Marxist historians. His focus is on the corrupting force of power, but the implications are more social than personal. We grieve for the destructiveness demanded by the policies of Lenin and his followers, but we do not grieve for the characters themselves.

Similarly depicting a leader at a turning point in Soviet history, Tariq Ali and Howard Brenton's 1990 drama of Mikhail Gorbachev's rise to power, *Moscow Gold*, subjugates biographical interest to social theme even more than Bolt's play. *Moscow Gold* acknowledges the influence of Gorbachev on events, but the style of the play diminishes the biographical dimension. The actions depicted function more on a metaphorical than a literal level; so we are invited to react to Gorbachev's position more than his personality. Brenton and Ali's Gorbachev converses regularly with the ghost of Lenin and with Andropov both before and after death. We see Gorbachev and his wife, Raisa, in bed but the topic of discussion is politics. Later a massage that Raisa gives Gorbachev provides an opportunity to catalogue the tension points in the dissolution of the Soviet empire:

Your body is full of knots. Relax, it hurts my fingers. Ah, here's Azerbaijan.

She rubs his shoulders going down slowly.

And Georgia. There. There. (*As she approaches his bum.*) And here are the Baltic republics. (*Massaging his bum cheeks.*) So you want independence, eh? Where would that leave him?[22]

Such a scene does not purport to reveal Gorbachev's domestic life, but satirically uses an imagined personal scene to illustrate a political problem. This Gorbachev may agonize about the responsibility of "making history," but biography is essentially a tool for revealing social problems that transcend the individual: the betrayal of a social revolution by the bureaucratic elite who have established new class privileges. Lenin, Andropov, Gorbachev, and Yeltsin all struggle to reform a corrupt institution. We will examine this drama later in relation to Marxist history plays.

In spite of critical griping about vacuousness, Bolt, along with Peter Shaffer, enjoyed the greatest commercial success of any of the modern writers of historical drama, perhaps because they projected a traditional sense of the individual's importance in shaping history. Peter Shaffer's *The Royal Hunt of the Sun* was produced by the National Theatre at the Chichester Festival, opening July 7, 1964, and subsequently at the Old Vic, December 8, 1964. Directed by John Dexter, this first new play staged by the National Theatre presented a highly spectacular dramatization of Pizarro's conquest of Peru. The response of popular press reviewers was generally positive, but the cult critics were highly negative, in the opinion of Charles Marowitz, an almost calculated reaction against the widespread praise.[23]

Shaffer's principal source was a Victorian history rather than any contemporary studies, but W. H. Prescott's 1847 book *The Conquest of Peru*, influenced by nineteenth-century notions of the noble savage, goes out of its way to emphasize the contrast between the native culture and the hypocritical Catholicism of the Spaniards. Although Shaffer exposes the violent bigotry of the Christian conquerors, thus allying the play with the colonial histories that we will discuss later, the play makes no modern political or social comment by emphasizing the genocide that occurred. Shaffer emphasizes Pizarro's personal struggle to escape his disillusionment with Spanish culture and religion and to find something in which he can believe. The Inca sovereign Atahuallpa is more a metaphor for personal commitment than the defeated ruler of an unjustly vanquished society. Shaffer recounts the basic details of the broader historical event, Pizarro's march over the mountains and defeat of the numerically superior Incas, but he invents details of characterization. The minor characters who surround Pizarro exist to embody specific points of view and to structure alternative models of behavior in order to highlight the choices that Pizarro makes. Desoto stands for liberal rationality; the Dominican friar Valverde, for the established church; the royal overseer Estete, the bureaucratic state; Young Martin, the romantic idealist.

Even more than Bolt, Shaffer, in *The Royal Hunt of the Sun*, utilized epic staging devices without using them for the alienation effects suggested by Brecht. A narrator, one of the conquerors many years later, gives background and relates portions of the story, but his commentary never serves to detach the audience from the action. Mountains are climbed in mime, battles are danced, an emblematic sun is stripped of its golden leaves to indicate the pillage of the country, but the impact is closer to Artaud than to Brecht. The visual images draw the audience into the illusion rather than encouraging an objective assessment of events.

Shaffer's *Amadeus*, a dramatization of the conflict between Mozart and Antonio Salieri, is one of a subgenre of biographical plays dealing with artists rather than political figures. The form presupposes a rise in the public status of the artist and emerges in the early twentieth century with plays like H. F. Rubinstein and Clifford Bax's *Shakespeare* (1921), Rudolph Besier's *The Barretts of Wimpole Street* (1930), and Alfred Sangster's *The Brontës* (1933). Of the

plays that we examine, Hugh Whitemore's *Stevie*, Liz Lochhead's *Blood and Ice*,
Pam Gems's *Piaf*, Edna O'Brien's *Virginia*, Michael Hastings's *Tom and Viv*,
Claire Tomalin's *The Winter Wife*, and Peter Whelan's *The School of Night* fit
into this category. Edward Bond's *Bingo* and *The Fool*, Ann Jellicoe's *Shelley, or
the Idealist*, Adrian Mitchell's *Tyger* and Howard Brenton's *Bloody Poetry* use
biography for other thematic purposes, but still deal with artists.

Amadeus, which opened on the Olivier stage at the National Theatre on
November 2, 1979, again places in a historical context the opposition between
an older disillusioned man and a younger one who is inexplicably blessed with
special gifts. As in *Royal Hunt*, the cynically more pragmatic older character
destroys the younger, to the loss of both. As with the tie between Pizarro and
Atahuallpa, Shaffer invents the relationship between Mozart and Salieri from
the flimsiest of historical materials. Shaffer textures the play with details from
eighteenth-century court life, but as Richard Allen Cave observed, he does not
use the historical setting to shape the action: "This is entirely a personal
dilemma, the individual self rebelling against the accidents of nature, that has
little to do with the process of history. . . . *Amadeus* is fundamentally about the
cruel ironies of chance rather than the way character is moulded by the
pressures of the times. . . . It is not Salieri's historical distance but his psychological closeness that preoccupies Shaffer."[24] *Amadeus* is staged with much of
the pageantry and many of the theatrical devices proved in *Royal Hunt*—masks,
mime, and music—but as in Shaffer's *Equus*, the narrator, Salieri, played by
that veteran of historical drama, Paul Scofield, is not a minor character, like
Royal Hunt's Martin, but the protagonist of the play. This makes the narrative
a device for developing the audience's awareness of the psyche of a central
character rather than a means of commenting on the significance of the
historical events.

Amadeus was very successful, the New York production winning a Tony for
best play and the film version an Oscar, but what little negative criticism the
play attracted centered on the characterization of Mozart as something of an
infantile oaf and on the play's language. James Fenton of *The Sunday Times*
found the characterization of Mozart "appalling" and B. A. Young of *Financial
Times* objected to his "coprophilous language."[25] Ultimately historical accuracy
is less important to Shaffer than the need to make Mozart personally unattractive in order to emphasize that his genius was unaccountable by the standards
of social success that Salieri acknowledged. Salieri is worthy but his work
mediocre; Mozart is unworthy and his work brilliant.

This dialectic between a disillusioned character and one who embodies some
inexplicable power is a thematic concern that runs through Shaffer's work and
transcends his historical sources. He seems less to discover this duality in his

sources than to find ways to structure the historical story so that it illustrates this particular theme. In spite of the strong biographical emphasis both on Salieri as the narrator and on Mozart as the subject of the play, characters are at the mercy of greater forces in Shaffer's world. Salieri addresses some perversely enigmatic god, but the power that accounts for Mozart's genius is, for Shaffer, certainly beyond the influence of social conditions and ultimately beyond the scope of either religion or psychiatry.

The continuing use of the biographical approach to history by politically radical playwrights like John Arden and Howard Brenton shows its resilience, but they adapt biography to serve their own ends. Arden used a historical setting for *Serjeant Musgrave's Dance* (1959) and *Armstrong's Last Goodnight* (1964), but these and Arden's later history plays avoid focusing on major players. *Left-Handed Liberty* at first seems to concentrate on the person of King John, but as might be expected with Arden, he places a new turn on the biographical format. The play was commissioned by the Corporation of the City of London to commemorate the 750th anniversary of Magna Carta, which may account for its being somewhat more conservative than Arden's other work. It premiered on June 7, 1965, with public performances at the Mermaid Theatre.

The play focuses more on the conflicts between John and the barons after the signing of Magna Carta than on the events leading to Runnymede, which occur in the third scene. John engages us more than Arden's usual characters, but the historical events still seem larger than the people involved. Arden's message is that Magna Carta assumes a significance not intended by either John or the barons. John realizes its potential as a document of individual liberty more than the brutal and self-serving barons do, but he makes a fetish of inconsistency and unpredictability. In contrast, the papal legate Pandulph tries to project an ordered universe. The church that he serves is a major, but somewhat clueless, player. Pandulph, who acts as player, narrator, and occasionally commentator, remains sitting on a corner of the forestage a good portion of the time but leaves when Arden wants to show an event outside Pandulph's reckoning.

Arden makes straightforward use of his historical sources:

There is very little in this play which cannot be justified historically. I have had to sandwich events here and there and transpose a few episodes, but I have only invented—as far as I can be sure—Pandulph's correspondence on behalf of the King with the Flemish recruiting agent; Young Marshal's love for Lady de Vesci; the episode at Dover with the Goldsmith and his Wife; and Lady de Vesci's relationship with John.[26]

The portions of the plot invented by Arden relate principally to a poorly developed line of conflict over the Lady de Vesci, the wife of one of John's Barons and the subject of attention by both John and the chivalric son of William Marshal, a loyal earl of the king's. Arden, in fact, devotes very little time to these romantic or domestic trappings and focuses largely on the public interplay between the king and the barons. Even the Lady de Vesci, citing the charter as a basis for her defiance of her husband's control over her, becomes a device for showing how the Magna Carta assumed meaning unintended by its drafters. Arden wants to concentrate attention on the theme rather than his characters. He has King John, pointing to the Lady de Vesci, say to the audience, "This play concerns Magna Carta, and Magna Carta only. The Lady is peripheral" (84). And to some extent even John is peripheral. The play assumes the guise of historical biography, but makes the point that individuals cannot foresee or control the effects of their actions, a denial of the "great man" approach to history.

Like Arden, Howard Brenton has written half a dozen history plays, but he rarely uses a straightforward biographic approach. His earliest historical drama, *Wesley*, comes closest. First performed on February 27, 1970, at the Bradford Festival by the Bradford University Drama Group, this sixty-minute play was designed to be the length of a Methodist service. It deals principally with John Wesley at university and his failed trip to America to convert the Indians. The play's presentational style mixes sermons, dialogue, monologues, an announcer to introduce scenes, and hymns by a background choir, which sings the play's resolution. Devils appear in black modern raincoats. Rather than dwelling on social ills as Brenton customarily does, the play moves attention away from the external obstacles that Wesley must confront and focuses on his internal doubts. Lacking much of the vitriolic quality of Brenton's later work, this is not a very satisfactory play.

Brenton's *Bloody Poetry* provides an example of prosopography—collective biography—the study of the careers of individuals connected by family, economic, or social relationships. This differs from social history, which we will investigate later, in that the actions are determined by the personalities of the people involved rather than by their identity as a class or type of individual. The events in *Bloody Poetry* occur because of the unique values of Byron and the Shelleys, not because they are literati or members of a certain social class.

Roland Rees, artistic director of the touring company Foco Novo, asked Brenton to write a play about the romantic poet Shelley. Brenton was wary of writing a stage biography, but as he explains, "I suspect that Roland's impulse was to present Shelley as a revolutionary hero. But I said 'yes' to the project, when I saw a different way of handling it, writing not just about Shelley, but about the quartet of Shelley, Byron, Mary Shelley and Claire Clairemont, Byron's mistress."[27] Shelley and his circle provided a parallel to the antiestablishmentarianism of radicals in the sixties and seventies. Ann Jellicoe had dealt with much the same material in her 1965 play *Shelley, or the Idealist,* which we will examine later in the context of feminist theatre. Jellicoe's play, though still dealing with a circle of people, is much more strongly focused on Shelley and closer to conventional biographic drama.

Performed by Foco Novo in 1984 and revived by the Royal Court Theatre in 1988, *Bloody Poetry* extends from the first meeting of the two poets in 1816 to the death of Shelley in 1822 and consists largely of a series of discussions, much like *The Symposium,* which Shelley is translating at one point in the play. The episodic structure organizes scenes largely around topics of discussion. Brenton interweaves verse into the dialogue, including passages from Coleridge and Wordsworth, about whom Shelley and Byron argue. The play presupposes that the audience has basic knowledge of the poets and their lives.

Brenton describes this as a "Utopian play."[28] The characters try to create a sexual utopia but ultimately destroy their children and one another. Brenton underscores this with a theatrical metaphor. The characters periodically join hands and form a circle, until late in the play after the women have been rejected by the men, "CLAIRE *steps forward, hoping they will form a circle, as in earlier scenes—they do not.*"[29] The conflict between the men is between Byron's cynical hedonism and Shelley's romantic idealism. Byron is a libertine; Shelley, a libertarian. Mary is a female version of Shelley, but her need to protect her children causes her to abandon her liberal idealism for the sake of security. The group falls apart because the men are unfaithful and unable to apply themselves to the practical matters of survival. Brenton emphasizes this ineffectualness not only in domestic matters but on a broader social scale by having Shelley comment on the massacre at Peterloo, about which he wrote a poem:

I can see it. St Peter's Field—the outskirts of Manchester. A great crowd, some 60,000 working men and women. Armed only with banners.

And then, from nowhere—the militia. The brutal attack. In ten minutes, a massacre. Eleven dead, four hundred and twenty-one cases of serious injury, one hundred and sixty-two men women and children with sabre wounds.

And where was I, the poet? Impotent in Italy, in the sun. (300)

Brenton uses two minor characters, Harriet, Shelley's first wife, and Polidori, Byron's biographer, to comment on the action. After her suicide, Harriet reappears as a ghost, an ironic reminder of Shelley's earlier betrayal of his first wife even as his fortunes decline, he wanders in exile, his children die, and his relations with Mary deteriorate. Narrative monologues by Polidori furnish some of the chronological context of the play, but Polidori also serves as a hostile reporter who reminds us that those who record events create history. In one scene the two couples have been debating about poetry and wind up in one another's arms as Polidori tries different ways of reporting what the audience sees:

Polidori: (aside) I entered the drawing-room of the Villa Diodati. Outside there raged the storm. No. Outside the storm raged. No. Outside, the storm abated. No. Outside, the storm I had just left, rolled around the gloomy house. No. No. I was wet and miserable.

He looks around the group. BYRON *and* CLAIRE *kiss passionately.* MARY *shifts toward* BYSSHE, *turning the pages of the Wordsworth. They do not respond to* POLIDORI's *presence.*

In a flash I saw them, a flash of lightning. The air in the room was heavy with their illicit sexuality, they had been at it, I knew it, I knew it, I knew it! They had thrown their clothes back on, the minute I came to the door! No. The two great poets, were, I observed, in contemplation, the women observing a discreet silence. (261)

Claire also recognizes the process of myth making and tells Mary, "We are privileged to stand on this beach, and see George Byron and Bysshe Shelley meet. It will be history" (242). After the meeting, Mary comments, "Now it has happened we can make it mythical" (250). Claire also observes, "Let us draw courage from our appalling reputations. How the world sees us, like it or not, how we are condemned to live. I think we have no choice in the matter" (244). A man who travels with his biographer must have some sense of playing for effect.

In the preface to his 1989 collection of plays, Brenton says that *Bloody Poetry* was among plays written from a left-wing perspective,[30] and we will examine other of Brenton's history plays in the framework of Marxist history, but *Bloody Poetry* shows few of the economic or class concerns that characterize that history. We see Byron as a wealthy nobleman, but those conditions do not define his behavior. Shelley, particularly, rails against the society that he has fled, but the failure of the group results more from personal weaknesses than from the social environment reacting on them. However, by dealing with a group of people rather than an individual, by presenting the characters in a relatively disjointed series of encounters rather than a clearly developing plot, and by making us aware of their role playing, Brenton obstructs the usual development of biographic detail.

Another biographical history with socialist overtones was David Pinner's *The Drums of Snow*, which began in 1968 as a television production and was staged in the United States at Stanford in 1970 and at Oxford in 1974. The English Revolution has been dramatized by recent English playwrights more than any other historical subject. These plays include Harry Waine's verse plays *Oliver Cromwell* (1958) and its sequel *The Lord Protector* (1963), Pinner's *The Drums of Snow*, David Storey's *Cromwell* (1973), Caryl Churchill's *Light Shining in Buckinghamshire* (1978), and *The World Turned Upside Down* (1978) by Keith Dewhurst. Treatment of the Civil War has always been a barometer of political orientation, and none of these plays takes the pro-monarchist position of nineteenth-century histories. Waine's biographical approach charts Cromwell's rise to power as an essential mediator between monarchists and levelers. Pinner, Storey, and Churchill all see Cromwell as betraying the more democratic impulses of the revolution. We will examine Storey and Churchill's plays later in the context of Marxist and of social history. Although *The Drums of Snow* is a "major players" history, both Charles and Cromwell become aware that they cannot govern the larger forces that contol them. Most of the characters are melodramatic stereotypes, and the characterization seems to be based less on concerns for historical accuracy than on dramatic expediency or topicality. Pinner describes this as "a modern play about modern dilemmas using historical syntax."[31] John Lilburne, "the first English Socialist," serves as the play's narrator, with the audience playing "The People." Lilburne points out that the revolution did not create a democracy or benefit the people, a regular socialist theme in the sixties and seventies: "Government will always be by the Select Few *for* the Select Few" (398). Pinner returned to historical settings for *The Potsdam Quartet* (1973) and *Hereward the Wake* (1974) but with invented actions and characters.

Peter Barnes, another writer of several history plays, frequently uses a biographical approach, but never for conventional purposes. *Noonday Demons* and *Leonardo's Last Supper* (1969), both one-act plays; *Laughter* (1978); and *Red Noses* (1985) all focus on historical characters, but Barnes develops their metaphoric and thematic value as much as any detailed or engaging personal portraits. For example, Leonardo da Vinci, the central character in *Leonardo's Last Supper*, is entirely Barnes's invention, as is the plot. An impoverished family of morticians, confronted with an apparently resurrected Leonardo, excitedly imagining the great works that he can yet create, drown him in a bucket of filth in order to assure their fee. Ivan the Terrible, who murders his son in *Laughter*, exists to provide an analogue to the 1942 Auschwitz bureaucrats who appear in the second act.

The Bewitched, produced by the Royal Shakespeare Company (RSC) at the Aldwych Theatre in London on May 1974, more clearly emulates the form of traditional biographical drama, but the central character, the mentally and physically defective King Carlos II, the last Hapsburg ruler of Spain, serves principally to expose the dynastic follies of the European court. This sprawling drama, which begins with Carlos's conception and ends with his death, depicts Carlos's efforts to engender an offspring. The play has a clear dramatic question, but incidents are selected to demonstrate the progressive entropy of the court rather than to develop a cause-and-effect sequence. Barnes has eliminated and simplified much of the historical background; characters are divisible into camps of influence, such as the queen mother's group versus the queen's group or medicine versus astrology.

Barnes develops his characters less through historically recorded events or conventional interaction with one another than through a series of vivid metaphors. The bulk of the dialogue remains relatively realistic but scenes move in and out of surrealistic effects. For example, the prologue shows the birth of the protagonist. When King Philip and Queen Marianna climb into bed,

there is the sound of heavy machinery creaking into motion from the bed. Massive wheels and screws turn laboriously and ancient pistons start pounding. The whole room shakes to a brutal thudding. It reaches a crescendo, a woman screams, Saint Isadore's skeleton jerks upright on the bier and collapses in a heap.

The scream turns into staccato cries of a woman in childbirth. They increase in intensity until drowned by a great tearing sound and the floor Down Stage Centre slowly splits apart.

Lights down to a Spot on the widening crack which seems full of dark, glutinous liquid. It stirs as something rises out of it. First a hand, then a shapeless body emerges completely wrapped in a pale, pink membrane. Hauling itself feebly out of the crack it flops onto the floor where it lies curled up tight.

A sharp slap is heard and a baby starts crying: the body stirs. . . . The body bursts through its membrane to reveal PRINCE CARLOS.

Carlos: Daa, dad-a...

PHILIP reacts in horror at the sight. He clutches his chest, utters a despairing cry and keels over backward off the rostrum, dead.[32]

The play fulfills this strong opening image of Carlos as a monster, but Barnes reveals Carlos's torment, gives him moments of lucidity, and makes him a pitiable if not a sympathetic character. At one point when the bickering factions at court enter, Carlos moans, Lear-like, to his fool, "They've come t'tear the skin fffffrom my soul. Tom. Tom, I'm the world's oldest living orphan" (231).

Asked to tell about death, the Torturer replies that he only knows about pain, and Carlos retorts, "I knnow pain, paaaa's my familiar tooo. Sleeping—waking paaa, eating—drinking paaa, all-the-time paaa; e'en when't doesn't hurt I feel paaaa. Whaaa cans't you tell me o' paaain?" (263). When told that Carlos is dying, his queen remarks, "his whole life's been one long dying" (331). Through the device of giving Carlos moments of lucidity after epileptic seizures, Barnes also allows him to voice the conscience of the play. Speaking in verse after one of these seizures, Carlos declares:

> Has Christ died that children might starve?
> Why shouldst wealth lie in usurer's pockets?
> And whole towns made poor t'raise up the merchant's walls?
> . . .
> Why shouldst some ha' surfeit, others go hungry?
> One man two coats, another go naked?
> Now I see Authority's a poor provider.
>
> No blessings come from 't
> No man born shouldst ha't, wield 't. (326–27)

Part of the impact of the play is Barnes's ability to reveal the heart of his monster.

Because of his importance to the succession, Carlos is central to the play, but in his role as king, not particularly as a character. The court that swirls around Carlos echoes his own idiocy and vulgarity, and *The Bewitched* exposes the corruption of a royal court as much as the corruption of one man. One device for conveying this is a strong scatological tone. The language is vulgar and business intentionally shocking. At one point Carlos and his queen vomit on the dying queen mother. The play's macabre pageantry and cynical world-view give it a Jacobean feeling. Barnes's technique of reducing historical material to a series of highly theatrical images produces a striking impact.

One of the most popular historical biographies in the contemporary British theatre was Tim Rice and Andrew Lloyd Webber's musical *Evita* (1979), about the Argentinean populist Evita Peron.[33] Even though spoken dialogue occurs only during the last two sentences of the production, the musical uses elements of biographical history, typically showing the connection between a political figure's personal life and public actions. Evita's youth as a poor girl who works her way to a position of power through a series of sexual liaisons underpins her sympathy for and appeal to the masses of Argentina. The musical, however, does not draw the audience into the personal life of Evita so much as it emphasizes her role as a cultural icon.

Rice and Lloyd Webber accentuate the artifice of the musical form in order to hold the audience at a distance from the material. We start with Eva's death, making the body of the musical a narrative flashback. The audience becomes further detached by its suspicions about the narrator, the Cuban revolutionary Che Guevara, who may have been in Argentina sometime during Eva's rule but whose interactions with her are entirely of Rice and Lloyd Webber's invention. Guevara is an unusually skeptical apologist for this musical heroine. The aristocrats, the military, and the masses all appear as impersonal groups, representatives of their class, never individuals. Even Juan Peron, the other major character, is a passive tool of forces that he cannot control, a paper cutout of a dictator. Guevara's orchestration of the mass rallies calls into question their spontaneity, and the repetition of lyrics in reprises emphasizes sloganizing. The musical makes its audience aware of the gender biases in Argentine society, but it deals with feminist issues in the same way that it presents Marxism: flattened into a theme for popular music. In a show about a show, *Evita's* mythic rags-to-riches heroine remains larger than life, never reduced to familiarity. Rice and Lloyd Webber, through the voice of their narrator, may call into question the process that societies use to create political myths, but the myth herself remains in place.

PSYCHOBIOGRAPHY

The most extreme biographical bias in history is psychohistory, the psychiatric analysis of the behavior of a major historical figure. Psychohistory uses the recognizable categories of a specific psychiatric approach, usually Freudian, to explain a person in terms of relations between parents and children, neuroses, and such behavior as repression and displacement. Although Freudian analysis of fictional characters occurred almost as soon as psychoanalytic theory emerged, the first systematic psychohistory was E. H. Erikson's *Young Man Luther* in 1958. The difficulty of documenting subconscious factors influencing behavior contributed to the late appearance and relative rarity of this approach.

John Osborne used Erickson's book and Roland Bainton's *Here I Stand*[34] as a basis for his play *Luther*, produced by the English Stage Company at Theatre Royal Nottingham, June 26, 1961, with Albert Finney as Luther, then in July at the Royal Court, and in September at the Phoenix Theatre in London. Osborne developed Luther more fully as a private man tormented by his own body and by his relations with his father than as a religious or political figure. This Luther extends his rebellion against his father to other authority figures, including the pope. Taking a lead from Erickson's observation "that a transference had taken place from a parent figure to universal personages, and that the central theme in this transference was anal defiance,"[35] Osborne presents a Luther who has an obsessive fixation on his own bowel functions. The result is the depiction of the hero of the Reformation as a neurotic.

The play covers a period of twenty-six years in twelve scenes from Martin's 1506 investiture as a monk until 1530. Osborne's "Decor Note" at the beginning of the second of three acts shows that he sees the play progressing from a psychologically interior to a more public level: "After the intense private interior of Act One, with its outer darkness and rich, personal objects, the physical effect from now on should be more intricate, general, less personal; sweeping, concerned with men in time rather than particular man in the unconscious; caricature not portraiture."[36] We see Luther posting his ninety-five theses at Wittenberg, confronting the papal legate, and appearing at the Diet of Worms, but his personal behavior dominates these scenes rather than the substance of his theological position. A knight reflects on the excitement set off by Luther at the Diet of Worms, but reminds us of the man behind the moment: "He'd sweated so much by the time he'd finished, I could smell every inch of him from where I was" (86).

Osborne suggests staging the play using a background of motifs from the work of sixteenth-century Northern European artists, including Hans Holbein, Albrecht Dürer, and Hieronymous Bosch. For example, the second scene calls for the torso of a naked man hanging across an oversized butcher knife suspended over the stage, an enormous cone from which Luther enters, and an oversized "bagpipe of the period, fat, soft, foolish and obscene looking" (25), all strongly echoing Bosch. This scene, which shows Martin about to perform his first mass, ends with Martin appearing in the intensely lit cone carrying a naked child. In the middle of the play, another child appears inexplicably on the steps of the Castle church at Wittenberg as Luther prepares to post his ninety-five theses. These theatrical metaphors for the child within Luther, at the play's end, transmute into his own child, whom he holds in his arms.

As with *A Man for All Seasons*, reviewers of the original production thought they saw the influence of Brecht. *The Guardian*'s Philip Hope-Wallace wrote that the "play is closely, almost slavishly, modeled on Brecht's 'Galileo.' "[37] Kenneth Tynan was even more explicit:

In form, the play is sedulously Brechtian, an epic succession of *tableaux* conceived in the manner of *Galileo*; and the graph of its development is likewise Galilean—a rebel against papist dogma publishes heresies, and is asked by velvet-gloved officialdom to recant. The difference is that Luther rejects the demand; all the same, Mr. Osborne's final scene is an obvious echo of Brecht's.[38]

Except for the use of a knight to announce the time and place of each scene, the staging does not seem peculiarly Brechtian. The early scenes appear more strongly influenced by expressionism, an appropriately solipsistic form for Osborne's dramatization of the inner workings of his protagonist.

Luther furthermore shows little of the social consciousness of Brecht's view of history. Ronald Hayman in his 1968 critical study *John Osborne*, continues to try to force Osborne into Brecht's mold, but points out their fundamentally different approaches to history: "Osborne makes exactly the same mistake as Bolt in thinking that a series of borrowed Brechtian tricks of styling and staging could be made to fit a completely different kind of play, which isolates the hero's personality from its social and historical context."[39] In the next to last scene, Osborne touches briefly on the social implications of Luther's personal choices. A now hostile Knight, standing over the body of a peasant killed during the brief Peasant's War, denounces Luther for siding with the ruling order against efforts to expand his idea of religious freedom to include personal freedoms as well:

Knight: . . . All you've ever managed to do is convert everything into stench and dying and peril, but you could have done it, Martin, and you were the only one who could have ever done it. You could have brought freedom and order in at one and the same time.

Martin: There's no such thing as an orderly revolution. Anyway, Christians are called to suffer, not fight.

Knight: But weren't we all of us, all of us, without any exceptions to please any old interested parties, weren't we all redeemed by Christ's blood? (*Pointing to the peasant*) Wasn't he included when the scriptures were being dictated? Or was it just you who was made free, you and the princes you've taken up with, and the rich burghers and . . . (89)

But Luther retreats into a religious justification: "If He butchers us, He makes us live" (92). Vera Denty, reviewing the original production for *Catholic World*, correctly summarizes Osborne's focus: " 'Luther' is neither a historical, nor religious play; rather it is a character study. . . . Each scene reveals Luther's character development, which is primarily that of a rebel and almost accidentally that of a social revolutionary."[40]

Osborne denied that his intent in writing the play was principally historical: "Historical plays are usually anathema to me, but this isn't costume drama. I hope it won't make any difference if you don't know anything about Luther himself, and I suspect that most people don't. In fact the historical character is almost incidental."[41]

Two plays that we will discuss later in relation to feminist drama, John Bowen's *Florence Nightingale* (1975) and *Virginia* (1981) by Edna O'Brien, both present their characters as subjects for psychiatric analysis. Bowen shows Florence as a neurotic whose behavior results from her parents' repressive influence. She uses her psychosomatically induced ill health to manipulate others and particularly to overwork the men who are devoted to her. O'Brien's play is a psychological biography of Virginia Woolf. As John Elsom observed in his review for *Listener*, "History and Virginia Woolf's literary career are rather perfuntorily handled, for Miss O'Brien concentrates on Virginia's internal history."[42]

Hugh Whitemore's *Breaking the Code*, which premiered at the Yvonne Arnaud Theatre, Guildford, September 15, 1986, and appeared subsequently at the Theatre Royal Haymarket, October 21, 1986, is a biographical drama based on Andrew Hodges's *Alan Turing: The Enigma*.[43] While depicting Turing's involvement in the British decipherment of the German Enigma code during World War II and the early development of the computer after the war, the play also dramatizes the public exposure of Turing's homosexuality and the reactions that followed. Structurally three time lines interweave: Alan's school days, the war years at the secret government code center at Bletchley Park, and events progressing from Alan's 1950s arrest for his homosexuality. The play begins in the middle of the chronology and alternately moves forward and back, progressively revealing information about Turing both from his past and from the unfolding of the case that begins with his reporting a burglary in his house.

The flashback is a particularly appropriate device for psychohistory, which concerns itself with the way that childhood experiences affect adult behavior. The leitmotif of Alan's attachment to and grief for Christopher Morcom, a bright school chum who died prematurely of tuberculosis, runs through the play and presumably explains some of Alan's behavior. However, any psychiatric cause for his homosexuality remains a matter for speculation. The play has some of the qualities of a who-done-it, moving from the question "Who burglarized Alan?" to "Why does Alan behave as he does?" to "Why does Alan commit suicide?" Alan's eccentric behavior—chaining his mug to the radiator, confessing a petty burglary that leads to the exposure of his own homosexuality, placing a towel on the bed before sex—manifest Alan's social naivete and also his scientific and mathematical desire for order that underlies his apparently careless personal demeanor. The idea of "breaking the code" is a theme on several levels: Turing is a professional cryptologist who breaks the social code by being homosexual, but he is also fascinated by the biological code of life, particularly of the brain. Alan's stutter and his sexual drive become signs for the embarrassment of the body that he hopes to escape by his suicide. Hodges suggests this dichotomy, dividing his biography into "The Logical" and "The Physical." In the play's final monologue, Alan explains, "Being a practical man as well as a theorist, I tend to look for practical solutions; in this case namely, viz., to dispose of the body and to release what is left. A mind. Or a nothing."[44]

Nicholas Wright's three-character play *Mrs Klein* dramatizes the conflicts among the 1930s psychoanalyst Melanie Klein; her psychiatrist daughter, Melitta; and Paula, also a psychoanalyst, friend of the daughter, and devotée of the mother.[45] The death of Mrs. Klein's son Hans is the play's inciting incident. The daughter uses her claim that her brother committed suicide as a device to expose the mother's apparent neglect of her children and exploitation of them for her acclaimed text *The Psycho-Analysis of Children*. Paula serves as an outside observer and subsequently discovers that the brother died accidentally. The idea of psychoanalysts analyzing themselves makes the characters very self-reflective.

Based on Phyllis Grosskurth's biography *Melanie Klein*,[46] the play premiered at the National Theatre's Cottesloe stage on August 5, 1988, and enjoyed a popular Broadway revival in 1996. Wright focuses on an episode that occupies only a few pages of Grosskurth's five-hundred-page psychobiography. The style is realistic, the action occupying twenty-four hours in Melanie Klein's London flat. Although the play makes some references to 1930s Germany, particularly to anti-Semitism, the historical period remains relatively unimportant. The historical fact of Melanie Klein's fame as a child psychiatrist adds irony to the interplay between mother and daughter, but audience interest centers on the battle of wits among three very intelligent and self-aware characters and how this conflict reveals both the artifice and substance of psychoanalytic methods. Klein's need to mother her daughter, whom she addresses directly as Melitta, conflicts with her professional rivalry with the same daughter, whom she refers to as Dr. Schmideberg in her professional role. Failing to reconcile herself with Melitta, Klein recognizes Paula as a surrogate daughter. Even though Grosskurth taught Women's Studies at the University of Toronto, neither her book nor Wright's adaptation reflects a particularly feminist perspective. Georgina Born, in a review for *New Statesman*, perceptively analyzed how the play tests Klein's own theories of parent–child behavior, noting that the play "raises also the reality of the destructive relations between women, an issue glossed over by idealist feminism."[47]

Alan Bennett's *The Madness of George III*, which premiered November 28, 1991, at the National Theatre, is, properly speaking, a medical history that specifically rejects a psychiatric explanation for the presumed insanity of

George III. Bennett, an Oxford-trained historian, reflects in the preface on the influence of Herbert Butterfield's *The Whig Interpretation of History*, which made him aware of the need to reexamine the assumptions of historians.[48] Bennett bases his interpretation partly on a 1969 book, *George III and the Mad Business* by Ida Macalpine and Richard Hunter. Hunter and Macalpine began research on George III for a history of psychiatry but concluded that George's problem was the result of a physical malady, porphyria, and not a mental disease.[49] According to Bennett, "Thus afflicted, he becomes the victim of his doctors and a tragic hero" (ix). Bennett's George is an eccentric, kind-hearted, somewhat bumbling king, who genuinely cares for his subjects, a star vehicle for the actor Nigel Hawthorne. George is droll but not particularly introspective; so the focus of the play tends to be more on the varying responses of minor characters to the king's malady than on any particular insight into the inner workings of the character.

In spite of the centrality of George, the play takes much time with the political maneuvering of surrounding characters. Bennett places George's madness in the middle of a political struggle between the Whigs Fox, Sheridan, and Burke, all aligned with a very self-serving Prince of Wales, and the Tory Pitt. This, however, serves less to advance a specific political point of view than to heighten the pathos of the relatively naive George III's vulnerability in the midst of all of these machinations. Bennett reflects, "Any account of politics whatever the period must throw up contemporary parallels. I think if I had deliberately made more of these it would have satisfied or pandered to some critics who felt that was what the play should have been more about" (xviii).

Bennett observed that what he had written was "more like a script for a film than a play" (xxi). A flight of stairs across the entire back of the stage, with curtains and large panels downstage of them, presented an arrangement that, Bennett observed, "is invariably described as 'Brechtian' by critics" (xxi). Except for the intrusion of the twentieth-century Dr. Ida Macalpine near the play's end, Bennett uses no narrative intrusion, only a straightforward episodic form. Also by an intertwining of George's recovery with his reading of the awakening scene in *King Lear*, George's suffering resonates with Lear's.

Bennett's primary concern is theatrical viability, not accuracy. He acknowledges in the introduction that "one casualty of the rewrites was strict historical truth" and proceeds to outline changes that he has made for dramatic effect (xi). He also expresses anxiety about his audience's vague knowledge of the historical context of the incidents that he dramatizes and voices a concern surely shared by all writers of history plays:

As I struggled to mince these chunks of information into credible morsels of dialogue (the danger always being that characters are telling each other what they know *in their bones*), I often felt it would have been simpler to call the audience in a quarter of an hour early and give them a short curtain lecture on the nature of eighteenth-century politics before getting on with the play proper. (xiii)

In spite of Bennett's disclaimer in the preface that he merely thought "George III might be fun to write about" (viii), the play does reflect on the role of kingship. George, in the midst of his raving, makes a connection between the king's throne and the chair that he is strapped to for his "treatment": "Thrown in the chair, enthroned in the chair, the chair a machine for punishing, a fastening chair, a fasten-in chair, a fashioning chair to fashion the King to the ordinary fashion. To fashion the King to the ordinary passion. This is the English way" (56). In other words, the English monarch is largely at the mercy of the uses that others make of him or her.

DOMESTIC BIOGRAPHY

From the beginning most biographical history plays show their protagonists at times "at home," in private moments that help to develop an understanding of the character. In Elizabethan drama these moments are one element in a matrix of principally public events, but through time, the primary focus shifts largely to the private, resulting in domestic biography. The development of romance in historical drama, beginning with Nicholas Rowe, continuing through the plays of Gordon Daviot in the 1930s and those of James Forsyth in the 1950s, usually entails deemphasis of the political events.

Contemporary attitudes about emphasizing domestic features in history are ambivalent. Plays like Robert Bolt's *Vivat! Vivat Regina!* and Peter Shaffer's *Amadeus* were criticized because they reduced important historical figures to the status of players in a domestic melodrama or failed to represent the social problems of the eras they depicted. Some feminists, however, see the exclusion of the domestic or personal as a way to exclude the influence of women on history, and social historians see domestic behavior as an inherently important dimension of history. Modern biographical plays dramatize private events in the lives of public figures for a variety of purposes other than romance: humanizing characters, downsizing historic incident for dramatization, developing psychiatric explanations for the behavior of historical personages, and exploring alternative ways of interpreting history. The amount of attention given to public events may also vary, depending on whether the protagonist operated principally in a public arena. The subjects of biographical drama differ, ranging from figures who have a high public profile; through persons, usually literary or artistic, known principally for their work; to individuals whose life and work are obscure to the audience until given prominence by the writer.

Terence Rattigan's *Ross*, a biographical drama of T. E. Lawrence, provides a good example of the use of a personal focus to reduce the action to a manageable scale on stage.[50] Though not precisely in a domestic setting, the play begins on an RAF base in 1922 where Lawrence is disguised as Airman Ross. Rattigan presents his protagonist in an "unofficial capacity," but still in a public setting that requires Lawrence to conceal his inner personality and thus remain largely enigmatic. We learn more about what he did in the past than why he is doing what he is doing in the play's present. In the third scene Rattigan uses Lawrence's malarial "dream" to introduce major figures from the past and as a device to move into the flashbacks. Of the play's sixteen scenes, the middle eleven deal with Lawrence in Arabia. All scenes except the third are played realistically, and the focus of the middle scenes is on character relationships before and after battles without any attempt to depict the larger actions.

Ross, with Alec Guinness playing Lawrence, opened at the Haymarket Theatre in London on May 12, 1960, two months before Robert Bolt's *A Man for All Seasons*. Bolt was already at work on a film script for David Lean's *Lawrence of Arabia,* released in 1962, and even though the film could depict the spectacular events that occur offstage in Rattigan's play, Bolt's Lawrence is more of a psychiatric study than Rattigan's. Rattigan's play, for example, indirectly makes much of the Turkish general who has captured Lawrence, but that Lawrence was actually raped remains unclear unless the audience already knows, and the impact of this on any later behavior of Lawrence remains undeveloped. Awareness of the censor may have forced Rattigan to underplay Lawrence's homosexuality on stage. His own potential for destruction terrifies Lawrence, but Rattigan does not develop this *Heart of Darkness* theme to the extent that Bolt does in the film. Rattigan has a talent for reducing epic events to stageworthy "backscene" proportions, but he also reduces his central character to a "nice guy" dimension.

Rattigan, who was the most prolific West End establishment playwright until his death in 1977, wrote several history plays, the first, *Adventure Story*, a dramatization of the life of Alexander the Great, which opened at the St. James Theatre, March 17, 1949, with Paul Scofield as Alexander.[51] Although typical of "great man" biography, the play's characterization of Alexander owes something to George Bernard Shaw: a well-known historical figure depicted in mildly flippant moods. Beginning with a prologue showing Alexander's death, the play's ten realistic "tent scenes" cover the period from 336 to 323 B.C. Alexander is tormented by the disapproval of his dead father, Philip, and driven to action by the influence of his teacher, Aristotle, who taught him that action defines a person's worth.

With *A Bequest to the Nation* Rattigan wrote a play closer to domestic biography, depicting Emma Hamilton as a foul-mouthed manipulator whose only hold on Admiral Nelson is her prowess in bed.[52] Opening at the Theatre Royal, Haymarket, on September 23, 1970, with Zoe Caldwell as Emma Hamilton, the play used a unit setting that included a staircase and different levels for the acting areas required by its eight scenes. This also allowed the occasional depiction of simultaneous action, contrasting scenes involving Emma with those showing Nelson's wife, Frances. The central conflict is between Emma's efforts to keep Nelson to herself in London and his desire to fight at Trafalgar. An attempt by his wife to get a letter delivered to Nelson through George, her nephew, provides a secondary plot. Nelson avoids the letter because it reveals Frances's inexplicable forgiveness of him, which he cannot endure. Something of a revisionist history because of its unsympathetic treatment of Emma Hamilton, a popular romantic heroine, the play possesses some of the worst features of domestic melodrama, reducing a major historical figure to a pawn in the conflict between a wronged wife and a predatory mistress. The social satire in John Arden and Margaretta D'Arcy's treatment of the Nelson myth, produced two years earlier, contrasts vividly with Rattigan's use of old formulas for the history play. We will examine Arden and D'Arcy's *The Hero Rises Up* in a later chapter on deconstruction.

Michael Dyne's *The Right Honorable Gentleman*, which appeared at Her Majesty's Theatre, London, on May 28, 1964, and the next year in New York, dealt with the scandal in 1885 involving Sir Charles Dilke, a leading Liberal and contender for prime minister. Seven scenes alternate between Dilke's study and two other settings. This realistic domestic intrigue seems uninfluenced by the sixties and could have been written thirty years earlier.[53] The famous—or in this instance near famous—are shown at home, but "at home" has public repercussions. Dyne leaves unanswered whether Dilke committed the specific impropriety for which he stands accused: a ménage à trois with the daughter of a former mistress.

The biographical bias in stage histories extends even to the use of that most impersonal of sources, the historical document. Writers who incorporated the language from historical documents directly into their plays tended to dramatize social unrest and deal with groups of people rather than prominent individuals, but a few wrote domestic biographies. These include William Francis's *Portrait of a Queen* (1963); John Bowen's *Florence Nightingale* (1975), discussed elsewhere; and several plays by Michael Hastings.

William Francis, in *Portrait of a Queen*, which opened at the Bristol Old Vic on March 2, 1965, and subsequently at London's Vaudeville Theatre on May 6, 1965, presents Queen Victoria's public acts in the matrix of her private life, using almost exclusively the language from surviving documents. In the first act, Victoria's correspondence with her uncle, King Leopold of Belgium, carries most of the exposition and reveals the personal feelings of a very insecure and inexperienced young Victoria. An opening tableau with Albert and Victoria at home, winding wool, sets the tone for a second act that conterpoints public events with their domestic relations. In the third act, after Albert's death, Victoria's journal writing serves to keep her personal responses in the forefront. A "Balladmonger" provides sometimes scurrilous narrative and commentary, linking very short scenes. He occasionally speaks dialogue for the actors, who mime major public events as well as the developing personal relations between Albert and Victoria. Characters at times address, in the first person, an abstract audience, with other unhearing characters on stage. Minor characters periodically function as a chorus, narrating the "public" response to events. With the frequent use of simultaneous action, the play is very fluid, more like a series of overlapping monologues with snatches of dialogue, producing a very distinct and effective style.[54]

Bernard Levin, reviewing the play for the *Daily Mail*, thought that Francis had failed to transmute his documentary sources into developed characters: "The selection of passages, sometimes of single phrases, has been designed to make quick thumbnail sketches of the scenes and characters and some of these are wearisomely cheap . . . you can almost hear the pages of the Dictionary of Quotations rustle."[55] Milton Shulman, in the *Evening Standard*, described the play as "unabashedly loyal, devoted, admiring and sympathetic to the memory of Victoria . . . an entertaining piece of hagiography."[56]

Michael Hastings's work included nondramatic biographies of Rupert Brooke (1969) and of Sir Richard Burton (1978). He developed a formula for enlarging a core of researched data into biographical plays, introducing his mixture of documentation and fiction with *Lee Harvey Oswald: A Far Mean Streak of Independence Brought on by Negleck*, produced at Hampstead Theatre Club, London, November 22, 1966, on the third anniversary of the assassination. It intermingles scenes from the Warren Commission investigation taken verbatim from the report, films, and scenes of "the Oswalds at home" invented by Hastings. A prologue presents a long narrative and film exposition of the public record. The domestic scenes present a fairly straightforward biographical drama with as much focus on mother and wife as on Oswald. Marguerite, Oswald's mother, is a "type": garrulous, sometimes near incoherent, self-centered. Lee remains enigmatic, something of a bully in his relations with Marina, but confused, paranoid and self-deluded. In *The Silence of Saint-Just* (1970) and *For the West* (1977), a play about Idi Amin, Hastings similarly mixed documentary and invented material, a method he describes as "an Aristophanic mould."[57]

In *Tom and Viv*, about T. S. Eliot and his first wife, Vivien Haigh-Wood, Hastings more clearly wove the documentary materials into a series of personal encounters between his principal characters. Research still underpinned *Tom and Viv*, as indicated by the four years of investigation, detailed by Hastings in his introduction, between the play's being commissioned by the Royal Court and its production there on February 3, 1984, under the direction of Max Stafford-Clark. Among other sources, Hastings drew heavily on four months of interviews with Maurice Haigh-Wood, Viv's brother, who died shortly after Hastings began work on the project and who appears as a character in the play.

The approach to his work described by Hastings synthesizes biography and fiction:

When I suggest that the past has to be regained, I mean that we have been thrown up various pictures of men and women, their work and happiness, but in too many cases shapes have not been fully drawn and certain figures are often only noticeable by their absence. And some quality of the past ought to be redeemed. A measure of what it was. . . . To return to the past a configuration of moment and place (as with a play) suggests a greater link, what perhaps Eliot meant by his "present moment of the past." The redeemed historicity.[58]

Similar to Aristotle in his argument for the supremacy of poetry over history, Hastings sees himself not slavishly reproducing reality but enhancing it.

With the exception of three medical functionaries, the characters are five members of the Haigh-Wood family. Eliot's work as a poet, the individuals in the Bloomsbury circle, and various outside events, including two world wars, are referred to, but what the audience sees is the disintegration of the Eliots' domestic relationship. The twenty scenes span thirty-two years with six actors playing eight roles. Having the actor who played Eliot also play the American doctor, who, in the final scene, accuses Eliot of having his wife falsely committed, tends to encourage the audience's detachment rather than emotional involvement. Eliot himself is neither introspective nor forthcoming about his personal relationships; so we see consequences without any attempt to articulate the causes. Eliot loses interest in Viv, but we don't know why; his circle of friends disapprove of her, but for reasons that we are never shown. At various times characters also step out of a scene to provide a brief narration to establish the setting, adding to the disengagement that we experience. The effect is to recreate domestic scenes without fully revealing the inner working of the characters. The play was highly controversial among Eliot aficionados, commercially successful at the Royal Court, and subsequently made into a film.

Brian Oulton's *Mr Sydney Smith Coming Upstairs*, which inaugurated the new Harrogate Theatre on Oct 12, 1972, dramatizes the domestic life of the witty and much quoted Anglican cleric Sydney Smith from 1814 until his death.[59] The public actions of Smith, who was probably known to the audience only by name at best, remain offstage. Oulton focuses on Smith's relations with family members, servants, his canon, and his noble neighbors. The subtitle, *A Happening in Two Parts,* hints that plot is a less important organizing factor here than character. The play covers a period of over twenty years, unified by the locale, a rectory in which moving in and moving out activities frame the action. Smith's son Wyndham serves as a stage narrator, addressing the audience, occasionally entering the action. At its conclusion, the play returns to its beginning, suggesting that Wyndham is continuing to try to be reconciled with his father, but that is a leitmotif. The central crisis comes after the death of Sydney's oldest son, which causes Sydney to question his role as a church jester. A somewhat surrealistic character who keeps appearing in a glowing light from the fireplace is "The Bishop He Will Never Be," who upbraids Smith for his unconventional behavior. This is a charming, somewhat lightweight play in the *Life with Father* vein.

The overt shift away from a public to a private focus is very apparent in Alan Bennett's two one-act plays about prominent British spies, *An Englishman Abroad* and *A Question of Attribution*, produced on a single bill at the National Theatre, Lyttelton, December 1, 1988, and later in the West End under the title *Single Spies*.[60] *An Englishman Abroad*, written originally as a script for a BBC film, dramatizes an actual encounter between the actress Coral Browne and the defected spy Guy Burgess in Moscow in 1958 as related to Bennett by Browne. Browne serves as a narrator in the play but otherwise the style is fairly realistic. Burgess emerges as an amusing, somewhat arrogant, unrepentant, and homesick man with aristocratic yearnings, forced to live a grubby existence in Soviet Russia. What we might call an "out of focus history," the play keeps the conventionally defined historic "moment" in the background and depicts instead a seemingly insignificant encounter, which, in fact, reveals much about the "man" as opposed to the "moment."

A similar redirection of focus occurs in *A Question of Attribution*, which deals with Anthony Blunt, an art historian and adviser to the royal household, who had been exposed as a spy only a few years before Bennett's play. Blunt, played originally by the playwright himself, is being quizzed by an art-loving counterespionage functionary while Blunt simultaneously tries to solve the attribution of a Titian painting. Bennett invents all of the material, interweaving an art history lecture given by Blunt, using projected slides, with a series of scenes in dialogue, including a humorous discussion between Blunt and Elizabeth II about art, forgeries, and life in general. Bennett even bases the issue of the attribution of the Titian paintings on the work of two art historians other than Blunt.[61] With little plot beyond reaching the conclusion that Blunt's spying must be publicly exposed, the play's theme is that counterfeits, whether spies or paintings, have their own kind of reality. Bennett manufactures his own counterfeit: Blunt's situation is real but the incidents presumably are not.

Peter Whelan, whose earlier history play *Captain Swing* will be discussed in the context of Marxist history, also wrote *The School of Night*, a biographical drama about the final days of Christopher Marlowe, based on Calvin Hoffman's *The Murder of the Man Who Was "Shakespeare"*[62] and produced by the Royal Shakespeare Company at The Other Place, Stratford, on November 4, 1992. Whelan incorporates some of the little material known about events surrounding Marlowe's death but invents most of the specific character encounters and dialogue. No evidence exists of actual contact between Marlowe and either Shakespeare or Sir Walter Ralegh. The eleven scenes are staged with minimalist scenery, act II somewhat gratuitously set backstage at plague-closed Rose Theatre, the ruins of which had been rediscovered just a few years before Whelan's play. Other than a few incantation scenes and a recurring vision that Marlowe has, the style is fairly realistic. Whelan uses the play as a vehicle for the very Shakespearean theme of the contrast between Ralegh's circumscribed world of realpolitik and Marlowe's Faust-like ambition for true intellectual freedom. Marlowe appeals to Ralegh:

There are two realms we can live in . . . one of power, the other of poetry. You can't live in both! The poets must always stand against the powerful . . . otherwise truth would die! I ask you to be the poet that you are and dare to be the philosopher that you can be. Turn your back on wealth and power. Pursue knowledge with me as you used to.[63]

Ralegh, who has abandoned his early intellectual promise for the sake of power and safety, finds his political ambitions threatened by his earlier friendship with Marlowe, an iconoclastic atheist who challenges conventions; so Ralegh has Marlowe murdered. Shakespeare, appearing as a young writer/actor using the nom de plume Tom Stone, is something of an onlooker, presumably acting as a spy of the queen, who is concerned about Marlowe's safety. Shakespeare becomes infatuated with Rosalinda, a black Italian commedia actress (the dark lady), who is hopelessly in love with the homosexual Marlowe. The play owes more to the detective/mystery genre than to historical drama, and Marlowe's death seems more the result of conspiracy than character choice.

Personal interchanges that reveal Marlowe's distinct personality, as developed by Whelan, are more important than the details of the plotting. The significant contrasting character, Ralegh, has no opportunity for self-revelation and remains, like Shakespeare, a mechanical foil.

Whelan's most recent history play moves even further into the realm of personal biography and away from his earlier interest in radical history. *The Herbal Bed* premiered at the Royal Shakespeare's Other Place at Stratford on May 23, 1996, subsequently moved to the Barbican, and finally continued its run in a West End theatre. The plot centers on the 1613 accusation that William Shakespeare's daughter, Susanna Hall, had committed adultery. The accuser was subsequently excommunicated by the consistory court in Worcester Cathedral, but the action focuses on the examination of Susanna, her lover, and her servant who witnessed the tryst. While based on a historical incident, the details are largely of Whelan's invention and develop a theme of personal freedom in the face of church and community pressure.

Of the eight new history plays by British writers running in London theatres in 1997, all were personal biographies except the musical *Martin Guerre* with lyrics by Herbert Kretzmer and Alain Boubil, music by Claude-Michel Schönberg, and the book by Boubil and Schönberg. The musical *Always* by William May, Jason Sprague, and Frank Hauser, which opened at the Victoria Palace on June 3, 1997, and the play *H.R.H.* by Snoo Wilson, which opened at the Playhouse Theatre on October 9, 1997, were both about Edward VIII, but dwelled principally on his attachment to his wife. *Always* treats the relationship romantically; *H.R.H.* demonizes the characters. British prime ministers are the subject of two other plays, Clement Attlee in Stephen Churchett's *Tom and Clem* and Harold Macmillan in Hugh Whitemore's *Letter of Resignation*. In the first, which opened at the Aldwych on April 15, 1997, the political events of the Potsdam Conference in July of 1945 disappear into the background of a personal encounter between the surprisingly droll Attlee and the flamboyant Tom Drilberg, a homosexual journalist and newly elected Labour Member of Parliament. Any serious issues are skirted for the sake of character studies by Alec McGowan as Attlee and Michael Gambon as Drilberg. *Letter of Resignation*, which opened at the Comedy Theatre on October 16, 1997, depicts events surrounding the Profumo scandal that brought down Macmillan's Conservative government in the summer of 1963. This public crisis precipitates flashbacks that replay the infidelity of Macmillan's own wife with another member of Parliament over a period of thirty years and expose the facade of the Macmillans' own marriage. Rather than being set in a public arena, the play takes place on a Scottish estate where the Macmillans are on holiday, which emphasizes the focus on the personal rather than the public dimension of the central character.

Pam Gems's *Marlene*, which opened at the Lyric Theatre on April 9, 1997, abandons Gems's serious inquiry into women's roles seen in earlier plays like *Queen Christina* and *Piaf* for the sake of a straightforward character study of Marlene Dietrich. Gems has long admired Dietrich, who appeared as a character in an early version of *Piaf* until Dietrich requested that Gems remove her from the play. Gems changed the character to Josephine Baker. *Marlene*, a star vehicle for actress Sian Phillips, dramatizes the idiosyncratic behavior of an aging Dietrich who cleans her own dressing room before a performance. The production culminates in a retrospective performance of some of Dietrich's better known songs.

Tom Stoppard's *Invention of Love*, which opened at National's Cottesloe Theatre on October 1, 1997, develops the character of the poet and classical scholar A. E. Housman. The play continues Stoppard's fascination with the manipulation of time by not only juxtaposing a young and an old Housman, but also interweaving a plot involving Oscar Wilde, whose homosexuality parallels Housman's. In spite of its postmodern structure, the play is the most purely biographical of any written by Stoppard.

Historians may deal in abstractions, but the allure of drama depends fundamentally on the personal appeal of characters vividly and engagingly created by actors. Theatre has an inherent inclination toward character studies whether they show their protagonists in known and documented public activities or develop largely speculative or even invented psychological and domestic behavior. But the techniques of characterization in history plays since 1956 range from character studies like John Osborne's *Luther* through plays, like Caryl Churchill's *Light Shining in Buckinghamshire*, that emphasize groups of people rather than prominent individuals, to the allegorical stereotypes in an agitprop like Steve Gooch's *The Motor Show*. Even in the face of assumptions that greater forces control individual choices, as in Trevor Griffith's Marxist play *Occupations*, depth of characterization continues to sustain dramatic interest. As we shall see, biography still holds a place in Marxist and feminist history as well as comic and deconstructionist treatments of historic materials. The emphasis on a prominent person does not in itself provide a litmus test for a specific attitude about history. Such an emphasis may, indeed, reveal the assumption, such as Robert Bolt makes in *A Man for All Seasons*, that the actions and values of prominent individuals shape history or even more extremely, as in *Luther*, that the very personal subconscious drives of one person can have a major impact on states and institutions. But a biography may also demonstrate, as in Arden's *Left-Handed Liberty*, that events develop in ways not suspected by their agents, or as we shall later see in Marxist, feminist, and deconstructionist plays, that agency itself is an illusion and that greater social forces victimize individuals. The persistent presence of a biographical bias in history plays may, therefore, reflect as much the perceived demands for successful theatre as it does attitudes about history itself.

NOTES

1. Herbert Lindenberger, *Historical Drama: The Relation of Literature and Reality* (Chicago: University of Chicago, 1975), p. 122.

2. *Home and Foreign Review* (January 1863), p. 219, quoted by Edward Hallett Carr, *What is History?* (New York: Alfred A. Knopf, 1962), pp. 58–59.

3. Cicely Veronica Wedgwood, *The King's Peace* (London: William Collins Sons, 1955), p. 17.

4. Both published with *Adelaise* in *Three Plays* (London: Heinemann, 1956).

5. Not discussed here is Olexander De's terribly written, unfinished, and unperformed, but published, blank verse play, *Stalin: Persona Non Grata* (London: Mitre, 1969). His Stalin talks to himself ("I have no friends . . . I need them not!" [5]) and confronts a variety of allegorical characters.

6. *The Saxon Saint* (St. Giles, 1950) and *The King of Scots* (Edinburgh: St. Giles, 1951).

7. Christopher Fry, *Curtmantle* (London: Oxford University, 1961), pp. 38–48.

8. Robert Bolt, *A Man for All Seasons*, First Vintage International Edition (New York: Random House, 1990), p. 91.

9. Kenneth Tynan, *A View of the English Stage, 1944–63* (London: Davis-Poynter, 1975), p. 283.

10. Quoted by Tynan, *A View*, 285–87.

11. Ibid., pp. 287–88.

12. Robert Bolt, *A Man for All Seasons* [1960] (New York: Vintage, 1990), p. x.

13. Ibid., p. xvii.

14. "Robert Bolt Interview," *Plays and Players*, Dec. 1963, reprinted in *Best of Plays and Players*, vol. 1, ed. Peter Roberts (London: Methuen, 1988): p. 164.

15. *New Statesman* 60, no. 1530 (July 9, 1960), p. 46.

16. *The Guardian*, July 2, 1960.

17. Richard Cave, *New British Drama in Performance on the London Stage: 1970 to 1985* (New York: St. Martin's, 1988), p. 250.

18. Ibid., pp. 249–50.

19. Robert Bolt, *State of Revolution* (London: Heinemann, 1977), p. 29.

20. F. Marcus, *Sunday Telegraph*, May 29, 1977.

21. D. Z. Mairowitz, "State of Revolution," *Plays and Players* 24, no. 11 (Aug. 1977): 17.

22. Tariq Ali and Howard Brenton, *Moscow Gold* (London: Nick Hern, 1990), p. 67.

23. Charles Marowitz, *Confessions of a Counterfeit Critic: A London Theatre Notebook 1958–71* (London: Eyre Methuen, 1973), p. 90.

24. Cave, *New British Drama*, p. 251.

25. James Fenton, "Can We Worship This Mozart?" *Sunday Times*, Dec. 23, 1979, p. 43; and B. A. Young, "*Amadeus*," *Financial Times*, Feb. 6, 1970, p. 15.

26. John Arden, *Left-Handed Liberty* (New York: Grove, 1965), p. 9.

27. Howard Brenton, "Preface," in *Plays: Two* (London: Methuen, 1989), p. xiv.

28. Ibid.

29. Howard Brenton, *Bloody Poetry* [1985, 1988, 1989], in *Plays: Two*, p. 302.

30. Brenton, "Preface," in *Plays: Two*, p. xv.

31. David Pinner, *The Drums of Snow*, rev. version, in *Plays of the Year*, vol. 42 (New York: Frederick Ungar, 1972), p. 313. Original version published in *New English Dramatists 13* (London: Penguin, 1968).

32. Peter Barnes, *The Bewitched*, in *Collected Plays* (Portsmouth, NH: Heinemann, 1981), 197–98.

33. Tim Rice and Andrew Lloyd Webber, *Evita* (New York: Music Theatre International, 1978).

34. E. H. Erikson, *Young Man Luther* (New York: W. W. Norton, 1958), and Roland Bainton, *Here I Stand* (New York: Abingdon-Cokesbury, 1950).

35. Erikson, Young Man Luther, p. 247.

36. John Osborne, *Luther*, 1st American ed. (New York: Criterion, 1962), p. 46.

37. Philip Hope-Wallace, "A Masterpiece with Flaws," *Guardian*, July 29, 1961.

38. Kenneth Tynan, 1961 review reprinted in *A View of the English Stage, 1944–63* (London: Davis-Poynter, 1975), p. 315.

39. Ronald Hayman, *John Osborne*, 2d ed. (London: Heinemann Educational, 1970), p. 49.

40. Vera Denty, "The Psychology of Martin Luther," *Catholic World* 194 (1961): 99.

41. "That Awful Museum," *Twentieth Century* 69 (Jan.–Mar. 1961): 216.

42. *Listener*, January 29, 1981.

43. Andrew Hodges, *Alan Turing: The Enigma* (New York: Simon & Schuster, 1983).

44. Hugh Whitemore, *Breaking the Code* (New York: Samuel French, 1987, 1988), p. 104.

45. Nicholas Wright, *Mrs Klein* (London: Nick Hern, 1988).

46. Phyllis Grosskurth, *Melanie Klein* (London: Hodder and Stoughton, 1985).

47. *New Statesman*, 116, no. 2995 (Aug. 26, 1988): 42.

48. Alan Bennett, *The Madness of George III* (London: Faber & Faber, 1992), p. v.

49. Ida Macalpine and Richard Hunter, *George III and the Mad Business* (London: Allen Lane/Penguin, 1969), p. vii.

50. Terence Rattigan, *Ross* [1960], in *Collected Plays*, vol. 3. (London: Hamish Hamilton, 1964).

51. Terence Rattigan, *Adventure Story* (London: Samuel French, 1950).

52. Terence Rattigan, *A Bequest to the Nation* (London: Hamish Hamilton, 1970).

53. Michael Dyne, *The Right Honorable Gentleman* (New York: Random House, 1966).

54. William Francis, *Portrait of a Queen* (London: Samuel French, 1963).

55. Bernard Levin, *Daily Mail,* May 7, 1965.

56. Milton Shulman, "Wit and Sympathy," *Evening Standard,* May 7, 1965.

57. Michael Hastings, *Tom and Viv* (Harmondsworth: Penguin, 1985), p. 41.

58. Ibid., pp. 42–43.

59. Brian Oulton, *Mr Sydney Smith Coming Upstairs* in *Plays of the Year,* vol. 42 (New York: Frederick Ungar, 1972).

60. Alan Bennett, *An Englishman Abroad* and *A Question of Attribution,* in *Single Spies and Talking Heads* (New York: Summit, [1988] 1990).

61. Bennett, *Single Spies,* p. 41, cites Erwin Panofsky, "Titian's Allegory of Prudence," in *Meaning in the Visual Arts* (London: Peregrine, 1974), and St. John Gore, "Five Portraits," *Burlington Magazine* 100, no. 667 (1958): 351–53.

62. Calvin Hoffman, *The Murder of the Man Who Was "Shakespeare"* (New York: Grosset & Dunlap, 1960).

63. Whelan, Peter. *The School of Night* (London: Warner Chappell, 1992), p. 24.

3

Social History Plays

In France in 1929, Lucien Febvre founded a periodical, *Annales d'histoire économique et sociale*. Over the next twenty years, he and Marc Bloch developed a new approach to historical studies that they called *mentalité* history, often referred to or the *Annales* school of history, or simply, social history. The *Annales* historians attacked what they described as "event history" (*histoire événemen-tielle*): texts focused on major political, diplomatic, or military episodes. Febvre characterized this as the "visible crust of history," the superficial surface.[1] *Mentalité* history rejected the idea that well-known persons make history and focused instead on "modes of thought" or "collective mentalities." Unlike Marxist historians, social historians placed no special emphasis on economic determinants or class differences. They tended to study impersonal determi-nants like climate, soil, or centuries-long cycles of change and to treat subor-dinate classes through "number and anonymity," in other words, through quantitative studies. Rather than recounting unique events and persons, social history attempted to describe the larger forces responsible for the dynamics of societies. It often highlighted external demonstrations of group behavior such as riots, fads, or church attendance and tended toward model building, econometrics, and cliometrics. However, the historian Harvey J. Kaye noted that after the student revolts in Paris in 1968, there was a marked shift by the *Annalistes* to ethnohistory dealing with individual experience at a particular time and place.[2] Critics of social history accuse it of undue concern with the minutiae of everyday life.

Social history shifts attention away from major players to groups of people, the disenfranchised or those simply ignored in the accounts of traditional history, but social history uses no particular political perspective in approaching its material nor advances an overt political agenda. This democratization of history underlies most of New History, and we will find the shift of focus away from major figures even in postmodern plays like Howard Brenton's *The Romans in Britain.*

Sociohistory was anticipated in England by J. R. Green's *History of the English People* (1877–80), which declared its intention to focus on the people more than their rulers, a tradition continued by H. G. Wells's *Outline of History* (1920), which set out to describe the world of "ordinary citizens" for "ordinary citizens."[3] The British also have a strong tradition of local and regional histories, beginning with William Lombarde's *The Perambulation of Kent* in 1570.[4] During the nineteenth century, this interest in local history produced county-by-county multivolume histories, the *Victoria History.* In his study *Local History in England,* W. G. Hoskins points out that, with few exceptions, these local histories tended to be the work of antiquarians rather than true historians, who collected facts rather than assessing causes and effects.[5] These local histories emulated national histories by centering on prominent figures, but they also often amassed data dealing with everyday matters unique to a locality, and they gained increased prestige with the advent of social history.

The community pageants that were particularly popular in Britain and America in the early decades of the twentieth century are an early theatrical expression of this interest in local history, but they at first followed the pattern of focusing on prominent figures, albeit of local importance, and never reached the commercial stage nor were treated as anything more than displays of local pride. With the ascendance of social history, local history plays attain new respectability, and we see a work like *Entertaining Strangers,* which begins as a local celebration, restaged at the National Theatre. Similarly, Alain Boublil and Claude-Michel Schönberg based their 1996 West End musical on Natalie Davis's *The Return of Martin Guerre,* a historical study that recreates sixteenth-century social life in France through the depiction of events in a single village, using contemporaneous court records.

A writer dramatizing ordinary persons confronts a lack of documentary material relating to specific individuals. With working-class subjects, even diaries or correspondence may be rare, so the traditional test of historical validity by reference to supporting documents may not apply. In traditional biographical history plays, the playwright creates minor characters; in social histories, the writer may need to invent all characters, obscuring the conventional distinction between history and fiction.

Social history has two major manifestations in the theatre: dramas of common life in a historically defined period and local histories with a geographically defined frame of reference.

COMMON LIFE HISTORY PLAYS

John Arden's *Serjeant Musgrave's Dance*, the earliest example of a play presenting a view of New History, premiered at the Royal Court Theatre on October 22, 1959. Arden utilizes some nonrealistic Brechtian staging techniques but sets the play in the north of England around 1880, giving his characters very authentic-sounding Yorkshire dialects and taking pains to establish period authenticity in costumes, music, and other staging. Arden, however, subtitled the play *An Un-Historical Parable*, meaning, presumably, that he had not fulfilled the then-prevalent standards of history, that he had placed invented characters and actions in a historic setting rather than reproducing "real" history.

In his earlier plays, particularly *Live Like Pigs* (1958), Arden had created gritty backyard realism. With *Musgrave*, he works much of the same texturing into a historical locale, and thereafter, most of his plays use historical settings. In *Musgrave* four army deserters arrive in a snow-blocked coal town to "recruit" followers. They arrive in the midst of a labor dispute and quickly become pawns in the mine owner's efforts to control the strikers. Arden is not, however, interested principally in the labor issue. The purposes of Musgrave and company gradually unfold as the first act progresses: as Musgrave says, to "make a whole town, a whole nation, understand the cruelty and greed of armies."[6] The deserters have returned with the body of a local soldier, which Musgrave somehow hopes to use to mobilize the town against militarism. However, the deserter's own violent impulses destroy their pacifist mission.

The reviewers accepted Arden's version of history, but objected to the play's gloom and darkness and to what they saw as its didacticism. Alfred Alvarez, writing for *New Statesman*, complained that Arden "insists so much on his own meaning that his characters never get a chance to develop. They have simple purposes, but no complexity of life, like so many puppets."[7] The play ran at only 30 percent of the Royal Court's capacity for its twenty-eight performances in 1959; by its revival in 1965, it played at 61 percent of capacity for thirty-two performances.[8] The play was revised and revived in 1972 and again by the National Theatre at the Cottesloe in 1981.

Charles Wood's antiwar play *Dingo*, which premiered at the Bristol Arts Centre on April 28, 1967, presents its case by showing the impact of war on the common man, using a macabre comic style. Influenced undoubtedly by Joan

Littlewood's music hall version of World War I, *Oh What a Lovely War*, staged four years earlier, Wood turns to World War II, using some of the same music hall techniques, but alternating satiric scenes with realistic depictions of the pain and suffering of warfare. Wood's play would never be accused, as Littlewood's occasionally was, of sentimentalizing war.[9] A screaming tankman burns to death, a fanatical soldier kicks to death a fellow-soldier, and an officer's men lead him into a mine field. The two principal characters, Mogg and Dingo, act as gamesters, commentators, and role players, reminiscent of Vladimir and Estragon in *Waiting for Godot*. Wood's play also shows the influence of an expressionist antiwar play like *The Good Soldier Schweik*. The officers who appear are identified abstractly as in an expressionist play: Hero Colonel, Hero Scot, the Navigator, Fourth Blonde, and so on. The burned up cadaver of the tanker Chalky appears onstage along with other corpses, who speak in the final scenes.

The play has no real plot, except for the completion of the war, just incident: Mogg returns to the prison camp as a battlefield non-commissioned officer and turns into a military fanatic; the Navigating Officer keeps reappearing, lost, to be further misdirected by Dingo. The progress of the war provides a rough chronological progression and each of the six scenes deals with a phase of the conflict: the North African desert, a prisoner-of-war camp, Normandy, another visit to the prison camp, Arnhem, and the postwar victory. At times Wood appears to organize the play around a series of music hall "turns": five hairy British officers in blonde wigs dance in a chorus line; Churchill appears as a hat and cigar, given voice by a ventriloquist. A character called "Comic," who seems to be entertaining the troops, often acts as the master of ceremonies. Wood served for five years in the military and filled his play with military patois, much of it nonsensical to the ear of the uninitiated. Characters occasionally step out of the play's time frame and address the audience directly, but the play contains no substantive narrative elements.

The play's final scene summarizes its iconoclastic treatment of World War II. Dingo explains why he will vote Socialist: "I have not come all this way to be pissed on twice by Mr. Churchill"[10]

Stephen Lowe's *Touched* also deals with the World War II years from the perspective of ordinary citizens, in this case civilians and in a much more realistic and serious vein than *Dingo*. *Touched* opened at the Nottingham Playhouse on June 9, 1977, and was revived on January 20, 1981, at the Royal Court Theatre.[11] The play dramatizes contrasting responses to the war by three sisters in England during the one hundred days between VE Day and VJ Day. With the exception of recorded broadcasts used to establish the wider historical background, the play is relatively realistic. The domestic plot set against these larger events centers around the imagined pregnancy of the middle sister,

Sandra, who has lost an earlier child to an automobile accident during a blackout, and the decision of Betty, the younger sister, to stop mourning the death of a young soldier with whom she had a fleeting relationship. Much of the forward movement of the play arises from unfolding exposition. Even though he focuses on women at home during war, Lowe's perspective is not particularly feminist. These women still define themselves largely in terms of their relationships with men.

Paul Allen in a *Plays and Players* review complained that if Lowe "has made a connection between the public and private worlds he doesn't pass them on,"[12] but the women's lives have been shaped by the war, and ironically, as the war ends on a public level, its personal consequences linger for the women who must find a way to end or minimize its impact so they can get on with their lives. Lowe lacks Wood's political agenda and vitriolic condemnation of the public figures in the background, but he nonetheless redirects our attention to the private repercussions of a major public event.

A much clearer connection between public events and their private impact emerges in Diane Samuels's *Kindertransport*, an exploration of the consequences of the transportation of Jewish children from Germany to England just before the outbreak of World War II. The Soho Theatre Company first performed the play at the Cockpit Theatre in London on April 13, 1993. The Manhattan Theater Club presented it the next year in New York and a London revival by the Soho Theatre Company at the Vaudeville Theatre occurred in 1996. Samuels indicates that she interviewed a number of the former "Kinder" as part of her research for the play, and that she wove many of their actual experiences into its fabric even though her characters are fictional.[13] She focuses her history on a study of one fictionalized child and her relations first with her natural mother and her foster English mother, and later, with her own daughter. Samuels interweaves two actions that occur forty years apart: events over an eight-year period surrounding World War II concerned with the child Eva's coming to England and one day four decades later when Eva's own daughter, Faith, discovers her mother's concealed background. Characters from both periods occupy the stage simultaneously. Different actors play the child and the adult Eva, but one actor plays Lil, her adopted English mother, in both time frames. The discovery of memorabilia from Eva's childhood precipitates the revelation of the past Eva had hidden from Faith. The preparations of Faith, who is in her early twenties, to live on her own away from home are juxtaposed against Eva's rejection of her own German mother, who she feels has betrayed her. Even though Samuels develops a psychiatric study of her protagonist, Eva's neurosis clearly rests in social causes, exposing the personal consequences of major political events.

Rather than World War II, David Storey and Caryl Churchill turn to the English Civil War as a backround for their social history plays. The title of Storey's *Cromwell* sets up an expectation for a biographical history, but Cromwell never appears, an overt disavowal of the "great man" approach to history.[14] Instead, we see the Civil War through its impact on civilians and recruits, a major historical event presented in terms of its effect on everyday characters. Staged at the Royal Court Theatre, where it opened on August 15, 1973, *Cromwell* takes an approach similar to that of *Rosencrantz and Guildenstern*, but rooted in a historical rather than a literary context, and like Stoppard's play, presents a familiar event from the out-of-focus perspective of minor participants. The plot centers on the wanderings of two picaresque Irish recruits who get caught up in a band of villagers escorting a casket that turns out to contain a murdered soldier. The Irish soldiers, O'Halloran and Logan, join first one side of the war and then the other. Storey's treatment of his material is also consistent with his own earlier plays such as *The Contractor*: terse vernacular language in short speeches counterpointed in near stichomythia, a cast of predominately working-class characters, and a lack of clear dramatic structure, resulting in a slice of life presented with almost documentary detachment. *Cromwell* disjoints the action even further by using short scenes sometimes needlessly interrupted by blackouts. Although the title and some costuming establish an expectation that this play concerns the English Civil War, Storey's sense of history is not specific to time and place. He keeps references as to the specific war swirling around his characters vague, and stage directions are equally inexplicit. Storey's apparent desire to stress his anti-war message also leads the play into a strange stylistic shift from realism to a spiritualist ending in which his characters cross what appears to be the Styx into a vision of light.

Caryl Churchill's *Light Shining in Buckinghamshire* dramatizes the Civil War from the perspective of Levellers, Diggers, and Ranters who felt betrayed because the revolution did not extend real property, voting, and religious rights to the common people. The subject provided a vehicle for developing the left-wing issues of the 1970s within the framework of the 1600s, and the play will be examined later in the context of Marxist history plays.

All of these plays develop the social repercussions of war, whereas Timberlake Wertenbaker's *Our Country's Good* uses the eighteenth-century penal system as a vehicle for exploring social behavior in a stressful and dehumanizing environment. Wertenbaker based her play loosely on Thomas Keneally's novel *The Playmaker*, an account of the First Fleet penal colony that settled Australia.[15] Even though the governor of the colony, Arthur Phillip, appears in the play and the action centers on one of the British officers, Lieutenant Ralph Clark, the true protagonists are the prisoners. Keneally and to a greater extent

Wertenbaker focus on the convicts' staging of George Farquhar's *The Recruiting Officer*. Wertenbaker's play, which premiered at the Royal Court Theatre under the direction of Max Stafford-Clark in 1988, appeared in repertoire with *The Recruiting Officer*. Governor Phillip sees the convict production as a civilizing influence, and the major dramatic conflict arises from the attempts of a group of officers to discourage the performance because they believe the prisoners incapable of civilized behavior. The play takes the perspective of a postcolonial history and advances the cause of the oppressed, but the relationships between groups result from faults in the penal system and class biases rather than colonial attitudes per se. Wertenbaker dwells principally on the redemptive power of art and the extent to which people respond to others' positive perceptions. In a note before the published version, she quotes from *Pygmalion in the Classroom*, which cites a study demonstrating that children learn better when their teachers *assume* that they are intelligent.[16] In the play Governor Phillip tells Ralph, who directs the prisoners' production, about Socrates's demonstration in *The Meno* that a slave boy can learn principles of geometry as well as a gentleman: "In other words, he shows that human beings have an intelligence which has nothing to do with the circumstances into which they are born" (24). Wertenbaker uses history here in the long tradition of parable.

LOCAL HISTORY PLAYS

We can think of social history as micro- as opposed to macrohistory—a concern for the smaller rather than the larger picture. Plays that develop local history usually do so at first for the benefit of a local audience, but several of these have attracted national audiences, not because of interest in the specific locale but because of their presentation of a type of history that focuses on everyday life.

Peter Cheeseman, who, in 1962, took over a theatre in a working-class neighborhood at Stoke-on-Trent, produced a series of plays dealing with the history of the Potteries, the region surrounding his theatre. Working with different playwrights or sometimes building a script out of group participation, Cheeseman fostered a dramatic form that he described as a documentary. In the introduction to *The Knotty*, a play that he developed with Peter Terson, he describes the ground rules: "The material used on stage must be primary source material. Words or actions deriving from the events to be described or participants in those events are the only permitted material for the scenes of the documentary. If there is no primary source material available on a particular topic, no scene can be made about it."[17] In addition to written sources, Cheeseman also used tape-recorded interviews with members of the community. His documentaries included *The Jolly Potters* (1964); *The Staffordshire Rebels* (1965), about the Civil War in the region; *Six into One* (1968), concerning the federation of the six Pottery towns; *The Burning Mountain* (1970), about Hugh Bourne and the Primitive Methodists; and *The 1861 Whitby Lifeboat Disaster* (1970), also by Peter Terson.

The Knotty, a "musical documentary" about the creation and demise of the North Staffordshire Railway, first presented at Stoke-on-Trent Theatre on July 12, 1966, and revived in 1967 and 1969, is typical of these plays, containing short scenes, often satirical, unified by songs and dances, and using a narrator and props to indicate changes of locale. The lyrics, usually folk songs, have a narrative function. As Cheeseman explains, "They stand outside the action and can if necessary, I feel, contain our own comments" (xvi). Cheeseman's plays, largely apolitical, have a clear working-class bias. In *The Knotty*, for example, a Chartist, demanding popular representation in government, recruits women who stand in a bread line before the background of the railroad's opening ceremonies, which involve much show of social affluence.

Cheeseman follows the published play with thirteen pages of "Notes on the Script" that detail the source materials used for each scene, a sort of long footnote to the production, but in spite of the concern for evidence, he often manipulates the source material for dramatic purposes. For example, concerning a scene between a landowner and an industrialist, Cheeseman comments, "We created a physical and private confrontation from one which so far as we know took place in the pages of the *Staffordshire Advertiser* and in the political arena. The two men may never have met" (87). The notes also reveal instances when the playwright invented a speech (88) and when a scene developed by improvisation enabled the actors to stitch together otherwise unrelated pieces of primary material (89).

The production also makes its own comments on the material in a manner similar to that of Brecht's epic theatre. For instance, the stage direction for a scene depicting the dedication of the railroad reads, "THE CROWD PERFORM AN UNKIND VERSION OF CEREMONY WITH RIDICULOUS VOICES" (26). In his "Notes on the Script" Cheeseman justifies this: "But I think though some other scenes were based on an ironic attitude to the event, this is the only one which actually abused the incident by describing it as a farce. The attitude in fact grew naturally from the pompous tones of the newspaper in contrast to the obviously disorderly chaos in the ceremony" (87).

Cheeseman believed that the documentaries required an acting style with "considerable restraint and objectivity in the playing of each part. There is a point perceptible where extravagance of characterization clearly begins to direct the attention of the audience away from the narrative line." The actor "must have a totally candid and honest basic relationship with the audience to start with. It is almost as if this permitted the audience to trace on him the shape of each character when they could see it so clearly standing out against his own openness" (xvii–xviii).

Inherent in the reliance on documentary sources is a striving for objective validation, almost a return to the old positivist call for the historian as a detached observer. Cheeseman, however, recognized the impossibility of true objectivity but saw in the collective nature of his production process a method for allowing errors to cancel one another: "The fact that the process of creation of the text of the documentary is controlled by a group of people, even under fairly strong leadership, rather than just one person, also tends to preserve the contradiction of viewpoint inherent in every historical event, controlled as it is by a number of people" (xiv–xv).

Don Taylor's documentary sources for *The Roses of Eyam* consisted primarily of names taken from the parish register. The play, which opened at the Northcott Theatre in Exeter on September 23, 1970, tells the story of a Derbyshire village stricken with plague in 1665–66 by a box of clothing shipped from London. Taylor calls for a cast in excess of fifty. Most appear on stage in the play's second scene, as a stage direction explains, to act as a chorus, but they mainly create a visual image for the impact of the plague on the village.[18] We see them assembling in diminishing numbers until only a handful remain at the play's end a year later. A unit set depicts the entire village and allows scenes to flow into one another. A village madman, identified only as Bedlam, functions as a prophet and provides some tie between scenes. He also serves as a theatrical element that allows the play to move at points beyond its predominantly realistic style. Set in the aftermath of the English Civil War, the play centers on the conflict between a new young clergyman, William Mompesson, and his Puritan predecessor, Thomas Stanley. The two finally unite to persuade the villagers to remain at home and not spread the plaque to neighboring towns. Even though the plague finally ends, most of the villagers die. Mompesson becomes thoroughly dispirited and the play's overall effect is strongly depressing. Although Mompesson clearly serves as the central character, the villagers in their collective identity act as the true protagonist, choosing to remain in Eyam so as not to spread the plaque.

Keith Dewhurst's dramatization of Flora Thompson's popular trilogy *Lark Rise to Candleford*[19] recreates village life in Oxfordshire in the 1880s, what Michael Coveney, reviewer of *Financial Times*, described as "a detailed and colourful mosaic of village rite, custom and gossip."[20] *Lark Rise* premiered at the National Theatre's Cottesloe stage on March 29, 1978, and its sequel,

Candleford, on November 14, 1979, both as "promenade" productions, intermixing performers and audience, an idea that Dewhurst traces to productions
of *Orlando Furioso* (1971), *1789* (1971), and William Gaskill's *The Speakers*
(1974) and *Passion* (1977). "When read, these plays may seem more like film
or television scripts than ordinary plays. That is because the promenade enables
one to cut away and, if the actors pull focus strongly, to achieve very brief effects
indeed."[21] In fact, Dewhurst makes nothing of the proximity of the audience,
which might as well not be present. As he explains in the plays' introduction,
"The actors are in 1880 and the audience is in the present" (15). The
simultaneous scenes do allow the action to flow quickly. The child Laura is a
thinly veiled autobiographical portrait of Flora Thompson, but the real protagonist is the village, and each of Dewhurst's plays occupies a day in the life
of the village: *Lark Rise*, a spring day; *Candleford*, a winter day. Laura provides
a few narrative introductions, and the company periodically sings to the
accompaniment of a band, but otherwise the style is realistic. The plays have
little action or plot, and scenes largely consist of disconnected events in the
daily life of the villagers. The primary appeal is to sentiment and nostalgia.

    The Roses of Eyam, Lark Rise, and *Candleford* are plays about communities
staged by professional actors, but Ann Jellicoe, beginning in 1978, devoted
herself to community history plays staged by members of the community. In
a preface to David Edgar's *Entertaining Strangers*, Jellicoe indicated that she had
discovered "a new form of Theatre" with the production of *The Reckoning*, a
play written for the Comprehensive School in Lyme Regis, Dorset, in 1978.
She describes it as a "promenade performance" about the landing of the duke
of Monmouth in Lyme Bay. After this she formed the Colway Theatre Trust,
which with foundation and Arts Council support, allowed her to devote seven
years to community drama. At the time of her writing in 1985, she was
resigning to protest a 50 percent cut in South Western Arts funding.[22] Her
second community history play, commissioned by the Southwest Music Theatre and produced in Exeter in 1979, was *The Bargain*, which dealt with Judge
George Jeffrey, the presiding judge at the trials of the Monmouth rebels. Jellicoe
wrote *The Tide*, which she produced at Axminster in Devonshire in 1980, and
in 1984, adapted a story by Fay Weldon, *The Western Women*, staged in Lyme
Regis, about the role of women during the siege of Lyme during the Civil War.
None of these plays was published. Jellicoe came to devote more of her energy
to directing, and she began to encourage other playwrights to develop scripts
that dramatized community history. She persuaded Howard Barker to write
The Poor Man's Friend for Bridport in 1981. John Downie wrote *Today of All
Days* for Crediton, and Shelia Yeger wrote a play for Ottery St. Mary.[23]

Allen Saddler, reviewing *The Reckoning* for *Plays and Players*, complained, "It is all action. . . . Events proceed so quickly that there is no time to examine the Catholic or Protestant case."[24] Jellicoe's objective, however, is not thematic. She writes in *Women and Theatre*:

It was extraordinary, the people of Lyme, in rehearsal and in performance, watching a play about themselves. There is a unique atmosphere. It's partly the promenade style of performance, partly that the play is especially written for the town, but it has never failed, that excitement, they just go wild. . . . What I love is that it is slowly building something in the community.[25]

Saddler described the degree of audience involvement encouraged by the promenade stage: "People rush by in terror, beg for mercy or confide strange secrets in your ear; . . . proclamations are read from various parts of the hall. Soldiers burst in. Bands play. Prisoners are dragged off screaming. Brawls break out just where you are standing."[26]

The most successful of the community dramas written under Jellicoe's influence was *Entertaining Strangers* by David Edgar, originally produced in St. Mary's Church, Dorchester, Nov. 18, 1985. As in *The Roses of Eyam, Entertaining Strangers* builds on a community response to an epidemic, in this case the 1854 cholera outbreak. The title is from Hebrews 13: "Be not forgetful to entertain strangers; for thereby some have entertained angels unawares." The play uses 169 named characters *plus extras*, most of whom we encounter on "promenades" through the town. These small roles do not call for intense emotion or elaborate character development, making them well suited for community performance. Even the principal characters are noted for their lack of emotionality. The play does focus on two figures: the breweress Sarah Eldridge (the production was underwritten in part by the Eldridge Pope Brewery) and the minister Henry Moule, who became a local hero during the epidemic and, as Edgar dramatizes events, consequently discovered his place in the community.

The play begins with three modern narrators who subsequently change into Victorian costume, but at various points, other characters deliver narrative passages, usually of a sentence or two, spoken in sequence, producing a choral effect. Edgar frequently has two actors play the young and old versions of a character, sometimes appearing simultaneously, with the older version aware of the younger. Children's songs in the background underscore many of the transitions.

One of the narrators comments in the beginning that even though sermons, pamphlets, and tracts by Moule survive, no information exists about his response to the suicide of his son. "So how we treat *that*, too, can't be how we know it happened, just how it could have done."[27]

Even though written as a community's history of itself, with extensive community involvement in its development and initial performance, the play's wider dramatic appeal led to its being restaged in a revised form by Peter Hall at the National's Cottesloe Theatre, where it opened on October 15, 1987, to a generally warm critical response.

Edgar came to Jellicoe's Dorchester project with a background of writing community history. After starting as a writer of agitprop plays, Edgar, in the midseventies, began to dramatize local history in order to make a political point. *The Case of the Workers' Plane*, produced in Bristol in 1973, presented the industrial issues surrounding the construction of the Concorde, and *Events Following the Closure of a Motorcycle Factory*, produced in Birmingham in 1976, dealt with the shutting of the Norton-Villiers-Triumph factory at Meriden. Both plays were written principally as documentaries.

Other socialist and Marxist writers also turned to local social histories. John McGrath's *The Cheviot, the Stag, and the Black, Black Oil* (1973) was written as a social history of a region of Scotland where his troupe, 7:84, toured. Steve Gooch developed *The Motor Show* (1974) with community theatre players in the auto factory city of Dagenham. *Taking Our Time* (1978) by Leeds-based Red Ladder Theatre dramatized the lives of local nineteenth-century weavers. Barrie Keeffe's *Better Times* (1985), written for the Theatre Royal, in working-class Stratford East, dramatized a 1920s tax revolt in the nearby London borough of Poplar. We will examine these plays in a later chapter.

Social history's diversion of attention from individual biography to group behavior underpins much of the Marxist and feminist drama that we will consider later. A large majority of those plays highlight oppressed or disenfranchised groups and differ from the plays discussed here only to the extent that they advance specific political agendas.

NOTES

1. Lucien Febvre, *Combats pour l'histoire* (Paris: Armand Colin, 1965), p. 62.

2. Harvey J. Kaye, *British Marxist Historians*, new ed. (New York: St. Martin's, 1995), p. 226.

3. Gertrude Himmelfarb, *The New History and the Old* (Cambridge, MA: Harvard University, 1987), p. 2.

4. William Lombarde, *The Perambulation of Kent* [1570] (Bath: Adams and Dart, 1970).

5. W. G. Hoskins, *Local History in England* (London: Longmans, Green, 1959), p. 23.

6. John Arden, *Serjeant Musgrave's Dance: An Un-Historical Parable*, in *Plays: One* (New York: Grove, 1978), p. 37.

7. *New Statesman*, October 23, 1959. Also see Harold Hobson's review in *Sunday Times*, October 25, 1959.

8. Richard Findlater, ed., *At the Royal Court* (New York: Grove, 1981), app. 2.

9. See, for example, W. A. Darlington, *Daily Telegraph*, June 21, 1963.

10. Charles Wood, *Dingo* (New York: Grove [1967] 1969), p. 96.

11. Stephen Lowe's *Touched*, rev. ed. (London: Methuen, 1981). First published by Woodhouse, Todmorden, 1979.

12. *Plays and Players*, 24, no. 11 (Aug. 1977): 19.

13. Diane Samuels, *Kindertransport* (London: Penguin, 1995), ix.

14. David Storey, *Cromwell* (London: Jonathan Cape, 1973).

15. Thomas Keneally, *The Playmaker* (London: Hodder and Stoughton and Sceptre, 1987).

16. R. Rosental and L. Jacobson, *Pygmalion in the Classroom* (New York: Holt, Rinehart, Winston, 1968), cited in Timberlake Wertenbaker, *Our Country's Good* (London: Methuen, 1988), p. iv.

17. Peter Cheeseman, "Introduction and Notes," in *The Knotty* (London: Methuen, 1970), p. xiv.

18. Don Taylor, *The Roses of Eyam* (London: Samuel French, 1976), p. 6.

19. Flora Thompson, *Lark Rise to Candleford* (Oxford: Oxford University, 1946).

20. *Financial Times*, March 30, 1978.

21. Keith Dewhurst, *Lark Rise to Candleford* (London: Hutchinson, 1980), p. 15.

22. In David Edgar, *Entertaining Strangers* (London: Methuen, 1986), p. 4.

23. Ibid.

24. Allen Saddler, "The Reckoning," *Plays and Players*, 26, no. 5 (Feb. 1979): 29.

25. Quoted in K. A. Berney, *Contemporary Dramatists*, 5th ed. (London: St. James, 1993), p. 333.

26. Saddler, "Reckoning," p. 29.

27. Edgar, *Entertaining Strangers*, p. 13.

4

Oppositional History Plays

Revision is a natural part of the process of writing history. New information and new ways of treating existing information cause revisitation and modification of the historical record, but the term *revisionist history* implies a more fundamental challenge to the way of doing business. Closely associated with the political values of the New Left that emerged in the United States and Europe in the 1960s, the revisionist historians set out to do more than reexamine: they sought to bring about a rejection of the prevailing historiography of the hegemony, the ruling powers, by directly contradicting the values of that official history. Where Old History, in the view of the New Historians, had actively distorted the past in order to uphold traditional values, New History actively sought to overthrow those values. Certainly some historians embraced the techniques of New History simply because it offered new and previously neglected methodologies, but the basic impulses driving change were political.

One method of reversing the values of the dominant political view was to take the perspective of the disenfranchised, the defeated, the outcast. To the extent that all of New History rejects the values of Old History, it is revisionist; so we will use the term *oppositional history* for a methodology that compensates for perceived biases in the established history specifically by creating an antithetical viewpoint.

Oppositional history is clearly a relative term. Opposite to what? A play that characterizes the English as unjust invaders in Ireland, like Brian Friel's *Making History*, may be an orthodox history in Dublin, but oppositional history in Belfast. Plays that show the working class victimized by an exploitative capitalist establishment would be oppositional histories if staged in West End theatres, but represent historical orthodoxy for the working-class audiences for which they are often written. That West End producers would never stage such plays shows the extent to which theatre depends on and reinforces the values of its particular audience. Theatre frequently appears to preach only to the converted, but as a public art, it necessarily depends on a climate of public opinion. Playwrights who wish to advocate an alternative history have a variety of strategies for dealing with the conservatism of audiences. They can seek a special, sympathetic audience; they can outrage their audience; they can temper a play's themes in order to appeal to the sympathetic if not the converted; or they can work through subterfuge and indirection to insinuate what the play, in safety, cannot declare directly. Ideally, they can change the values of the audience itself or those values can change in response to other pressures. The contemporary British intellectual climate has called into question attitudes about history itself to a sufficient extent to precipitate some skepticism about orthodox Whig or positivist histories. If this process were complete, oppositional history would become orthodox history.

Oppositional history includes both Marxist and feminist plays that we will examine in separate chapters, but here we will look particularly at a group of what we may loosely describe as "loser's histories" and at postcolonial histories, plays that advance the cause of politically oppressed cultures.

The idea of dramatizing the outlook of the losing side of a historical encounter is as old as *The Persians*, written about 472 B.C., but whereas Aeschylus's play encourages our sympathy for the defeated, it leaves uncontested the official version of events. Euripides's *Trojan Women* (415 B.C.) comes closer to revisionist history in its challenge to the prevailing political orthodoxy. Such treatments of history remain rare because contesting the status quo entails risk and a social environment that will tolerate unorthodoxy, but supporting the dominant order invites reward and popularity.

The presence of official censorship in Britain until 1968 certainly discouraged some of the defiance of establishment history. Edward Bond's *Early Morning* and John Osborne's *A Patriot for Me* were among the history plays initially denied public performance by the Lord Chamberlain's Office. The Licensing Act, which since 1737 had given the government the power to require changes in scripts or even to prohibit production of plays considered politically or morally unacceptable, was finally revoked by the Theatres Act of September 28, 1968.

Even apart from official censorship, economic and political pressures could work to suppress plays that threatened the orthodox history. For example, in 1967, when Kenneth Tynan, a respected critic and the National Theatre's literary manager, wished the National Theatre to stage the German playwright Rolf Hochhuth's *Soldiers*, which portrayed Churchill as an accomplice to the 1943 assassination of the Polish anti-Communist leader General Wladyslaw Sikorski, the production was blocked by the chairman of the National Theatre board, Oliver Lyttelton, Lord Chandos, who had been a member of Churchill's wartime cabinet. It was produced at the New Theatre in London in December 1968, following the abolition of stage censorship.[1] Similarly, late in 1968 after the rescission of the censorship laws, the National Theatre Board discussed staging Conor O'Brien's *Murderous Angels*, but concern about being sued for libel prevented production.[2]

Historians must contend with the often traditional values of publishers, but they escape the economic dependence of theatrical production on the traditionally monied, well-educated British theatregoer. The emergence of revisionist history in drama, like other themes of the New Left, was linked to the development of alternative audiences and, in some instances, new modes of production. The advent of fringe theatre in the sixties, devoted to radical theatre, in both form and content, provided a venue for histories that challenged the establishment. As we shall later see, both Marxist and feminist theatre developed by instituting their own production companies and by seeking to generate new audiences. And importantly, because of their relatively greater staging resources, conditions were, for a time, conducive to experimenting with alternative histories at the Royal Court Theatre, the Royal Shakespeare Company, and the National Theatre. The association of the Royal Court Theatre first with New Wave and then with New Left theatre resulted partly from the progressive political views of a succession of artistic directors beginning with George Devine and continuing through William Gaskill, Oscar Lowenstein, Stuart Burge, and Max Stafford-Clark. The Royal Court was willing to defy censorship, chance economic disaster even as a nonprofit theatre, and develop in the Theatre Upstairs, a venue for limited productions of very experimental plays. The Royal Shakespeare Company (RSC) after 1971 had an alternative theatre space and even the National Theatre (NT) responded to incentives during the early seventies from the Labour-controlled Arts Council to broaden the social appeal of their work. Both the RSC and NT at times had an administration sympathetic to left-wing causes. As a consequence we find oppositional history plays staged in every type of venue in Britain ranging from state-supported theatres to fringe groups.

LOSER'S BIOGRAPHY

Obviously, not all prominent historical figures met with success, and failure holds a continuing allure in historical drama, perhaps because we find recompense in the fall of persons of high rank or because such falls are the raw material for tragedy.[3] Traditional tragedy usually implies some degree of culpability on the part of the protagonist, and compensation results from his or her growth or acquired knowledge. In oppositional history, the failure of the protagonist results principally from external causes and calls into question the legitimacy of the dominant social order.[4] A play like Michael Hastings's *Lee Harvey Oswald* (1966) deals with a failing character but upholds the values of the dominant society and is therefore not an example of oppositional history. In contrast, the five examples to be discussed use personal failure to question historically held standards of success.

John Whiting's *The Devils*, commissioned by Peter Hall and produced by RSC at the Aldwych Theatre, February 20, 1961, stands at the juncture between the old humanistic biography and the politically conscious New History.[5] Set in France and depicting events occurring over a period between 1623 and 1634, the play, an adaptation of Aldous Huxley's *The Devils of Loudun*, resonates with themes similar to those developed by Arthur Miller in *The Crucible*, which had been a popular play in London when it appeared there in 1956. With a more corrupt, more articulate, but less introspective protagonist than *The Crucible*, *The Devils* develops much the same anticlerical witch-hunt subject through the dramatization of the destruction of the libertine priest Urbain Grandier, on charges of diabolism, an accusation made by a sexually frustrated nun whom he has rejected. The church and government authorities under the influence of Richelieu quickly seize these accusations as a means of destroying Grandier, whom they see as a threat to a variety of orthodox opinions. Whiting uses secondary characters in fixed groups of two or three to represent the antagonistic orthodoxy: Mannoury, a surgeon, and Adam, a chemist, are voices for the prevailing science; the bishop of Poitiers and the exorcist priest Barré represent the church; de Laubardemont and Richelieu, the state. D'Armagnac, the governor of Loudun, and DeCerisay, the chief magistrate, are enlightened rationalists who try to protect Grandier, but they are powerless in face of the combined forces of church and state. Grandier is simultaneously a victim of the destructive forces of his society and of his own appetites for both sensual and spiritual gratification. J. D. Hurrell, in his study "John Whiting and the Theme of Self-Destruction," notes an important change that Whiting made in this respect in his source material:

Huxley sees the whole series of events leading up to Grandier's execution as no more than a concatenation of circumstances with a chronological but no causal connection, whereas Whiting portrays Grandier as committed by both logic and desire of a way of life that is a deliberate flirtation with spiritual and physical death, an engagement with the sense that it is so complete and so intense that it amounts to a kind of spirituality.[6]

However, Grandier's arrogance, insensitivity to a young girl whom he has impregnated, and final thirst for his own self-destruction prevent the audience from maintaining their initial sympathy for him.

The Devils lacks an obvious political target for its British audience such as McCarthyism provided for *The Crucible* in the United States. Like Peter Shaffer's *The Royal Hunt of the Sun* three years later, *The Devils* denounces examples of religious and social oppression in history that the establishment had already denounced; so although the play dramatizes an event from the perspective of the victim, it is not really revisionist history and emerges less as a protest against a specific social or political ill than a generalized condemnation of any pressure for social conformity.

The first new play produced by the Shakespeare Memorial Theatre in its eighty-two years of existence, *The Devils* inaugurated the newly named Royal Shakespeare Company's decision to add a London season to its Stratford repertory and was given an appropriately elaborate send-off with a company of fifty-nine. Locale changes occur in Shakespearean fashion with overlapping groups of characters entering and exiting. H.A.L. Craig, reviewing the play for *New Statesman*, wrote:

Mr. Whiting's construction of *The Devils* is also of deep cunning. It is made up of many short scenes that sometimes follow, sometimes overlap, and sometimes climb over each other. A word at the end of one scene may prompt the next, or dab its meaning. This gives the kind of fluidity that avoids the stilting of historical style.[7]

In one instance Grandier makes love to his young student while the nun Jeanne, presumably in her cell in another part of Loudun, describes their actions as if they were part of her own personal dream. Whiting uses no narrator in the play, but a character known as "The Sewerman" acts as a confidant for Grandier and as a spokesman for the cynical materialism that underpins much of the play. The use of onstage torture to emphasize the cruelty of the church is a technique reminiscent of Jacobean drama, which *The Devils* resembles in tone. The play provided the basis for a 1968 opera by the Polish composer Krzysztof Penderecki and for a 1971 film.

James Saunders based *Next Time I'll Sing to You* on *A Hermit Disclosed* by Raleigh Trevelyan, an investigation of the life of the Canfield Hermit, James Mason (1857–1942), who lived alone for the last thirty-six years of his life, sustained by daily food drops from his brother. Questors Theatre, Ealing, produced the play initially in late 1962, and it was revived at the New Arts

Theatre, London, on January 23, 1963, with Michael Caine as Meff, in a production later transferred to the Criterion Theatre. Four actors, hired by the "director" Rudge, who is obsessed with the life of the Hermit, meet nightly in an attempt, through dramatization, to understand the Hermit's motives. This is less a history play than a dramatization of a historian's search to understand the past. Dust, one of the actors, reminds Rudge that the Hermit's life that they attempt to recreate is actually a figment of Rudge's mind: "*You* are the engineer of this lopsided once-nightly little dreamworld. It's *your* brains they're gawping at. . . . You sit there like some fragmentary Hamlet, complaining of a martyrdom you dreamt up out of your own head. Let's get on for God's sake, you say, where's the Hermit, you say, and who lost him? You, you, you!"[8] However, near the play's end Rudge realizes that he cannot impose order on what he increasingly discovers to be the inexplicable past of his Hermit:

To impose order on nature, this was to be my life's work. A hill or two there—a lake there—with ducks swimming on it—not deep enough to drown in. . . . And when I try for this, when I begin to follow that winding magic path leading through a beautifully ordered park of knowledge to the tea gardens of illumination—what do I find?
    Slight pause.
A *zoo*; a zoo with all the cage doors left open by an idiot keeper, where the animals roam at will. (55–56)

The little company of actors eventually realizes that all persons are to a large extent hermits, trapped alone in themselves.

    The self-consciously theatrical play, which includes direct references to the audience, alternates between seriousness and fooling. The recreation of the events of the Hermit's life consumes relatively little of the play's time, most of which is spent with discussion and game playing, reflecting the influence of *Waiting for Godot*. Characters treat one discussion like a cricket match with points made for a good argument, and the actress Lizzie claims to be her identical sister who has the same name.

    John Arden, the most prolific writer of historical drama after 1956, describes himself as an anarchist and, understandably, writes oppositional history. All of his history plays pit an oppressive structured society against a disorganized, impulsive individual, what he characterizes as a dialectic between the "rectilinear" principles of government and the "asymmetrical curvilinear" individual.[9] The individual almost always fails, but the conflict calls into question the legitimacy of the established order. Arden's first major history play, *Serjeant Musgrave's Dance* (1959), discussed earlier as an example of social history, explodes the Victorian myths of colonialism and industrial expansion by taking as his central characters a group of army deserters. Arden had three separate history plays published in 1965, all dealing with historical figures who were failures: *Ironhand, Armstrong's Last Goodnight*, and *Left-Handed Liberty*.

The first, *Ironhand*, an adaptation of Goethe's romantic robber drama *Goetz von Berlichingen* (1773), was produced in Bristol in 1963. With a large cast and thirty-nine realistically treated scenes, this is historical pageantry in the best nineteenth-century tradition. Love interest develops around the unful-filled passion between Goetz's sister and his former friend who has turned enemy, Adelbert von Weislingen, a knight in the service of the bishop of Bamberg. Goethe presented the rebellion of the German free knights, led by Goetz, as an early failed attempt at German nationalism. Arden was attracted to the play because it provided a vehicle to dramatize the destruction of an anarchist advocate of personal freedom by an ordered feudal society, a theme similar to that soon developed by him in *Left-Handed Liberty*, discussed previously as an example of biographic history. Common law that favors the German free knights led by Goetz conflicts with the more hierarchal Roman law that favors the emperor. The action, set in the sixteenth century, revolves around the struggle between Goetz and representatives of the emperor. A serf rebellion develops toward the end of the play and mirrors some of the same issues surrounding the rights of the Free Knights. The moral does not become overt until the final scene: "Freedom. And no warfare. Freedom. And good order."[10] Arden made a fairly straightforward adaptation but spread the "fault" more evenly between sides than did Goethe. Arden tempers Goethe's heroic aggrandizement and adds an element of pacifism. Arden's Goetz tells one of his mercenary followers, "You should have asked them all why, you should know *why* you are fighting!" (157).

Arden returned to the same theme in *Armstrong's Last Goodnight*, which premiered at the Glasgow Citizen's Theatre May 5, 1964, opened at the Chichester Festival Theatre, July 6, 1965, and was restaged at the National Theatre at the Old Vic, October 12, 1965, under the direction of John Dexter with Albert Finney playing Armstrong. The play depicts the events leading to 1530 the execution of Johnny Armstrong of Gilnockie, a Scots bandit living by the border between Scotland and England. Armstrong's execution was manipulated by Sir David Lindsay of the Mount, poet and herald to the court of James V of Scotland. Arden cautioned in an introduction, "This play is founded upon history; but it is not to be read as an accurate chronicle."[11] The connection of Lindsay with Armstrong is, by Arden's own admission, an invention of the playwright.

The first act establishes the basic conflict quickly—James the Fifth of Scotland needs Gilnockie to stop raiding England to prevent giving Henry

VIII justification for raiding Scotland—but the play bogs down in act II with an affair between Gilnockie and Lindsay's mistress, another character invented by Arden. Lindsay, the diplomat sent to tame and ultimately to destroy Armstrong, emerges as a polished and charming Machiavellian: "serpent eneuch to entwine the Armstrangs in your coil" (253). Armstrong, a somewhat infantile character with a stammer, can be impulsively violent or charming, but neither he nor the suave Lindsay develops into a complex or sympathetic character. This is not a drama of character but an almost allegorical enactment of the conflict between the primitive and the civilized man.

Even though the power of the English Henry VIII lingers in the background, *Armstrong's Last Goodnight* is not a play about colonial oppression. A Scottish king destroys Armstrong. This is also no Whig history bemoaning the royalist defeat of a democratic rebel. Armstrong's actions are self-gratifying, and his only political consciousness is a fantasy of himself as king.

While crediting the influence on the play of Conor Cruise O'Brien's narrative history of the Congo crisis, *To Katanga and Back*, Arden points out that he has based neither characters nor episodes on the Congo conflict but rather adopted "a basic similarity of moral" (239). Arden subtitles his play, *An Exercise in Diplomacy*, and in both the twentieth-century Congo and sixteenth-century Scotland, diplomacy, or the "doubleness of the world" (237), ruthlessly destroys the aberrant rebel in order to maintain the political power structure. The audience responds with divided sympathies to this dialectic with reason and order on one side and on the other, emotion and anarchy.

Lindsay also acts as the play's principal narrator although other characters occasionally address the modern audience directly. The staging uses the medieval convention of simultaneous mansions, with Armstrong's castle stage right and the king's palace stage left. The somewhat episodic play, divided into forty-two French scenes, is chronologically structured with sixteen actors playing the thirty roles.

Arden introduces numerous ballads, with his own lyrics, used for entertainment value rather than as a commentary in any Brechtian manner. Once a song covers an onstage journey. Crediting Arthur Miller's invention of an early American stage dialect for *The Crucible* (239), Arden creates a patois of old Scots dialect, complete with an eighty-three-word glossary in the published version. The dialect was apparently not a problem for the English audience and critics responded positively to the production.

John Osborne's 1965 play *A Patriot for Me* uses a minor historic incident to develop a drama about homosexuality, which was consequently denied a license for performance by the lord chamberlain.[12] It was nonetheless staged as a for-members-only production at the Royal Court, June 30, 1965, with Maximilian Schell as Redl and became the most successful production of the Royal Court's season, running for fifty-three performances at 92.5 percent of capacity.[13] The play follows the rise and fall of Albert Redl, an Austrian officer who gradually recognizes his own homosexuality. While rising to be a major officer in Austrian counterespionage, he falls victim to blackmail and becomes a spy for the Russians. Finally discovered, he commits suicide. To create authenticity, Osborne uses a large projected blowup of the *Times* article of May 30, 1913, reporting Redl's death. The play spends a good deal of time establishing the social formality and masculine bravura of the Austrian army that provide an important context for Redl's homosexuality, but outside historical events do not figure significantly in the plot. The play is biographical, but Redl is not particularly articulate in his introspection. Unlike *Luther* four years earlier, this play advances no psychiatric explanation for its protagonist's behavior and appears more interested in the way that society punishes him for his nonconformity. Set in Lemberg, Warsaw, Prague, Dresden and Vienna, the twenty-three scenes cover a period from 1890 to 1913. The play uses a large cast, but except in a gay ball at the top of act II, only a few people appear in each of the realistically treated scenes, which are staged with simple furniture pieces such as desks, beds, and chairs.

POSTCOLONIAL HISTORY

The largest group of plays based on oppositional history are those that dramatize events from the colonial era, but present them in terms of postcolonial history, which involves "rewriting Eurocentric and other imperialist perspectives from indigenous viewpoints."[14] The British colonial experience held a naggingly prominent place in public consciousness in Great Britain after World War II in the same way that the Vietnam conflict later did in the United States. Even though Britain was withdrawing, often painfully, from the control of its colonial possessions, the process was not as rapid as some wished. Whereas the development of nationalism had held a central place among the concerns of the Whig historians, that same nationalism became the evil spirit of oppositional history. Where once colonial expansion had been seen as a historically inevitable manifestation of the superiority of the European state, it became a symptom of cultural oppression. Even though the legacy of colonialism lingered with such public issues as the Suez crisis in 1956, relations with Southern Africa throughout the 1970s, and the Falklands War in 1982, colonialism per se was largely a moot issue and not the principal target of these plays. The "exposure" of colonial exploitation in the historical record could, however, provide a basis for calling into question the legitimacy of the entire hegemony. All of the colonial history plays written after 1956 are oppositional histories, presenting events or developing character from the point of view of the subjugated colonials.

The term *colonial* is itself fraught with valuative connotations. The inclusion of plays by Irish or Scots nationalists, for example, accepts at face value their contention that the incorporation of the Irish or Scots into Great Britain was forceful and illegitimate, making Scotland and Northern Ireland, in effect, colonies—obviously a debatable position.

Terence Rattigan's *Ross* in 1960, discussed with reference to biographical history, provides a good example of the more traditional jingoistic view of colonial history. Like Robert Bolt's film *Lawrence of Arabia*, released in 1962, *Ross* to some extent lionizes T. E. Lawrence. Although the British establishment does not immediately see the value of encouraging Arab nationalism, Lawrence's actions assume importance because they contribute to the British war effort and "bring civilization" to the Arabs.

Conor Cruise O'Brien's *Murderous Angels* (1968) is unusual in being to some extent an autobiographical history play.[15] O'Brien, a noted historian, critic, and Irish statesman, was a minor United Nations official involved in the incidents surrounding the Congo crisis in 1961, which he subsequently dramatized. Although he does not actually appear as a character on stage, other characters refer to his offstage involvement. O'Brien had treated the same subject earlier in his best known work, the narrative history *To Katanga and Back* (1962), which John Arden credited as an inspiration for *Armstrong's Last Goodnight*. *Murderous Angels* is less a play than a history in play form, complete with extensive notes documenting sources and a scholarly appendix. This rather long play dramatizes UN Secretary General Dag Hammarskjold's sacrifice of the Congolese revolutionary Patrice Lumumba in order to appease European politicians and ends with Hammarskjold's apparent assassination in an airplane crash. The dramatic form permits O'Brien to recreate events but also allows for some degree of speculation about causes. He writes in the introduction that this is not a realistic play: "My Hammarskjold and my Lumumba, then, are not to be thought of as the 'real' characters of that name, but as personages shaped by the imitation of a real action associated with their names" (xxxi). After a somewhat ritualized prologue that provides the historical context with the aid of slides and film, O'Brien treats individual scenes realistically, although the characters are more stereotypical spokespersons for various political positions than developed personalities. Although the central conflict is dramatic, and O'Brien makes his point that the Congolese were victims of colonial manipulation, the overwritten dialogue and polemic tone hurt the play, which was published without prior performance. Interest in producing the play had been expressed by the Nottingham Playhouse, by Laurence Olivier at the National Theatre, and by the Abbey Theatre in Dublin, but the first performance was not until 1970 at the Mark Taper Forum in Los Angeles.[16]

Edward Bond's pseudohistory play *Narrow Road to the Deep North*, first performed at the Belgrade Theatre in Coventry on June 24, 1968, parodies British colonial intervention, but the play's principal theme is the artist's corruption by involvement in politics, even when motivated by good intentions. Bond's central character, the seventeenth-century haiku writer Matsuo Basho, was a real historical figure, but Bond invents other characters and events, setting the play vaguely in "Japan about the seventieth, eighteenth, or nineteenth centuries."[17] The British, in fact, played only a minor role in Japan before the late nineteenth century. Bond casts his Japanese plot in a style that blends traditional Japanese material with Gilbert and Sullivan. Basho rescues an abandoned infant, who later becomes the enlightened despot Shogo, a peasant ruler eventually overthrown by British intervention. The Commodore, a British officer who arranges Shogo's fall, and his missionary sister, Georgina, are Gilbertesque parodies of British colonialism. Bond even uses some of Arthur Sullivan's music (222).

Charles Wood's *'H'* focuses on debunking the Victorian myth of Britain's colonial destiny. Produced by the National Theatre at the Old Vic on February 13, 1969, the play dramatizes Sir Henry Havelock's march to relieve Lucknow during the Indian Mutiny in 1857. A Raj version of *Oh What a Lovely War*, *'H'* uses a toy theatre staging motif to counterpoint ironically its demonstration of the savagery, butchery, and social disintegration at the core of this colonial war. Irving Wardle, the *Times* reviewer, also pointed out the possible influence of American playwright Arthur Kopit's *Indians*, which had premiered in London the previous year, "another work that handles national myth in terms of a vaudeville show of the period."[18]

In the "Author's Introduction," Wood comments that the stage should be considered a road for a march that stops or slows when a painted front cloth drops across it.

The front cloth is very important and must be painted by a good scenic artist in the best trompe l'oeil manner on old or soft canvas so that it hangs from a batten with the curves of a sail. It is used to stop dangerous sharp action from spilling into the auditorium where paying people have a right to feel safe from bayonets and involvement; it is used to shut off the din and let us hear ourselves speak, not easily done in battle; it is used, to paraphrase an apt phrase . . . to give style and description to what might otherwise be vulgar sprawl. It fails in all these things, I hope.[19]

The first stage direction describes the opening act drop: "British India 1857; golds and reds and superb illustration. Elephants, English Ladies, English Soldiers, Parasols, Horses, Carriages, Children that are white, the whole supported left and right by smiling Johnny Sepoy" (p. 21). During the play Wood required this curtain to be "so abruptly dropped that bayonets tear into it, men skid underneath it" (p. 17). This violation of the painted image of colonial India functions as a theatrical metaphor for Wood's debunking of the myth of the British Raj. The characters struggle unsuccessfully to fulfill some Victorian stage artist's image of what a colonial war should be: a picturesque composition with brightly colored uniforms and dynamically arranged bodies. At one point near the end of the play, corpses rise and wounded men struggle to find their place in front of a stagedrop reproducing a familiar Victorian engraving of the relief of Lucknow. The danger of the toy theatre staging is that the comedy undercuts Wood's serious message. He objected that in the National Theatre production, the toy theatre staging, beautiful though it was, "introduced a note of archness I never intended" (17).

The staging techniques owe much to the Artaud-influenced theatrical hieroglyphics introduced into England by Peter Brook and John Dexter. Rather than realistic business, a series of stage pictures and surreal activities convey a metaphorical image of the action. For example: "The BOMBARDIER and the SEPOYS make the noise of each shell that is sent at the British. . . . The MONKEY GOD HUMAYON comes out of the tight press of SEPOYS under the ELEPHANT. He dances an obscene and insulting dance." When one of the British soldiers comes to watch, the monkey god "squirts him with water from its oversize phallus" (82), a graphic image for the contempt that the Indians felt for their British masters. Mimed battles culminate in five "tableaux vivant," used to show the disintegration of the idealized image of Queen Victoria's little war. Wood's stage direction emphasizes the awkwardness with which the first tableau forms, creating some tension from the beginning. After everyone has found a place, anticlimatically, "There is no sound at all, just a little coughing. Silent puffs of smoke and flame in the sky, like cotton wool. Some men crumple slowly to remain in the arms out, mouth open, body on its way to the ground position beloved of print makers." Two speeches follow and then Wood deconstructs the image:

SUDDEN NOISE and horror, the carefully composed and slowly moving forward tableau becomes a thing of horror and confusion—terrible noise of shot and shell and screams of dying men rolling their agony into the ground. A great surge of HIGH-LANDERS pelts forward and HARRY HAVELOCK throws himself with them staggering to his knees at front of a front cloth come down just in time to prevent the

78th from entering the stalls. Their bayonets rip into the cloth and there is silence. (67–68)

The tableaux become increasingly desperate until the final one, which Wood describes with a stage direction in verse:

> Compore,
> and the Grand Trunk Road sprawled across
> the ground, tumbled amongst the scenic
> debris of two acts, the Camp of the
> Mutineers, Havelock's Tent, the Field
> Hospital swags from the sky, hangs
> limp as a flag, is spread as covering,
> a tumble of cloth and silk among trenches,
> mines, saps, revetments, parapets,
> fascines, iron hoop gabions, . . .
> abbattis, chevaux de frise, trous de
> loups and simple holes scraped in the
> earth are full of SOLDIERS,
> covered with SOLDIERS,
> impale SOLDIERS, bury SOLDIERS, expose
> SOLDIERS as on the palm of a gigantic
> theatrical hand for inspection as the
> Triumph of Havelock. (135)

This last act depicts the dying of Havelock, but inserted throughout this scene five other scenes replay, at times surrealistically, earlier events. In one of these, Captain Jones Parry, who is something of a Raj Everyman, reunites with his wife, a typical memsahib, who has survived rape and humiliation at the hands of the rebelling native troops. Simultaneously with this reunion, the physician attending Havelock carries on a monologue about the effect of diet on the fighting man: "SOOTER talks through all of the following dialogue, his voice out of sync with his lip movements while he tends HAVELOCK" (162). As Havelock dies, his son, also his aide-de-camp, "sits with him while everything is taken away, the mattress, his clothes, everything, until he is left on the bare boards of the stage" (178). Havelock dies of dysentery, a fact kept before the audience by other characters' strong reaction to the smell throughout the act.

Subtitled *Monologues at Front of Burning Cities*, the play begins many of its thirty-one scenes with soliloquies and embeds others in the dialogue. The play's free verse gives Wood considerable latitude to depart from realism, but he uses colloquial speech rhythms to differentiate character and give a sense of period.

The reviewer Wardle said that Wood rivaled John Arden in "recapturing the demotic speech of another age." He noted that the language often reflects the same "stilted heroic convention" as the tableaux. "The intention, I think, is to contrast the barbarity of the military action with the verbal convention that masked its real character from Victorians in Britain."[20]

Wood deflates the myth of the British Raj, but he does so not so much to expose imperialism as to advocate pacifism, a more significant statement in the midst of the Vietnam War than denouncing colonialism twenty years after the end of the British Indian empire. In this respect, Wood transfers to Victorian India many of the themes and staging techniques that he had developed two years earlier in his World War II play *Dingo*, which we will examine later as a deconstructionist history. He also worked in the same nineteenth-century period with much the same iconoclastic approach to a piece of military history when he wrote the script with John Osborne for the 1968 film *The Charge of the Light Brigade*.

In the final analysis, Wood manages to debunk the heroic myth of the British presence in India without losing sympathy for his characters. Havelock emerges as a good-hearted Christian man trapped by Victorian values that are too much a part of his makeup for him to call into question. The epilogue shows the Parrys visiting Havelock's tomb at Lucknow eleven years after the battle, accompanied by Indian servants holding sunshades over them. Captain Jones Parry sees the place as a shrine: "Are not the English of / the truest aristocracy, inasmuch as / they can fight like tigers and die / without a murmur?" (183). But a very brown child also accompanies them, the product of Mrs. Parry's rape, who nonetheless carries the Parry name: Timothy Jones Parry. Mrs. Parry revises her husband's view of history when she says the final words of the play: "Timothy, here is where your father was shot and died in agony" (183). We will examine the narrative structure of this play in more detail in the final chapter.

Where Wood's play used panoramic effects and a large cast that only one of the state-supported nonprofit theatres could afford, Simon Gray's postcolonial history *The Rear Column* uses a cast of eight and was produced at the Globe Theatre in London's West End on February 22, 1978, under the direction of Harold Pinter. Gray's play shows the disintegration of five Victorian gentlemen waiting in the Congo to support H. M. Stanley's expedition to "rescue" Emin Pasha in 1887. Barttelot, the officer in charge, while aware of his own inadequacies, is a martinet and a sadist (and given to monologues). Bonny is addicted to morphine. Jameson, a gentleman naturalist played by Jeremy Irons, seems the most rational but ultimately buys a slave child so he can have her eaten and make sketches of the cannibal ceremony. Except for two minor black characters who serve as victims, the native presence remains offstage, an ironic counterpoint to the barbarism onstage.

In a preface to a 1986 collection of plays, Gray commented that Vietnam atrocities lay at the background of the play and noted that it was based on a true event that was the source of not only Conrad's *The Heart of Darkness*, but also Francis Ford Coppola's 1979 film about the Vietnam Conflict, *Apocalypse Now*.[21] The play was staged very realistically with a single setting and each of the three acts occurring six months apart. A central action that consists principally of waiting allows a tight focus on a small group of characters, deviating from the historical and chronological sprawl of many history plays. This also accounts for the involvement of Pinter rather than the directors usually associated with the more spectacular productions of history plays. Clearly drawn personality conflicts among the men sustain dramatic tension, but even though the characters are complex enough to hold interest, the play exposes no psychological depths; although it reveals the worst of colonial exploitation, the characters' circumstances are too extraordinary to support generalization to broader social ills.

John Spurling's *The British Empire, Part One*, which opened as a promenade production at the Birmingham Repertory Studio Theatre on February 14, 1980, interweaves five major nineteenth-century colonial episodes in forty-one scenes, using a cast of only nine principals. The play derives its novelty largely from the scope of its subject matter, which Spurling manages adroitly. The explorer Richard Burton and his wife, Isabel, in the 1880s act as a frame for the actions, which occur principally from 1820 to 1850: India, Gordon Laing in the Sahara, Zululand, George Arthur in Tasmania, and Burton in Africa. To avoid taking time to fill in the sweeping historical background, Spurling presupposes the audience's familiarity with the major players. The courtship of the Burtons and maturing of their relationship provides the most sustained plot element. Each plot line roughly observes chronology but not the movement from one to the other. The individual situations develop realistically with only a few players. In all instances the natives, who are unwilling subjects, betray the British, who exact their revenge. Spurling indicates that he had Vietnam in mind when he wrote the Afghan scenes,[22] but by implication, the play exposes the destructiveness of colonialism everywhere. The action develops from the point of view of the dominant powers, but with an overriding sense of irony.

In the introduction to the published version of the play Spurling harks back to a positivist view of history: "In writing history plays today, we have to do rather better than Shakespeare on the score of accuracy. There are far more sources; infinitely more is known about the past and audiences are better informed." Spurling acknowledges that the playwright's "prejudices and beliefs naturally colour his interpretation, but one should also feel a pull the other way, that the discovery of the facts has coloured his beliefs and prejudices."[23] Spurling clearly rejects the "great man" approach: "There is no single, grand figure whose fatal flaw carries him to disaster, but a series of lesser figures, whose small individual failings and setbacks combine to form a national or rather international disaster" (xvii). Spurling adapted the play for BBC radio, which then commissioned *Part Two*, broadcast in 1982, and *Part Three*, broadcast in 1985, carrying the narrative up to 1911.

One of the more unusual dramatizations of the impact of colonialism on native Africans was Peter Brook's adaptation of Colin Turnbull's anthropological study *The Mountain People* about the progressively asocial behavior of the Ik, who were displaced in 1946 when the British made their homeland in Uganda into a national park. Produced first in French in 1975 by Brook's International Center for Theatre Research and in London in 1976, *The Ik*, was developed as a company piece, with Colin Higgins and Denis Cannan doing the final adaptation.[24]

The dialogue seems simple, straightforward, and fairly realistic, with a narrator used occasionally but unobtrusively. The script, however, gives the barest hint of the Grotowski influence on the production. The intervention of Europeans, for altruistic purposes, sets up the situation that leads to the decline of the Ik, but Colin Turnbull does everything possible to prevent it. Because of the passiveness of the Ik themselves, the play has less of a plot than a series of episodes centered on Turnbull, which provide opportunities for the audience to see the deterioration of the Ik's situation. Disaster results not because exploitation by a colonial power has continued but because displacement in and of itself destroys the social structures of these people.

Victorian Africa was also the setting for Caryl Churchill's 1979 play *Cloud Nine*, but in this case the absurd exaggeration of Victorian colonialism became an image for sexual chauvinism, so we will deal with the play as an example of feminist history. Timberlake Wertenbaker's *New Anatomies* (1984), a biographical drama of the Russian Arabist Isabelle Eberhardt, who toured French Morocco dressed as a young Arab male, also contrasts the narrow-mindedness of European men with the open-minded attitudes of the Arabs, but Wertenbaker focuses on gender issues, not on colonial history.

In *Poppy*, Peter Nichols uses the popular English pantomime or "panto" to satirize Victorian involvement in the Chinese Opium Wars. The first new play staged by the Royal Shakespeare Company at the Barbican Theatre, *Poppy* opened on October 5, 1982, and transferred, with some modifications, to the Adelphi for next year's Christmas season, the traditional times for pantos. Even though *Poppy* won the Society of West End Theatres (SWET) award for best musical, Nichols was not altogether satisfied with the RSC production and later wrote, "My simple, subversive idea—to use the favorite Victorian entertainment form to tell a story of imperial hypocrisy and wickedness—was lost among the grandeur."[25] A later version was staged more simply at the Half Moon Theatre in 1989.

Nichols described the Victorian pantomime as "an expansionist imperial spectacle that matched the Victorian mood of fantasy, trans-sexuality, opulence and jingoism" (407). Even though the postwar panto has become largely a provincial form of winter entertainment, its highly developed conventions are well known to British audiences: a set of stock characters including a "Dame" played by a man, a "Principal Boy" played by a woman, and a horse performed by two actors; direct interaction with the audience; heavy reliance on spectacular scenic "transformations"; forced rimes; music; and dance. The pantos often made a direct appeal to patriotism; so Nichols's exploitation of panto conventions to subvert Victorian colonialism has special irony. Inherent in the form are the romantic sentimentalism, moral certitude, and chauvinism that Nichols exposed in the Victorian treatment of China.

Queen Victoria herself serves as a narrator and something of a cheerleader. She frequently addresses the audience, referring to them in panto fashion as "boys and girls" and implicating them in the action:

Victoria: (to audience)
   I'll need to know you're firmly on my side.
   So if you are, shout "Yes" when I count three
   One—two—three—

Audience: Yes!

Victoria: Yes who?

Audience: Your Majesty!

Victoria plays a variety of chauvinistic characters—opium auctioneer, English schoolmarm in India, missionary in China. She also has a series of combative exchanges with the Chinese emperor, who appears as a stage conjurer with diminishing powers of magic. Both the Victorian grande dame, Lady Dodo Whittington, and her son, Dick, crossdress, Dick in the high cut tights and high-heeled shoes traditionally worn by the "Principal Boy." "Dick Whittington" is an English rags-to-riches fairy tale based on the true life of a fifteenth-century lord mayor of London and a subject for pantomimes since the eighteenth century. Nichols's Whittington shares the same entrepreneurial spirit but begins as and remains a toff. The "Principal Girl," usually the romantic interest, becomes an opium addict, and the panto horse, Randy, is eaten during the blockade of Canton.

The panto today serves ostensibly as family entertainment, but with an adult audience, Nichols stresses double-entendre and latent sexuality in order to deflate further Victorian utopian and romantic fantasies. The traditional ballet sequence ends the first act:

The Garden of Eden appears, a Douanier Rousseau paradise where animals appear with humans—elephants, birds, crocodiles, RANDY.

DODO *and* UPWARD *swing on a great trapeze, make love.* SALLY *in flowing draperies makes love to* DICK *and* JACK *in turn. The animals couple with naked men and women.* (452)

This culminates with the nude wedding of Victoria and Albert.

Even though Nichols points out that the Chinese characters are historical and that others are often given speeches and sayings of the time (409), this is less a history play than a satiric commentary on history. In the introduction to the 1991 published version, Nichols makes clear his intent to undercut popular misconceptions "that the Opium Wars had been about Britain trying to 'cure' China. I'd believed this too till an essay by Robert Hughes put me straight and showed me what a black comedy had been overlooked" (409). Critics were intrigued with the production but complained about its handling of the historical material. Michael Billington, reviewing the Half Moon revival, said that Nichols whisked the audience briskly through twenty years of history and concluded that "panto is not the best vehicle for historical analysis."[26]

In an introduction to the play Nichols lists six books on the Opium Wars for "further reading," which we may presume to have influenced his writing. Of these, the contrast between two provides a good example of the strong divergence between old and new histories. Maurice Collis, in the introduction to *Foreign Mud*, written in 1946, writes of the Opium Wars, "When all has been said, there will be found little malice, little cause for moralizing, but a great deal of humanity."[27] Jack Beeching in *The Chinese Opium Wars*, written in 1975, opens with the dedicatory phrase "A nation that oppresses another cannot itself be free."[28]

From the perspective of revisionist historians, England's affairs with her Celtic neighbors represented a form of colonial oppression, a position taken by a number of history plays that deal particularly with relations between the English and the Scottish or the Irish. John McGrath's *The Cheviot, the Stag, and the Black, Black Oil* (1973) makes such an appeal to Scots nationalism, but it takes an economic tack, and we will discuss it as a Marxist play. Brien Friel's dramatization of Irish history comes closer to pure oppositional history.

Although he was born and received most of his early education in Northern Ireland and still lives there, Brian Friel considers himself Irish. However, he has shown particular concern to develop Irish English as a literary language, and many of his plays have been popular in England. *Translations* was produced originally by the Field Day Theatre Company, which Friel founded. It premiered in the Guildhall, Londonderry, on September 23, 1980, and the next year in London, first at the Hampstead Theatre and then at the National's Lyttelton Theatre. No clear factual basis exists for the specific incidents invented by Friel, but the situation needs the historical context, and Friel works to establish the feel of period authenticity. The action takes place in an informal classroom, a "hedge-school," in Baile Beag, Donegal, in 1833. An English surveying team mapping Ireland, and in the process replacing all of the local Gaelic names with new English ones, provides a vivid metaphor for the use of language for cultural genocide. One of the English surveyors, Yolland, falls in love with an Irish girl, Maire, who is also sought by Manus, the lame son of the local teacher, Hugh. Hugh's other son, Owen, serves as a translator for the English. Yolland is murdered after being seen at a dance with Maire, and in retaliation, the English Captain Lancey promises to devastate the county. The English are clearly depicted as invaders, but the point of Friel's star-crossed lovers is that personal relations should be able to bridge national barriers or language differences.

In some respects, this is a play about language, which Friel uses as a metaphor for both entrapment and escape. Hugh, who teaches Latin, Greek, and, if necessary, English, says, "It is not the literal past, the 'facts' of history, that shape us but images of the past embodied in language."[29] In the play, Gaelic speaking characters in fact use English, a stage convention that Friel cleverly exploits, including a charming love scene in which the lovers are both speaking English so the audience can understand, but presumably Yolland cannot understand Marie's Gaelic, nor she his English. Secondary characters include the mute Sarah, whom Manus teaches to speak but whose only significant use of language turns destructive when she tells Manus of Maire's infidelity. The unwashed Jimmy Jack, who at first appears to be a stereotyped Irish derelict, turns out to have a fascination for Greek mythology, which he reads in Greek. Latin and Greek passages are spoken in the original, exploding the image of the Irish as backward and uneducated.

Friel returned to the history play with *Making History*, which the Field Day Theatre Company opened in the Guildhall, Derry, on September 20, 1988, with a subsequent performances at National's Cottesloe Theatre. At one level a conventional biographical history showing the failed attempt by Hugh O'Neill, the Earl of Tyrone, to free Ireland from English dominance in the late sixteenth century, Friel's play covers over twenty years in O'Neill's life, from his failed attempt, with Spanish assistance, at defeating the English occupiers until his exile in Rome near the end of his life. The first act develops around the love conflict between O'Neill and his young wife, Mabel, daughter of the Queen's Marshal, one of the "New English, or as the Irish describe them, 'Upstarts,' planted by Elizabeth I in Ireland to pacify and control the country. This romantic interest provides a vehicle for Friel's theme of reconciliation. Tyrone has spent nine years being educated in England, and Mabel, even as an Englishwoman, demonstrates a loyalty to Tyrone that wins the begrudging respect and love of his strongly nationalist cohorts.

On another level, the play, as its title states, develops the idea that history is a fabrication used to support political ends. Christopher Edwards in his *Spectator* review described Friel as a "revisionist and writer of historical fiction," who "deliberately sets out to 'reread' a period of Irish history."[30] Early in the play we discover that Peter Lombard, the Bishop of Armagh, has arrived to gather information for a history about O'Neill:

O'Neill. Have you begun?

Lombard. No, no; only checking some events and dates.

O'Neill. And when your checking is done?

Lombard. Then I suppose I'll try to arrange the material into a shape—eventually.

O'Neill. And interpret what you've gathered?

Lombard. Not interpret, Hugh. Just describe.

O'Neill. Without comment?

Lombard. I'll just try to tell the story of what I saw and took part in as accurately as I can.

O'Neill. But you'll tell the truth? . . .

Lombard. If you're asking me will my story be as accurate as possible—of course it will. But are truth and falsity the proper criteria? I don't know. Maybe when the time comes my first responsibility will be to tell the best possible narrative. Isn't that what history is, a kind of story-telling?[31]

O'Neill remains suspicious. As he later tells his wife, Peter believes "that art has precedence over accuracy. I'm beginning to wonder should we trust historians at all!" (43). Lombard, however, has developed a clear historiography for himself:

I don't believe that a period of history—a given space of time—my life—your life—that it contains within it one "true" interpretation just waiting to be mined. But I do believe that it may contain within it several possible narratives: the life of Hugh O'Neill can be told in many different ways. And those ways are determined by the needs and demands and the expectations of different people and different eras. What do they want to hear? How do they want it told? (28)

An argument between O'Neill and his young wife, who wants him to make peace with the English queen, demonstrates this subjectivity of history:

Mabel. You are not united. You have no single leader. You have no common denomination. At best you are an impromptu alliance of squabbling tribesmen—

O'Neill. Careful!

Mabel. —grabbing at religion as a coagulant only because they have no other idea to inform them or give them cohesion. (*Pause*)

O'Neill. Is that a considered abstract of the whole Gaelic history and civilization, Mabel? Or is it nothing more than an honest to goodness, instant wisdom of the Upstart? . . . For you to suggest that religion is the only coagulant that holds us together is to grossly and ignorantly overlook an age-old civilization. (57, 59)

At the end of the play, with Tyrone defeated and exiled, Lombard more specifically describes the kind of history he intends to write:

People think they just want to know the "facts"; they think they believe in some sort of empirical truth, but what they really want is a story. And that's what this will be: the events of your life categorized and classified and then structured as you would structure any story. No, no, I'm not talking about falsifying, about lying, for heaven's sake. I'm simply making a pattern. . . . Ireland is reduced as it has never been reduced before—we are talking about a colonized people on the brink of extinction. This isn't the time for a critical assessment of your "ploys" and your "disgraces" and your "betrayal"—that's the stuff of another history for another time. Now is the time for a hero. (93–94)

Friel has given Lombard a perception of the function of history that accurately reflects sixteenth-century attitudes. The play's end places the two views of history in sharp contrast. While Lombard reads from his hagiography, O'Neill recites his oath of submission to Queen Elizabeth: "When O'NEILL speaks HE speaks almost in a whisper to counterpoint Lombard's public recitation. HIS English accent gradually fades until at the end his accent is pure Tyrone" (98).

Although Friel's plays may secondarily support nationalist goals, his histories do not aim at problems specific to Northern Ireland, but appeal rather on more humanistic grounds for mutual understanding between people of different cultures.

None of the plays examined in this chapter advances a specific social agenda so much as they make an argument against any dogmatism that fails to recognize the right to difference. The Marxist and feminist dramas that we will examine in subsequent chapters also redefine history from an oppositional perspective but with a more specific agenda for revision.

NOTES

1. Tim Goodwin, *Britain's Royal National Theatre: The First 25 Years* (London: Nick Hern, 1988), pp. 12–13.

2. Donald Harman Akenson, *Conor: A Biography of Conor Cruise O'Brien*, vol. I (Montreal: McGill-Queen's University, 1994), p. 212.

3. The first earl of Shaftesbury first suggested that tragedy functions to compensate the low born in *Characteristics*, vol. 1, 4th ed (London: J. Darby, 1727), p. 143.

4. Arthur Miller, "Tragedy and the Common Man," *New York Times*, Feb. 27, 1949, sec. 2, pp. 1, 3, develops a theory of tragedy in which the fall of the hero implies a wrong or evil in the environment. For a more detailed discussion of this question see Richard H. Palmer, *Tragedy and Tragic Theory: An Analytic Guide* (Westport, CT: Greenwood, 1992).

5. John Whiting, *The Devils* (New York: Hill & Wang, 1961).

6. J. D. Hurrell, "John Whiting and the Theme of Self-Destruction," *Modern Drama*, 8, (1965): 141.

7. H.A.L. Craig, *New Statesman*, 61, no. 1563 (Feb. 24, 1961), 318.

8. James Saunders, *Next Time I'll Sing to You* (London: Heinemann Educational [1963] 1965), p. 17.

9. John Arden and Margaretta D'Arcy, *The Hero Rises Up* (London: Methuen, 1969), p. 5.

10. John Arden, *Ironhand* (London: Methuen, 1965), p. 156.

11. John Arden, *Armstrong's Last Goodnight*, in *Plays: One* (New York: Grove, 1978), p. 238.

12. John Osborne, *A Patriot for Me* (London: Faber & Faber, 1966).

13. Richard Findlater, ed., *At the Royal Court* (New York: Grove, 1981), p. 248.

14. Francis Barker, Peter Hulme, Margaret Iversen, eds., *Uses of History: Marxism, Postmodernism and the Renaissance* (Manchester: Manchester University, 1991) p. 4.

15. Conor Cruise O'Brien, *Murderous Angels* (Boston: Little, Brown, 1968).

16. Akenson, *Conor*, pp. 211–13.

17. Edward Bond, *Narrow Road to the Deep North* [1968], in *Plays: Two* (London: Methuen, 1978), p. 172.

18. Irving Wardle, "British India of 1850s," *Times*, Feb. 14, 1969.

19. Charles Wood, *'H'* (London: Methuen, 1970), p. 17.

20. Wardle, "British India."

21. Simon Gray, *The Rear Column*, in *Plays: One* (London: Methuen, 1986), p. xi.

22. John Spurling, *The British Empire, Part One* (London: Marion Boyars, 1982), p. xvii.

23. Spurling, *The British Empire*, p. ix.

24. Colin Higgins and Denis Cannan, adapters, *The Ik* (New York: Dramatic, 1984).

25. Peter Nichols, *Poppy*, in *Plays: Two* (London: Methuen, 1991), p. 408.

26. *Guardian*, Sept. 1, 1988.

27. Maurice Collis, *Foreign Mud* (London: Faber & Faber, 1946), p. 9.

28. Jack Beeching, *The Chinese Opium Wars* (New York: Harcourt Brace Jovanovich, 1975), p. 5.

29. Brian Friel, *Translations*, in *Selected Plays* (Washington, DC: Catholic University of America, 1986), p. 445.

30. *Spectator*, Oct. 12, 1988.

31. Brian Friel, *Making History* (London: Samuel French, 1989), pp. 18–19.

5

Marxist and Socialist History Plays

American and British New Historians differ in their degree of political emphasis. As Howard Felperin explains in his analysis of their work in Renaissance
studies, American and English New Historians share an understanding that
literature and history depend on constructed textuality and reflect an inevitable
political context; however, the Americans incline toward cultural poetics,
focusing on the past while attempting to avoid contact with contemporary
politics. The British, building on the strong postwar Marxist tradition in
English history and theory, tend toward cultural materialism, which always has
a contemporary political perspective.[1]

Although Marxism provided the most fully developed left-wing political
theory in Britain, other socialist and labor movements emerged at the same
time. Through the influence of the Labour party, these other radical political
philosophies exercise more influence than classical Marxism, which was often
burdened by associations with Soviet communism. Doctrinaire Marxism
defined the extreme of radical politics in Britain, but adaptations of Marxist
ideas were interwoven into socialist thought. On a theoretical level the Marxist
envisioned the eventual demise of the state upon the ascendance of a classless
society. The socialist saw the state as the principal tool for redistribution of the
wealth to the working classes. The Marxists were associated with the Communists who advocated the overthrow of capitalist states; the socialists wished to
modify the capitalist economy and control the state for their own purposes.

Even if we could neatly separate socialist, Communist, and Marxist ideas,
few if any historians or British playwrights would fit neatly into any one
classification to the exclusion of others or remain in one category over time.

In the discussion that follows, therefore, the political labels reflect the uses of the writers being examined more than any set of clearly defining criteria.

Marxist historians provide the first examples of history admittedly written from an articulated political position. Karl Marx's political philosophy was rooted in his view of history as an economic dialectic driven by class struggle. He shared with nineteenth century Whig historians confidence in the progressiveness of history, but where the Whig historians saw the historical process confirming the ascendancy of the ruling culture, Marx saw it as progressing through a series of revolutions against the dominant culture, leading to the eventual prevalence of communism.

No distinct socialist historiography exists without a Marxist core of dialectic materialism. The socialists may substitute evolution for revolution and differ in the remedies prescribed for economic ills. They usually reject the Marxist idea that socialism is merely the penultimate stage before communism.

More recently the term *neo-Marxist* has been used to describe the application of selected Marxist principles to fields as wide ranging as economics and literary criticism. Neo-Marxism is less politically dogmatic and more humanistic than traditional Marxist approaches.

Although Marxist histories vary in the details of their approach, they share a central *Weltanschauung*. Rejecting any spiritualism, their materialistic outlook sees a world organized into opposing forces that interact through conflict and revolution. All insist on an economic interpretation of events and explain human behavior in terms of class conflict with capitalism as the pervasive antagonist in this economic drama. Although imperialism was evoked as an accompanying social evil, the Marxist viewed it as an inevitable stage in the evolution of capitalism and had little interest in the plight of the victims.

The issue of historical determinism, hotly disputed among Marxists, shaped their varying attitudes toward the importance of the individual in history. Early Marxists espoused determinism and placed very little stress on the contributions of individuals to the historical process, but in Britain after the Second World War, the Marxist historians defined determinism to be both the setting of limits and the exertion of pressures that precipitate reaction rather than a force directly controlling human behavior. This allowed a place for human agency, if not by individuals, at least by collective groups, in driving the forces of history. Concentrating more than traditional histories on the political role played by the lower classes or by organizations of people, the British Marxist historians insisted that the lower classes had been active participants in the making of history, not merely passive victims. Their histories emphasized struggle as a necessary corollary of social and political change.[2]

New Marxist historians still debate this question of how to characterize and evaluate individual agency. The American historians Elizabeth Fox-Genovese and Eugene Genovese, who ally themselves with the British Marxist historians, objected to social histories that dwell on the daily lives of people instead of class struggle, that romanticize ordinary life, denying the theory of immiseration that provides the Marxist impulse for revolution.[3] Harvey J. Kaye in his study *British Marxist Historians* differentiates Marxist history from what he labels "Radical-populist history," focusing on the private rather than political experience of the subordinate classes and depicting resistance and struggle without showing the harsh realities of accommodation in lower-class experience.[4] This tension between the personal and the political appeared as a frequent theme in Marxist drama, but regardless of the degree of emphasis placed on the individual, Marxist history is ultimately political, always seeking causes and remedies in the structure of social governance.

Marxist history in many ways resembles the "from the bottom up" social histories that we discussed in Chapter Three, but the social historians treat subordinate social groups without depicting class or economics as principal determinants of behavior. The Marxist historians always presuppose a political remedy; the social histories are apolitical.

The Marxist historians also dwell less on common people in general and more on the ancestors of the Communist movement such as Chartists, trade unionists, and labor militants. John McGrath, a playwright of working-class theatre, uses audience appeal to justify the popularity of this self-reflective historical drama:

Some kinds of general area of subject-matter work better with a popular audience than others. The actual history of the working class, its formation, centuries of suffering and pride, the victories as the people moved towards a greater degree of emancipation, the distortions of purpose as they approached complete power, the lessons of the political struggles, the divisions within the people today and the mystification that prevails as the ruling class pretends it no longer rules. All this history has been suppressed, and needs to be shown to the people: it is rich history, full of vivid episodes, songs, strong characters and plenty of action.[5]

Trevor Griffiths, Alan Plater, Steve Gooch, McGrath, Caryl Churchill, and Peter Whelan all dramatize working-class political history.

Marxist historians were active in England as early as the 1930s, but they attained full prominence in 1946 when Maurice Dobb published *Studies in the Development of Capitalism* and the same year helped to found the Cambridge-based Communist Party Historians Group, which in 1952 began publishing the journal *Past and Present*. British playwrights often derived their material directly from the published works of these Marxist historians. Dobb explored peasant uprisings as a principal cause in the decline of feudalism, a point of view at the base of Steve Gooch's *Will Wat? If Not, What Will?*[6] Trevor Griffiths acknowledges the influence of E. P. Thompson's history of popular movements, *The Making of the English Working Class* (1963), and Raymond Williams's *The Long Revolution* (1961). Peter Whelan's play *Captain Swing* (1978) was influenced by E. J. Hobsbawn and George Rude's *Captain Swing* (1969). David Hare, Trevor Griffiths, Howard Brenton, and Ian McEwan were all influenced by Angus Calder's *The People's War* (1969).[7] Christopher Hill's *The World Turned Upside Down: Radical Ideas During the English Revolution*[8] was adapted by Keith Dewhurst for a production at the National's Cottesloe Theatre in 1978. Hill approached the English Civil War as a failed democratic revolution and focused on the Levellers, who espoused political equality; the communism of the Diggers; and the notions of free love advanced by the Ranters, all groups developed in Caryl Churchill's *Light Shining in Buckinghamshire*. Feminist playwrights have been influenced by the work of English Marxist feminists: Juliet Mitchell's *Woman's Estate* (1973) and Sheila Rowbotham's *Woman, Resistance, and Revolution: A History of Women and Revolution in the Modern World* (1972) and *Woman's Consciousness, Man's World* (1973).

The use of theatre as a vehicle for socialist proselytizing is as old as the works of George Bernard Shaw, whose Fabianism owed as much to the Whig view of history as to the Marxist. Although the iconoclastic Shaw, in plays like *The Devil's Disciple*, *The Man of Destiny*, *Saint Joan*, and *Caesar and Cleopatra*, undercut romantic treatments of history, his "superman theory" left intact the Victorian assumption that shakers and movers are the principal historical forces for change. The underclasses may be the designated beneficiaries, but Shaw's historical interest was in the reformers. Although Shaw contributed to a general skepticism regarding establishment history, his specific approach was without British followers, certainly not among socialist playwrights, who largely rejected the "great reformer" model.

Bertolt Brecht, of course, provided a model for the dramatization of Marxist history. In his "A Short Organum for the Theatre," he described a place for a "historical field of human relations" within his concept of epic theatre:

This field has to be defined in historically relative terms. In other words we must drop our habit of taking the different social structures of past periods, then stripping them of everything that makes them different; until they all look more or less like our own, which then acquires a certain air of having been there all along, in other words of permanence pure and simple. Instead we must leave them their distinguishing marks and keep their impermanence always before our eyes, so that our period can be realized to be impermanent too.

The ultimate purpose for what Brecht called "historification" was to create an alienation effect: "If we insure that our characters on the stage are moved by social impulses and that these differ according to the period, then we make it harder for our spectator to identify himself with them." The process could also be applied to the present: "And if we play works dealing with our own time as though they too were historical, then perhaps the circumstances under which he himself acts will strike him as equally odd."[9]

The Marxist playwright Steve Gooch complained that British adapters had missed the political point of Brecht's epic theatre: "His principal concept of 'alienation,' that of seeing events on stage as something *un*-natural in order to sharpen an audience's awareness of the social and political motives behind them, was too much for the insular, chauvinistic and anti-intellectual British tradition."[10] Brecht's own Marxist orthodoxy has been questioned,[11] and, as we have seen, writers influenced by Brecht adopted his epic staging without subscribing to his politics. Epic staging does, however, dominate the British Marxist history plays even when the same playwrights use a more realistic style for plays that are not historical.

Brecht's narrative theatre underscores the Marxist assumption that art must tell a story that illustrates the Marxist worldview. Individualism, truth, even life itself were subservient to this end. Any conflict for the historian between Communist orthodoxy and observed "facts" was avoided by making the assumption that historical events would inevitably justify party objectives; any failure to do so must mean that the historian had observed badly. For the artist, the directive is even more certain: the story must have a message that supports Communist orthodoxy. We can therefore expect Marxist playwrights to select and rearrange historical material in order to emphasize their political point. As Edward Bond stated in an introduction to a collection of his plays, "Socialist art is a weapon in the struggle to create good government."[12]

A large proportion of the socialist and Marxist history plays in Britain were written during the 1970s. This brief flourishing of socialist drama resulted from many of the same factors that made the Labour party with its socialist core a viable political force. A sufficient audience existed to support a number of successful socialist or Marxist playwrights, many of whom moved from the fringe theatres to state-supported theatres during the years of Labour Government strength before 1979.[13]

Before 1970, left-wing theatre was largely relegated to agitprop, workers' theatre, or the fringe, but in the seventies, beginning with the Royal Court Theatre Upstairs, the more established state-subsidized theatres began to stage some Marxist plays along with other experimental forms. These subsidized theatres were partly reflecting the liberal inclinations of their own management, particularly at the Royal Court, but they also embraced alternate theatre seasons in order to silence accusations of being establishmentarian and to protect their Arts Council subsidies, which the fringe theatres had begun to share with them in 1970. In 1970 the Royal Court Theatre held a festival of twenty fringe theatres under a title derived from a Beatles lyric, "Come Together." The next year the Royal Shakespeare Company initiated an alternate space at the 330–seat The Place with a nine-week season of three plays, including *Occupations*, a history of the 1920 Turin strikes, written by the Marxist playwright Trevor Griffiths. Two other playwrights with Marxist leanings, Edward Bond and Howard Brenton, were increasingly making inroads into the large established nonprofit theatres. In 1965 Bond had replaced John Osborne as theatre's enfant terrible with the Royal Court production of *Saved* in which, notoriously, a gang of young hoodlums stone an infant in a baby carriage. In the decade following, Bond became the principal playwright at the Royal Court and in 1978 his play *The Woman*, directed by him, was the first new play on the Olivier stage at the National Theatre. Howard Brenton's work, like Bond's, was being done at the Royal Court, the Royal Shakespeare Company, and the National Theatre throughout the seventies and eighties. The first original play produced at the National Theatre was Brenton's call for a return to Marxist orthodoxy, *Weapons of Happiness*, staged in 1976 by David Hare, another playwright with Marxist leanings. The 1979 victory of Margaret Thatcher's Conservative party over the Labour party dispirited the left wing, resulted eventually in reduction or withdrawal of Arts Council subsidies to radical theatre groups,[14] began a period of gradually increasing political caution by the state-subsidized theatres, and forced the more successful Marxist playwrights to find approaches acceptable to mainstream theatre.

The writers of Marxist history plays fall into two groups: those who adapted biographical histories for Marxist purposes—Griffiths, Bond, and Brenton—and those who wrote social histories that focused on groups rather than individuals—Steve Gooch, John McGrath, Caryl Churchill, and Peter Whelan.

The failure of the Paris students' strikes in 1968 and Labour's loss to Edward Heath in 1970 precipitated something of an ideological crisis among socialists, and Trevor Griffiths was the dramatist of left-wing self-assessment. Rather than focusing on the revolutionaries' clash with the establishment, the more usual subject of Marxist plays, Griffiths concentrated on conflicts among the revolutionaries over strategy and motives. He set many of his dramas against the background of significant moments in the history of radicalism: *Thermidor* (1971) against the Stalinist purges of 1937; *The Party* (1973), the Paris strikes; *Country* (1981), a television drama, against the 1945 Labour victory; and *Real*

Dreams (1984), the American student protests of the sixties. But even though the surrounding events are grounded in actual events, all of the characters in these plays are fictionalized minor participants and onlookers except in *Occupations*, which contrasts the styles of leadership of Kabak, a Bulgarian representative of the Soviet Comintern, and the important Marxist thinker Antonio Gramsci, leader of the 1920 workers' strike against Fiat. In this one case Griffiths comes close to the focus of more traditional historical drama on prime movers, even to the extent of developing the personal lives of his major characters. Griffiths could draw on a good deal of biographical material on Gramsci, principally Fiori's *Life of Gramsci*[15], but the playwright enlarged Kabak from a historical figure, Khristo Kabakchiev, about whom little is known beyond his public speeches on behalf of the Comitern at the Congress of Livorno, where the Italian Communist party was founded in 1921. Griffiths developed not only the private dialogue of his characters, but also the specific content of the public speeches made on stage by Gramsci, which Griffiths fabricated from ideas presented in Gramsci's writings at the time.

Occupations premiered at the Stables Theatre Club in Manchester on October 28, 1970, a year before its appearance at The Place, RSC's alternative theatre in London. As in most of Griffiths's later plays, theatrically staged exterior events frame a realistic central action placed in a single room, a private space surrounded by public actions, an effective metaphor for Griffiths's concern for the interaction between private and public behavior. *The Party*, for example, takes place in the home of a young radical couple, but throughout, television news coverage of the 1968 Paris riots appears on large wall screens and an onstage TV. The majority of *Occupations* occurs in a hotel room where Kabak's mistress, the Countess Angelica, lies dying. Kabak uses the room as something of a command center for his behind-the-scenes machinations, and the plot moves forward through a series of visitations by representatives of the outside world, including Gramsci, the hotelier, a government official, and a Fiat representative. The exterior action is represented largely through a series of epic devices including projections, recorded voices, and two long speeches to the workers by Gramsci. The projections show "future" images as well as those of events contemporaneous with the play.

The plot moves forward on three interwoven levels. The public plot centers on the rise and fall of the Fiat strike. As the play progresses, it becomes apparent that the strike will fail, and we realize that Kabak is the tool of the Soviet leadership, who have reached an accommodation with the Italian industrialists in order to further Soviet trade needs. Although Kabak is the agent, the forces actually controlling events are in Moscow; so the second plot level, the very subtle struggle between the idealistic Gramsci and the cynically practical Kabak for the soul of the nascent revolution, unfolds through their reaction to the strike, but this conflict has no practical influence on the outcome of the strike. This tension between compassion for the individual and the need to sacrifice personal concerns for the benefit of Communist goals is an old standard of Marxist literature, most clearly dramatized in Brecht's play *The Measures Taken*, but Griffiths gives the topic an ironic twist by transforming the usual group benefit into an economic ploy perpetrated for questionable ends by a foreign state. Kabak's parting words to Gramsci are "You still love them too much, comrade."[16] Kabak's own melancholic sadness about his duplicity adds further moral weight to Gramsci's attitude, but the third and most personal plot level reinforces this contrast in principles. Kabak's relationship with his dying mistress, a small domestic tragedy invented by the playwright, counterweighs the public events. Angelica, slipping in and out of sleep induced by the morphine taken for her pain, overhears the sexually frustrated Kabak making overtures to her nurse, Polya, and encourages Polya to satisfy his demands. Kabak, called back to Moscow when the strike fails, abandons Angelica in spite of her imminent death. Gramsci, in contrast, goes to Sardinia to be with his dying sister, highlighting the different human values of the two characters.

That Griffiths was concerned more with delineating conflicting values than with documenting a historical event is apparent in a prologue to the 1980 edition of the play, "In Defence of Occupations," an answer to criticism by Tom Nairn published in *7 Days*:

It's important to respond to historical plays as art-works, not as selected documentary accumulations containing historico-political speculations valuable largely in terms of a "known," historical and political reality. And we must learn to look for "historicity" more as Lukács finds it in the histories of Shakespeare. As for example when Lukács says: "Shakespeare states every conflict, even those of English history with which he is most familiar, in terms of typical-human opposites; and these are historical only in so far as Shakespeare fully and directly assimilates into each individual the most characteristic and central features of a social crisis."[17]

Kabak and Gramsci embody these opposite and conflicting social values.

Nairn also criticized the play for being romantic, even sentimental, and pessimistic, thus undermining its revolutionary intent, and for using a naturalistic form that devalued the promise of its content and themes. Griffiths retorted:

Occupations was written as a sort of Jacobinical response to the failure of the '68 revolution in France. *What it asserts* is that courage and optimism do not, of themselves, ensure the success of revolutions, unless they are harnessed, disciplined, tightly organized; in a word *led.*"

And what it *asks*—because it's a play that, characteristically, asks rather than asserts—is whether the courage and optimism aren't in some way necessarily damaged, distorted, in that disciplining process. (And that's a meaning for Kabak that Nairn barely smells, he's so often so far away from the play's muscle, skin and sinew.) (9)

Griffiths effectively fused the domestic drama with the historical context in the final moments of the play when Angelica is left alone on stage:

Angelica: The Tsar was in residence in the early spring a ball every night for a month Faberget [*sic*] swore he'd never seen such costumes such diamonds such . . .

(*She screams once, sharp, anguished, then holds her breath. The scream cues an image on the wall behind her: the corpse of Nicholas II. Cut the image as she speaks again.*)

(*Shouting*) Bolsheviks Bolsheviks Bolsheviks bread riots strikes bread peace land they were underneath here now here . . .

(*She screams again, cueing a second image: Lenin embalmed in the catafalque. The image is cut on her next word.*) All things will bend all things the iron brain of Lenin hammering the future will will will what will stop them stop them who . . .

(*She screams again: Tato's March on Rome. She screams again: Mussolini embracing Hitler. She screams again: Stalin in profile stares across a black gap at Hitler, who stares back. She screams again: the gap is filled with an image of Molotov and von Ribbentrop signing non-aggression pact. She screams again: cut to black.*) (72)

If this seems an indictment of communism, Griffiths rejoins by quoting Gramsci, " 'It is a revolutionary duty to tell the truth,' even where there is little comfort to be had from it" (8).

Griffiths's play is not just a biographical history about a Marxist; it is a Marxist assessment of a historical stage in the development of world communism; so even though Griffiths may mourn the personal sacrifices demanded by the advance of communism, he wishes to present it as part of a necessary process. In response to Nairn's criticism that he had conflated different epochs of Communist history, Griffiths acknowledged, for example, that the decree on which he had based Kabak's interchange with the Fiat boss had actually occurred five weeks after the scene in the play took place, but, he retorted,

the decree simply served to crystalize a whole strand of Soviet foreign policy that had been nursed (quite correctly in my view) since the summer of 1918.

After the autumn of 1920, however, with the failure of the Italian Revolution, the emphasis on the defence of Soviet national interests toughened, as the retreat from a policy hostile in principle to all capitalistic governments (while the prospect of proletarian revolution remained alive) got under way. As far as I can see, the play simply states that emphasis as a pragmatic, unavoidable fact. (8)

The Marxist playwright gives a nod to the Marxist view of history.

Edward Bond uses historical material in nearly half of his plays, and his attitude toward history, as toward everything else, is iconoclastic. We will discuss his 1968 send-up of Victorian England, *Early Morning*, in the context of deconstructionist history, but two of his plays develop an overtly Marxist view of history: *Bingo* and *The Fool*.

Bingo: Scenes of Money and Death, dramatizes Shakespeare's final days at New Place shortly before and up to his death. The play premiered at the Northcott Theatre in Devon on November 14, 1973; appeared at the Royal Court on August 14, 1974, and was revived by the Royal Shakespeare Company at the Other Place in Stratford in 1976. The Royal Court production starred John Gielgud as Shakespeare and played at 89 percent of capacity, making it one of Bond's most popular plays.[18] Given the scanty documentary evidence about Shakespeare's life, any writer of a biographical play has considerable latitude for invention, but as might be expected from Bond's proclivity for shock effect, he avoids most of the mythic material about Shakespeare and instead does a Marxist analysis of Shakespeare as a bourgeois property owner: "His behavior as a property-owner made him closer to Goneril than Lear. He supported and benefitted from the Goneril-society—with its prisons, workhouses, whipping, starvation, mutilation, pulpit-hysteria and all the rest of it."[19] Bond focuses more on Shakespeare's conjectural complicity in the enclosure of the commons at Welcombe than on any aspect of his artistic life. Even though he bases the central situation in the play on a legal document that Shakespeare signed, Bond develops the characters and action from his own imagination.

To "protect the play from petty criticism," Bond, in his introduction, asserts its accuracy: "It is based on the material historical facts so far as they're known and on psychological truth so far as I know it." Concerning his depiction of Shakespeare's death as a suicide, Bond portrays himself as the historian/detective, recreating events from fragmentary evidence: "I'm like a man who looks down from a bridge at the place where an accident has happened. The road is wet, there's a skid mark, the car's wrecked, and a dead man lies by the road in a pool of blood. I can only put the various things together and say what probably happened." He bases his final assessment, however, on his own moral sensibility: "If he didn't end in the way shown in the play, then he was a reactionary blimp or some other fool." Ultimately, Bond admits, "I'm not really interested in Shakespeare's true biography in the way a historian might be. Part of the play is about the relationship between any writer and his society" (4).

Rather than trying to replicate a historical event, Bond uses history as a metaphor for his vision of social disintegration. The style of the play is fairly realistic, but the characters function largely in an emblematic fashion. Shakespeare represents a seeing, knowing artistic vision that detaches itself from social responsibility. In the middle of the play Bond creates a long drinking scene between the taciturn, externally composed Shakespeare and the garrulous, tormented, and cynical Ben Jonson, from whom Shakespeare obtains a vial of poison that he uses to end his life. Bond also shows aspects of Shakespeare's domestic life, largely through his interactions with his estranged daughter Judith and his dying wife, present only as an offstage cry unheeded by Shakespeare, but these glimpses of the dramatist's private life only serve to emphasize his withdrawal from personal as well as public matters and his consequent abrogation of human responsibility.

Like other Marxist histories, this play depicts class conflict, the rebellion of the small farmers and laborers against the attempts to enclose common lands by large landowners represented by Combe, a local magistrate who leads the local enclosure effort, but rather than being the focus of the play, this revolution serves only as a background to reveal Shakespeare's lack of involvement in social issues. Bond melds public and private matters by making the leader of the yeoman opposition the son of Shakespeare's housekeeper, who, with her simpleminded husband, represents a kind of nurture that may be self-interested but is uncorrupted by money, the ultimate defiler of human values (8). Another subplot involves a young woman whipped by Combe for begging and finally garrotted for being an arsonist. Twice Shakespeare stirs from his ennui in an attempt to aid her, but each time his charity is too late and ineffectual. For Bond, even charity is an inadequate gesture as long as the giver retains his wealth and as long as the social structure that created the poverty remains in place.

Bond's Shakespeare kills himself in remorse because he sees his own complicity in the sufferings of life. In the play's introduction, Bond writes, "I wrote *Bingo* because I think the contradictions in Shakespeare's life are similar to the contradictions in us. He was a 'corrupt seer' and we are a 'barbarous civilization' " (10).

Bond continued to use historic material to explore the impact of economics on the artist with *The Fool*, which premiered at the Royal Court on November 18, 1975. With twenty-three actors needed, this was the most expensive production undertaken at the Royal Court in its twenty-year history and with the box office at 53 percent of capacity for its thirty-eight-performance run added to the Royal Court's growing deficit. Essentially a biographical play, *The Fool* dramatizes the life of John Clare, an early nineteenth-century yeoman poet who was institutionalized for the last twenty-three years of his life. As with *Bingo*, Bond focuses more on economic oppression than on Clare's artistic life, but Clare, unlike Shakespeare, is a victim rather than a victimizer. His poetry fails to sell, according to Bond, because he refuses to expunge verses critical of class oppression. A potential patron, Admiral Lord Radstock, and a fan, Mrs. Emmerson, interview Clare:

Admiral. Those remarks in—poem named after your village—

Mrs Emmerson. Helpstone

Admiral. (You see we've discussed it)—which criticizes the landowning classes—smack of radicalism.

Mrs Emmerson. (*reciting*): Accursed Wealth!—

Admiral. That bit.

Mrs Emmerson.   O'er bounding human laws
                           Of every evil then remainst the cause.

Admiral. And so on.

Mrs Emmerson. Including lines from "Winter".

   (*Reciting.*)   What thousands now half pined and bare
                        Are forced to stand thy—

   (*Explains.*)   That is, Winters—

   (*Reciting.*)   —piercing air.

Admiral. Now now, sir

Mrs Emmersson. All day near numbed to death with cold
                            Some petty gentry—

Admiral (*shaking his head*) At it again.

Mrs Emmerson.   —to uphold.

Admiral. Tut tut!

Clare's only retort is, "On't see no nymphs in our fields but I seen a work-house."[20]

   As with *Bingo*, Bond sets the main action in *The Fool* against class conflict: rural wage riots. Clare stays largely in the background through the first four scenes of the play, which deal with the riots in a fairly realistic fashion. The fifth scene begins to concentrate on the biographical drama but also introduces an epic technique of playing a foreground encounter between Clare and his patrons against a simultaneously staged bare-fisted boxing match, an image of a predatory society exploiting human pain for money. The next scene shows the domestic suffering caused by Clare's obsession with poetry, which prevents him from working as a laborer. His insanity increases partly because of his obsession with two characters: Darkie, a worker hanged for participating in the riots, and Mary, a quasi-gypsy servant dismissed from domestic service because the house-keeper has seen Clare masturbating outside the mansion. Clare has romanticized Mary as his "real wife," in contrast to the nagging Patty, who cannot understand the utility of his writings or appreciate his poetic sensibility. Scene seven becomes an expressionist journey into Clare's mind, where he confronts Mary and the boxer, who turns out to be the blind Darkie, who is dead.

Class differentiates the play's supporting characters. The working-class characters, all of whom speak with an East Anglian dialect, struggle with economic hardship and possess little time or capacity to understand Clare's poetry. The middle-class Mrs. Emmerson, a well-intentioned devotée of Clare's poetry, confronted with the poverty of Clare's family as he declines into insanity, comments, "A widow of my social standing can't risk any suggestion of want. . . . Society is so intolerant" (135). Charles and Mary Lamb appear, with no direct effect on the plot, merely to illustrate that economic oppression extends to the middle classes as well. Mary Lamb ends the play as a fellow inmate in the insane asylum. The upper-class characters, Lord Milton, who owns the land on which Clare's village stands, and the Admiral, a potential patron, are not depicted harshly, but they express the economic and moral views of their class. Even though he apparently pays for Clare's care for decades and visits him toward the end of his life, Milton expresses what, to Bond, seems the inevitable capitalist values of a landowner: "The war made us all prosperous but prices have fallen with the peace. Wages must follow. Not because I say so. That is a law of economic science. Wages follow prices or civil institutions break down" (88). The Parson serves as the most extreme spokesman for capitalist values, but after being seized and stripped during the riots, even he discovers humility and becomes more sympathetic. Bond succeeded so well in softening the black and white characterization of his usual polemic style that one critic described *The Fool* as "an unashamedly snobbish right-wing play. . . . In contrast to this adulation of the well-born Mr. Bond represents the common people as brutal, vindictive, sadistic, and perverted."[21]

Bond prefaced the play with an essay on capitalism, culture, and art, arguing that capitalism is not truly culture but only an organization. Culture, which functions in part through art, helps to create a *rational* order for society, telling how we *ought* to live. Bond does not, however, forward a romantic conception of the artist as a visionary individual, an idea that he dispels by an unflattering characterization of Clare as a man of crude sexual infidelities whose scribblings lead to the neglect of his wife and child. Clare's authority arises from being a member of his social and economic class, an individual speaking for the collective (77).

If Griffiths and Bond gave a Marxist twist to biographical histories, Howard Brenton did a Marxist deconstruction of a political hagiodrama with *The Churchill Play*, produced at the Nottingham Playhouse, May 8, 1974, and revived with major revisions by the Royal Shakespeare Company at The Other Place in Stratford on August 8, 1978. This is less a history play than a play *about* a history play. It begins with what appears to be Churchill's lying in state, complete with a coffin, catafalque, stained glass window, candles, and a military guard. Brenton shortly lets us know that we are not watching a routine history play, when we hear knocking from the coffin, followed by Churchill bursting out, swirling the Union Jack. A monologue ensues but just as Churchill asserts, "I can say I bludgeoned my way, through many jarring blows and shocks, bludgeoned (*With a great pout of his jaw and a gesture with his cigar hand.*) Onto . . . History's stage!"—he sees that his cigar isn't lit. When a sailor from the color guard crosses with a lighter, any illusion of historical semblance disappears as Churchill says to him, "Give us a kiss, Jolly Jack Tar."[22] This opening turns out to be a dress rehearsal by the inmates of a military prison in an aircraft hangar used as a recreational area, and we see much of the same action replayed in the final act. Inmates in a British military prison are producing a short play about Churchill under the direction of the prison doctor, Captain Thompson. The framing action takes place in 1984, the future to its original audiences; the play within the play occurs in 1965, the year of Churchill's death. The style of the framing action is largely realistic, but the amateurism of the prisoners' inner play allows a variety of alienation devices: characters breaking out of roles, providing side comment, using a "gong" in place of profanity, providing a slide show, and so on. Within the interior play, we see one scene played twice: as Churchill reported it and as it "actually" happened according to the prisoners.

The prison officers debate the characterization of Churchill in the first act to determine whether they will allow the performance of the play for a parliamentary delegation, and in the second act the prisoners argue whether their participation in the production makes a mockery of them. The prisoners have written the iconoclastic inner play to show their rejection of "Ruling Class values." The conflict over the production pits the principally lower-class victim–prisoners against the exploiting prison regime with Thompson in the middle. The guilt-ridden Thompson and his wife, who longs for an idyllic middle-class life in the suburbs, afford a degree of domestic drama. A short and otherwise extraneous third act moves to the prison yard to show two officers and their wives discovering a dying prisoner killed by the guards.

Brenton establishes the class consciousness of the prisoners early in the play. When the marine guard hears knocking from Churchill's coffin, he exclaims, "He'll come out, I do believe that of him. Capable of anything, that one. (*Fiercely.*) To bugger working people" (113). They depict the Churchill of Angus Calder's *The People's War*: detested by the working man as a union buster and defender of aristocratic privilege, but tolerated for the duration of World War II because of his effectiveness as a war leader.[23] When one of the prisoners says that he learned a trade in "their Army," a newcomer asks, "Their Army?" and the prisoner explains, "Ruling Class" (131). Class alone does not, however, guarantee righteousness in Brenton's world. The most savage representative of the establishment is the prison sergeant, and Reese, the new prisoner, lacks the lower-class accent of the others. When the government delegation arrives, we find that government is a coalition of the Conservative Party and part of the Labour party. A character who represents the "other part" of Labour and promises that his investigation of the prison will "go through this place like . . . like . . . a hot turd in an outside loo on a frosty morning" (171) turns out to be totally ineffectual.

The play has funny moments, most provided by cockney comments on the establishment, but its violent undercurrent finally erupts when the prisoners try to escape by taking hostages. In the initial version, Brenton left the ending somewhat ambiguous with the lights going out and a character's final line interrupted: "I don't want the future to be . . . "; in the 1978 rewrite of the ending, Brenton adds a more explicit counterattack from the prison forces; "Outside the revving engines of motorbikes. Blinding light from searchlights," and the final line is by one of the rebelling prisoners: "The Third World War" (176–77).

In a 1986 collection of plays including *The Churchill Play*, Brenton forwards his "Marxist view of the world" and justifies his own concern for the individual within the framework of the Marxist idea of historical determinism: "The great socialist leaders wake in their cells in South Africa, in South America, as do the cadres in Soweto and Nicaragua, confident that history is moving as surely as the planet moves. But millions do not have that vision, confidence and heroism, and some are traumatized by defeat. It is they whom I want to write about."[24]

The Churchill Play was a victim of history's moving in ways that Brenton had not anticipated. Michael Billington, reviewing the 1978 revival, writes, "In 1974, . . . the combination of rampant inflation and confrontation between Government and unions made its vision of England peppered with concentration camps in 1984 seem not wholly fanciful. But after four years of

Sunny Jim [Prime Minister James Callaghan] and growing financial stability, Brenton's notion of a collapsing England now looks slightly alarmist."[25] By 1986, in the middle of Margaret Thatcher's government, the situation had changed again, and Brenton writes, "[*The Churchill Play*] is at its root a satire against the erosion of civil liberties and union rights that began under Edward Heath's Government and spread apace under Margaret Thatcher's. But! A good red must keep the knives sharp in such times" (xv).

Brenton frequently used historical material, in plays such as *Wesley* (1970), *Scott of the Antarctic or What God Didn't See* (1971), *Hitler Dances* (1972), *The Romans in Britain* (1982), and *H.I.D. (Hess is Dead)* (1989), all of which we will discuss in the context of deconstructionist and postmodern historical drama, but *Moscow Gold*, which he wrote with Tariq Ali, returns to a specifically Marxist subject matter. This play about Mikhail Gorbachev's rise to power was staged by the RSC at the Barbican on September 20, 1990. The setting consists of a huge oval table where the Politburo meets, which also has traps for entrances, for exits, and for the introduction of furniture so that a variety of scenes can be played on top of it. Using epic staging techniques, along with devices borrowed from Meyerhold and from the English music hall, the play dramatizes Gorbachev's ascendancy within a framework of struggles by the Soviet leadership from 1917 to 1990. The first act opens with a tableau scene of 1917 and the second with a tableau of 1990. The stage direction makes clear that "in contrast to the 1917 pageant at the beginning of Act One, the 'PERESTROIKA pageant' is chaotic, unfocused, bad tempered."[26] One episode from the beginning of the second act illustrates both the play's satiric tone and its theatricalism. A Baltic Man and three Baltic Women enter "in national costumes, dancing, each with their National flag. They sing, in exquisite folk-song harmony":

> Happy proud and free.
> 'Til Stalin talked to Hitler
> And stole our countries three—
> Now our flags fly high again
> Oh please oh please oh please
> Don't let it be in vain.
>
> *And they are drowned by the Leningrad rock group who screech a punk song.*
>
> Freedom is a load of piss
> I don't see no way out of this
> (*Chorus*) Fucked fucked fucked
> Fucked in Leningrad
> Fucked fucked fucked
> With all the shit I've had

Fuck fuck fuck
Fucked in Leningrad. (48)

Although the play mimics a biographical history, the action is concerned less with a realistic portrayal of Gorbachev than with emblematic use of characters to illustrate thematic points. Brenton staged the progression of leadership from Brezhnev to Gorbachev as a ritual. In early scenes first Brezhnev and later Chernenko pops out of a coffin to vote at Politburo meetings for his successor. The Romanian dictator Ceausescu appears as a talking corpse and later as a ventriloquist's dummy. The ghosts of Lenin and Andropov carry on political discussions with Gorbachev. Gorbachev has soliloquies, and music includes a song by Boris Yeltsin, who keeps turning up in various states of undress. Minor characters serve symbolic functions, such as a Pepsi vendor and "a heavily tanned" Chernobyl Man (56–57). At the play's end, three members of the Russian mafia, a subchorus appearing throughout, kill Gorbachev, but a minor character appears and announces, "At this stage, the two authors decided it could not end like this" (84). A brief comic "happy" ending follows with Gorbachev and Raisa in retirement, commenting on the fact that America must buy wheat from Russia.

Brenton and Ali show the impact of political choices on the common people by using three maids to serve as a chorus as well as to move props and to appear in crowd scenes. One of the three, Zoya, provides a subplot. Married to a torturer of the secret police, who is also a Gorbachev liberal, she loses one son in the Afghanistan War and the other, after a futile attempt to create a reformed Socialist party, flees to the West in pursuit of "happiness and light."

In the preface, Ali and Brenton describe *Moscow Gold* as "a song of history as it *is*, not as it should be." The purpose of the play is "to understand the very real human needs of the Soviet people as well as the dilemmas which confront the Soviet leader Mikhail Gorbachev" (6–7). The play demonstrates the betrayal of the revolution by the bureaucratic elite that has established new class privileges that Andropov, Gorbachev, and Yeltsin try to eliminate. The development of Gorbachev as a character is secondary to what Brenton described as "the unprecedented attempt of a decayed, authoritarian system to reform itself."[27] The playwrights have an ambivalent view of the capacity of an individual, Gorbachev, to affect history. At one point they have him say, contradictorily, "It's a sad business, making history under circumstances out of your control" (69). They simultaneously highlight the importance of his choices and recognize the extent to which conditions beyond his power shape events.

Brenton's plays are certainly not traditional biographical histories. The prisoners as a group are really the protagonists in *The Churchill Play*, and the maids in *Moscow Gold* provide a working-class counterpoint to the Soviet leadership. To this extent, these plays relate to the Marxist social histories that deal with collective protagonists, including those by Alan Plater, Steve Gooch, John McGrath, David Hare, Caryl Churchill, and Peter Whelan. The documentary history play influences all six, and Plater, Gooch, and McGrath use the more overt style of agitprop and Brechtian staging, while also drawing on techniques from the English music hall and Gaelic *ceilidh*. These three writers also made separate decisions to work outside the London commercial theatre and to direct their energies on performances for or by regional or community-based theatres. McGrath and Gooch wrote books justifying this focus: McGrath's *A Good Night Out: Popular Theatre—Audience, Class and Form* (1981) and *The Bone Won't Break: On Theatre and Hope in Hard Times* (1990) and Gooch's *All Together Now: An Alternative View of Theatre and Community* (1984).[28]

In their attempts to develop a theatrical form particularly suited for working-class audiences, they followed in the footsteps of Joan Littlewood at the Theatre Workshop, first in Manchester and after 1953 at the Theatre Royal, Stratford East, in London, and Peter Cheeseman, at the Victoria Theatre, Stoke-on-Trent. Littlewood was a committed socialist who began work with alternative theatre in 1933 when she founded a street theatre company called the Manchester Theatre of Action. She created the Theatre Workshop in 1945 to present plays that were relevant to contemporary social and political issues. Influenced by the documentary style of the Living Newspapers produced in the late thirties by the American Federal Theatre Project, Littlewood and her husband, Ewan McColl, in 1947 produced *Uranium 235*, which traced the history of scientific investigation from the discovery of the atom to the development of the atomic bomb and left the audience with the question of the uses to which they should put atomic power. Littlewood was one of the earliest producers of Brecht in England. She directed and took the title role in an English translation of *Mother Courage* in 1955, the year before the Berliner Ensemble first appeared in London. She produced new plays, most notably those of the Irish radical Brendan Behan, and developed a method of working with an ensemble to develop new materials, the most successful of which was *Oh What A Lovely War* (1963), which combined the documentary techniques of the Living Newspaper with Brechtian devices to satirize the military and political motives for perpetuating World War I. McGrath in *A Good Night Out* pays tribute to the influence of this production on young writers in Britain in the sixties, including himself.

Peter Cheeseman at Stoke-on-Trent developed a form of historical documentary using a narrator, folk ballads, mime, dance, and humor. Throughout the sixties, these productions dealt with issues in local history such as the closing of the steel mills, the pottery industry, and various attempts by local workers to overcome exploitation. Although oriented toward the working class, Cheeseman's plays were not particularly political, but his very presentational style of staging historical material influenced a number of later political writers, including Peter Terson, Alan Plater, Steve Gooch, and John McGrath.

Alan Plater had five plays produced by Peter Cheeseman at Stoke-on-Trent between 1963 and 1965. In his introduction to *Close the Coalhouse Door*, which premiered at the Newcastle Playhouse, April 9, 1968, Plater acknowledges the influence of Littlewood and Cheeseman.[29] Plater, himself from a working-class background, writes principally about and for the working classes in Northeast England. Much of his large output has also been staged for theatres in this region, particularly the 150-seat theatre in the Hull Arts Centre. Plater says that he based *Close the Coalhouse Door* on "a shelf-load of un-Establishment history books," chiefly the stories of Sid Chaplin (vii). A golden wedding anniversary celebration for an old pitman and his wife serves as a springboard for reenactments of major events in the history of the labor movement in the coal mining districts of Tyne and Wear beginning with the formation of the first union in 1831. The first act deals with nineteenth-century oppression, the second with chaos between the two world wars, and the last act with what Plater calls "post-Nationalisation non-Utopia" (vii). In the present-day action, a domestic conflict between a stay-at-home miner and his educated-away-from-home brother over a girl provides romantic interest. A core of ten actors play a variety of roles. An "Expert" acts as occasional narrator and establishment spokesman. Two characters play the "feed and tag" duo of music hall routines. Alex Gasgow wrote original songs, including the theme song with the title refrain "Close the coalhouse door, lad, / There's blood inside." Plater commented on the degree to which Brecht influenced the production: "The music-hall element is very important. One of the pleasant side-effects was that I was asked by a journalist whether I had been influenced by Brecht: and was able to reply, with total honesty, not so much Brecht as Jimmy James, Norman Evens, Dave Morris, and Harry Mooney" (viii).

Plater is very frank about his polemical uses of the historical material in the play's introduction:

Finally, of course, there is no such thing as cold objectivity, in theatre or anywhere else. We set off with inbuilt attitudes towards the subject and the stated aim of creating "an unqualified hymn of praise to the miners, who created a revolutionary weapon without having a revolutionary intention." We selected those areas of history which confirmed our attitudes—though, as it happens, there were plenty to choose from." (ix)

An alphabet song sung by one of the miners most clearly states the play's political point of view:

> A is for Alienation that made me the man I am
> and B's for the Boss who's a bastard, a bourgeois who don't give a damn.
> C is for Capitalism, the boss's reactionary creed. . . .
> O is for Over-production that capitalist economy brings
> and P is for all private property—the greatest of all sins.
> Q is for Quid pro quo that we'll deal out so well and so soon
> when R for Revolution is shouted and the Red Flag becomes the top tune.
> (10)

Near the play's end the cast sings the ironic "It Couldn't Happen Here":

> We've made a little Eden so it couldn't happen here.
> We need no revolution to achieve the things we've planned,
> No fighting in the streets for us, we've got the promised land. . . .
> There are no idle rich men who profit from the poor,
> There are no landed gentry shooting grouse upon the moor. (70–71)

The play became something of a cult piece among working-class audiences in Newcastle, but when it moved that same year to London, it failed to attract audiences.[30]

Steve Gooch's approach to working-class theatre also owed much to Cheeseman, who in 1972 produced one of Gooch's early plays, an adaptation of Voltaire's *Candide*. Gooch's play of the 1381 Peasants' Revolt, *Will Wat? If Not, What Will?*, which premiered at London's Half Moon Theatre, May 27, 1972, presented, according to its author, "the peasant's side of the story."[31]

Gooch depicted events clearly from a Marxist perspective. Class affiliation and economic motives drive the action rather than characters' personalities. First the royalty and then the rising bourgeoisie are shown to exploit the commoners through high taxation, low compensation for labor, and legal restraints limiting the laborers' mobility and consequently their bargaining power. When the common people revolt against this exploitation, they are ruthlessly suppressed.

Gooch, unlike Griffiths, but more like the social historians, diminished the importance of the individual character in this drama and emphasized the agency of the group or class. Gooch made this choice clear in his discussion of the play in *All Together Now*:

Wat Tyler is shown fleetingly on stage, but the eventual victors of the Peasants' Uprising of 1381, the rising merchant class, are shown gaining their advantage through a number of different characters and in a wide variety of situations. The peasant class is shown in a similarly anonymous way, and the interest for the audience lies not so much in rediscovering a piece of the East End's history (the original reason for doing the show) through identification with an individual, but through individuals who, variously and from time to time, carry the advance of the interests of the common people on their shoulders. (82)

Even Wat Tyler, rather than precipitating a revolution, serves more as a bearer of responsibility assigned to him by the other laborers and as the victim of social forces greater than he.

The first half of the play deals with events from 1340 to 1377; it consists largely of a series of cutout scenes used to establish the social background. The plot involving the Wat Tyler rebellion does not begin until almost half way into the play. A devious and dishonest King Richard enslaves the common people, arrests them for petty infractions, and taxes them to death. The play ends with a predictable catastrophe for the commoners but contains a good deal of comedy along the way: hapless Pythonesque knights prepare for an offstage jousting match, the dying King Edward III is picked clean by his mistress, a comic bishop sells dispensations, and an extraneous scene shows Chaucer writing *The Canterbury Tales*. Gooch clearly tried to make his history lesson entertaining.

Without adhering to Cheeseman's insistence that a play use only documented material, Gooch employed many of the staging devices developed by Littlewood and Cheeseman for workers' theatre. One of the ten actors announces the locale and date of each of the nineteen scenes. The four women in the company, of necessity, play many men's parts, contributing to the epic distancing of characterization. Staging is simple and largely emblematic. All court scenes appear on a balcony; other interiors are represented by a platform. A huge reproduction of the Westminster Abbey portrait of Richard II looks down on the action. Songs provide transitions, and "a musical apparatus corner" furnishes a kabukilike area for musical instruments. The actors interact with the audience. For example, when a narrator comments that the Black Death killed one third of the population, the actors hand out undertakers' cards to every third audience member. Gooch intentionally uses anachronisms such as a reference to the pub next door to the theatre.

In a "Writer's Note" prefacing the published play, Gooch stated that his object was not to present a traditional play but rather to have his actors "telling and showing the audience what happened to the peasants and artisans in 1381."

"They should be like people getting up at a family party and doing their turn" (iv). According to D. Keith Peacock, in *Radical Stages*:

This simulated party atmosphere was Gooch's solution to the problem apparent to all creators of documentary histories, that of finding a theatrical style that would both communicate the documentary material in an effective and unpatronising manner and promote that sense of group solidarity which, above all, the theatre could offer the political propagandist." (89).

In spite of the Brechtian devices, the individual scenes within this theatrical matrix are fairly realistic. Speaking of political-fringe theatre in the seventies, Gooch wrote in *All Together Now*, "Even the parameters of an aesthetic consensus emerged, based on a realism that took seriously the predicaments of its characters' lives yet also attempted to relate these to broader social or historical events and a political analysis of them" (56). Consistent with this, Gooch created a Brechtian context for *Will Wat?*, but still developed characterization to have emotional appeal.

Gooch's next history play, *Female Transport*, produced the next year at the Half Moon Theatre, limited the epic material to ballads sung between fairly realistic scenes in the hold of a prison ship.[32] Maintaining Gooch's Marxist perspective, all of his female prisoners are lower-class and have been deported because of economic crimes: petty theft against bourgeois victims. The ship's doctor, forced by financial need into making the voyage, makes a Marxist analysis of the situation: "In peacetime the Navy has a surplus of surgeons. It's hard to find a use for them and their market value is low. So just as the Government is dumping its surplus criminality in New South Wales now America's no longer available, so the Navy's dumping its surplus medical expertise on the ships that take it there" (13). The play contains no villains. Gooch makes clear that economic incentives drive everyone. The captain explains his reasons for not laying over at the Cape: "I'm sorry. I'm being paid nine pound ten a head for these girls. With a hundred and three heads, that's nearly a thousand pounds. Over six months that's six pounds a day. Every day we're in Cape Town I lose six pounds" (54). We will discuss the play in more detail later in the context of feminist history.

The reaction of many Marxist playwrights against commercial theatre was also a reaction against the traditional way of producing theatre, both the economic arrangement and the hierarchal organization of the production staff. Most left-wing theatre groups in Britain used some form of collective process to develop or stage productions so that the organization became a model of the classless society that the company was advocating. The artistic and economic implications of this arrangement produced some strains on most of these groups, but also gave them the organizational persistence needed to take productions to working-class audiences outside the normal venues for theatrical presentation. In *All Together Now*, Gooch explains his commitment to amateur community theatre as a logical extension of this model of collective theatrical production. Other theatre companies that were not specifically political such as The Joint Stock Theatre Group and several feminist groups adopted the collective model for other reasons, some artistic, some ideological.

Gooch's next history play, *The Motor Show*, was written in collaboration with Paul Thompson and developed with community theatre players in the auto factory city of Dagenham. This dramatization of the sixty-year class struggle against Ford Motor Company was first performed in Dagenham to an audience of carworkers and later transferred to the Half Moon Theatre, London. The style of the play reverts to the flat characterization and music hall presentationalism of agitprop. "Mr. Big," who has a lower class American accent ("dat's good tinking"), is a parody of Henry Ford, who keeps calling on the ghost of his "Pappy." Tommy Toyota enters with a great cry and a karate leap, then does calisthenics. Johann Volkswagen comes on goose-stepping with weights on his feet and arms. Sir Merciful Merry, "a real English Lord," used as a front to legitimize the industrial land grab, is a ventriloquist's dummy. The twenty-four titled scenes develop more of a chronology than a plot. Gooch justifies the style as a means of commenting on the material: "Shows that deal with broad contemporary issues like . . . my own *Motor Show*, . . . often portraying facts and figures as well as decades of historical process, may well rely on the techniques of documentary, caricature, cartoon-style depiction, songs, music and cabaret-style patter to indicate the general trends behind the particular incidents."[33] The agitprop staging in this case serves not just as a concession to working-class taste, but as a device for avoiding realistic characterization that may be difficult for less experienced amateur actors.

As in his earlier plays, the protagonist here is not an individual but a group of people responding over time to economic exploitation. In *All Together Now* Gooch justifies this diversion of focus away from individual agency:

The attempt is to create a dramatic excitement and involvement in the shared fate of a group of people—as with the convict women in *Female Transport* or the pirate crew in the second half of *Women Pirates*. Within this dramatic context the unities of time, place, action and character are secondary to the unity of collective interest. Plays which range over forty to sixty years, move location from country to country and in which characters grow up, die and are replaced by others as in *The Motor Show* or *Passed On* (about the history of the Lollards) attempt to appeal to a core of common interest rather than pin identification on a particular, necessarily fallible individual. (82)

Gooch ties his dramatic focus on a group in with his mode of staging:

No longer are an author's private vision and an actor's personal enthusiasm the object of the audience's voyeuristic attention; instead, the publicness of the occasion is acknowledged, and knowledge of particular events and incidents is shared and related to that common forum, "the floor," as it were, "of the house." All the methods of "taking out" a show to its audience, so common in community theatre, share this function—be they songs, asides, monologues, narration or direct audience address. . . . It is as if everything said by one character to another can be overheard and shared by anyone and everyone. . . . Values are held in common and so characters come to complement each other collectively, and it is the *sum* of their words and deeds which is most important. (82–83)

This is an excellent justification for social history, motivated in this case by Marxist concern for the effect of economic oppression on the working class.

Gooch has continued to write history plays, including *Made in Britain*, a *Motor Show*–format exposé of British Leyland, also written with Paul Thompson; *The Woman Pirates*, to be discussed in the context of feminist history; and *Taking Liberties* (produced London, 1984), which deals with John Wilkes's populist politics in late eighteenth-century England.

John McGrath presents his Marxist view of history to working-class audiences in a theatrical form even more dependent on the music hall techniques of agitprop than Steve Gooch's plays. McGrath began writing plays as an undergraduate at Oxford in the late fifties. During the sixties he established a career for himself in British television, but he abandoned this in the seventies in order to devote himself to a producing company known as 7:84, named to remind others that 7 percent of the population in Britain owned 84 percent of the wealth. Like so many leftist playwrights, McGrath was energized by events in May of 1968 in Paris, where he went to take part, in the students' uprising. His wife, Elizabeth MacLennan, one of the principal actresses and cofounder of 7:84, states that the failure of the Paris revolution was a major incentive for founding the company.[34] McGrath developed two 7:84 companies touring among working-class audiences: one in England and another in Scotland, both presenting plays written principally by McGrath. *The Cheviot, the Stag, and the Black, Black Oil*, which in 1973 inaugurated the Scottish 7:84 Theatre Company, was McGrath's first and most successful history play.[35] The play shows three instances of historical crisis when Scottish Highlanders were sacrificed to profit: the Clearances in 1813 when small crofters were evicted from land that they rented in order to make way for more lucrative large-scale sheep raising ventures, mid-nineteenth century depopulation to support colonial expansion, and the American exploitation of oil in the 1970s.

The Cheviot is fundamentally an economic history. Economic considerations affect all major character decisions, and financial data permeate the dialogue of both characters and narrators. There is no ambiguity about McGrath's position. He has one of the company members say, "Until economic power is in the hands of the people, then their culture, Gaelic or English, will be destroyed. The educational system, the newspapers, the radio and television and the decision makers, local and national, whether they know it or not, are the servants of the men who own and control the land" (55). At the play's end all company members appear on stage and call the audience to action: "We too must organise, and fight—not with stones, but politically, with the help of the working class in the towns, for a government that will control the oil development for the benefit of everybody" (73). In an afterword, McGrath writes, "This play tries to show why the tragedies of the past happened: because the forces of capitalism were stronger than the organisation of the people. It tries to show that the future is not pre-determined, that there are alternatives" (77).

This company piece, with actors playing multiple roles, used the form of a *ceilidh*, a Gaelic community gathering in which everyone does something for the others. This style has elements of the English music hall, agitprop, docudrama, and Brecht. At one point in the middle of a speech a character removes his hat and the actor makes a one-sentence comment before returning to character: "Believe it or not, Loch and Sellar actually used these words" (7). Scene changes are done with a giant version of a child's pop-up book. Songs and dialogue are sometimes in English and at other times in Gaelic. Narration both advances the story and comments on the action. Characters are a mixture of music hall types (Lady Phosphate of Runcorn, Texas Jim) and historical figures (Patrick Sellar, James Loch, Harriet Beecher Stowe). McGrath cites John Prebble's, *The Highland Clearances*, about nineteenth-century land policy, and Ian Grimble's *The Trial of Patrick Sellar* as sources of historical material (vi).

The Cheviot attracted the audiences that McGrath wanted; so he returned 7:84 to the same format the next year with *The Game's a Bogey*, a play about the early Scottish Marxist economist and activist John Maclean.[36] The action switches from 1907 to 1973 and back to 1913, the two periods in ironic contrast. *Joe's Drum*, built around an eighteenth-century character who lived in the Cowgate in Edinburgh and assembled a mob with a drum to protest any injustice done to the poor, appeared in 1979 in direct response to the Tory's government's rejection of a popular vote to create a Scots Assembly.[37] *Border Warfare*, produced in Glasgow in 1989 and available only in manuscript, is an episodic depiction of centuries of Scotch/English border conflict.[38] McGrath returned infrequently to documented history among his prolific output, but he continued to use the *ceilidh* staging approach.

In *A Good Night Out* McGrath articulated the connection between his political philosophy and approach to history and his search for a new type of theatre. As a Marxist he takes a skeptical approach to establishment history: "In order to begin to write a play today, one needs first to redefine our inheritance from the history of Western civilization. . . . You have to question all your assumptions about life and society, and try to find out where they came from, and evaluate them in a new way according to the demands of your own and your contemporaries' situation" (87). His Marxist view extends to an assessment of the theatre establishment itself: "Ours is a class society. . . . The British state and its institutions are organized in the interests of the ruling class. . . . I see the bourgeois theatre in all its forms as part of that legitimating ideology" (20–21). He therefore posits a "working class culture," "which is simply *different* from the bourgeois culture emanating from Sir Peter Hall's emporium" (61). McGrath catalogues what he sees as the unique characteristics of this culture as it affects theatre for working-class audiences: directness, heavy reliance on comedy and music, emotionality, variety, emphasis on theatrical effect, immediacy, localism, and a strong sense of identity with the performer (54–58).

McGrath also emphasizes theatre as a public event related to matters of public concern. "Theatre launches even the most private thought into a public world, and gives it a social, historical meaning and context as it passes through the eyes and minds of the audience. . . . How could it remove itself from the other public acts of recognition, evaluation and judgement known as politics? How could it ignore the study of past interaction of human beings and social forces known as history?" (83) McGrath recognizes that the theatre by itself can never cause a social change. "It can articulate the pressures towards one, help people to celebrate their strengths and maybe build their self-confidence."[39]

Theatre collectives were not all politically motivated. The search, originating in the United States during the sixties, for alternative theatre styles generated the practice of developing scripts out of company rehearsals and improvisations. One of the earliest uses of this method was the Traverse Workshop in Edinburgh, which from 1968 until its collapse in 1972 developed company-built pieces under the direction of Max Stafford-Clark. In 1973 Stafford-Clark was one of the founders, with the Royal Court's William Gaskill, of the Joint Stock Company, a larger London-based company that used the same script-building techniques as Traverse. One of Joint Stock's early successes was David Hare's *Fanshen*, a 1975 dramatization of William Hinton's book about his experiences in the Chinese village of Long Bow between 1945 and 1949. In the play, which was about a collective, Gaskill and Stafford-Clark used a collective approach in developing the script, even though Hare claims to have been influenced only by the spirit of these workshops when he went away for four months to write the actual script. The play was revived by Joint Stock in 1977 and by the National Theatre in 1988.

Hare's initial stage direction contends that "*Fanshen* is an accurate historical record,"[40] but he indicates his awareness of an underlying political point of view when he reports on a meeting with Hinton after the play's tryout in Sheffield:

He consulted with his daughter who had been a Red Guard and then with officials from the Chinese Embassy before insisting that the play must be altered if its life was to be prolonged. He had a list of 110 changes most of which—I am using shorthand here—sought to rid the play of what he called my "liberal" slant and to give it more of what I would call his "Marxist" emphasis. (ix)

Hinton's book provides a good example of microhistory, which focuses on the specific local impact of historical events. From the six hundred-plus pages of Hinton's work, Hare concentrates on characters and incidents that occupy only a few pages, but he conveys the overall sense of the villagers' struggle to get the revolution "right."

The plot of *Fanshen* relates the efforts of the Communist leadership of Long Bow both to find a way to redistribute the meager resources of the village and to develop a style of leadership that balances popular participation with the need of the party to exercise control. The cast of nine, playing over thirty parts, performs on a bare stage without lighting cues, but costumes and props are realistic. Signs with slogans indicate changes in the action or the passage of time: "They talked for Eight Hours. . . . They talked for Three Days. . . . They Stopped Paying Rent" (17). Characters periodically narrate the story, and on several occasions a "series of tableaux" illustrates narrative passages. The techniques are Brechtian without Brecht's use of a third-person acting style, and even though the characters adjourn for discussion sessions with almost ritual regularity, they never directly engage the audience in these discussions in a Brechtian manner.

Submerged in *Fanshen* are plot lines involving a Cinderella-like conversion, wife abuse, and the overthrow of a corrupt bully, but these concessions to the Western theatregoer are turned into Communist parables: the woman who learns to criticize becomes a leader, "Women Are Half of China," and even a bully may be redeemed and serve the party. The play leaves several questions unanswered because it ultimately advances a process rather than a product. We see a number of missteps, corrections, and reversals, but a process emerges for participatory correction: the right way can be found as long as participants will examine themselves, the effects of what they are doing, and how their actions

fit into Communist theory. Hare creates a vivid theatrical image for this at the
play's end:

(As they talk the musical note turns into a superb massive groundswell of music that consumes
the stage. Banners flood down so that the whole stage is surrounded in red. At the centre the
cadres mutter on, gesturing, explaining, trying to hold the peasant's attention, getting a
variety of first responses. Just before they are drowned out each cadre gets to the question.)
I'd like to know what you think.

Tell me.

Let me know what you think.

What do you think about this?

(*Then they drown in sound and light.*) (80)

David Hare frequently writes what he describes as history plays with
fictional characters placed in an early twentieth-century context. In *Writing*
Left Handed in 1991 he explained:

For five years I have been writing history plays. I try to show the English their history.
I write tribal pieces, trying to show how people behaved on this island, off this
continental shelf, in this century. How this Empire vanished, how these ideals died . . .
if you begin to describe the undulations of history, if you write plays that cover passages
of time, then you begin to find a sense of movement, of social change.[41]

Caryl Churchill was also influenced by the improvisational technique used
to develop scripts by Joint Stock, which produced more of her plays during the
seventies than those of any other playwright. During this period, Churchill
began a series of plays that experimented with the uses of history. The first of
these, *Light Shining in Buckinghamshire*, was written after a three-week workshop with actors, then produced at the Traverse Theatre in Edinburgh in
September 1976, followed by performances at the Royal Court Theatre
Upstairs. The project at first centered on the Crusades but when the company
had difficulty finding documentary material, they shifted attention to the
English Civil War. According to Churchill, "The company discovered that
their somewhat traditional history book perception of the English Revolution
was turned upside down. . . . We found that we had been sold the idea of
English history's continuity. . . . By our reading in those early stages we
discovered how the history we are taught at school keeps us all in ignorance."[42]
The production was influenced by Norman Cohn's *Pursuit of the Millennium*,
which found an economic basis for religious millennial revolutions, and by
Christopher Hill's *The World Turned Upside Down: Radical Ideas During the*

English Revolution.[43] Hill, a Marxist historian who viewed the English Revolution as a failed democratic revolution, concentrated on the Levellers who espoused political equality; the Diggers, communism; and the Ranters, free love.

Churchill created an episodic collage of sermons, debate, narrative accounts of battles, announced titles for scenes, a few songs, and simultaneous dialogue, along with traditionally constructed dramatic scenes. The technique resembles that of Peter Cheeseman's documentaries and at times the source material seems obtrusively unabsorbed in the drama. Four actors and four actresses played many roles, and more than one actor played a single character. Churchill explains her reason for dividing a role among several actors: "The audience should not have to worry exactly which character they are seeing. Each scene can be taken as a separate event rather than part of a story. This seems to reflect better the reality of large events like war and revolution where many people share the same kind of experience."[44] The availability of documents partly determines the cast of characters and scenes, with real historical figures intermixed with fictionalized characters. Dramatic interest is dispersed among a number of participants, major and minor, and important historical figures such as Cromwell appear only briefly, a marked contrast with most other Civil War plays. Churchill also brings female participants into focus more than with most history plays, anticipating her feminist histories, which we will discuss later. Churchill directs attention onto the broad social consequences of the Civil War rather than its impact on a few individuals. As David Mairowitz observed in a *Plays and Players* review: "The play's history is rooted wholly in a *collective* consciousness which is its protagonist and hero. . . . Churchill does not feel constrained by the preeminence of personality in our culture (and in our theatre) and twists our comprehension of interrelationships in her view of events and in her operation of the stage."[45] He sees the play as a dramatization of the beginnings of class consciousness in English history.

Churchill establishes a definite economic and class basis for the political and religious turmoil of the Civil War. Claxton, something of a common man character in the play, brings home Hoskins, a Leveller who has been beaten by a church congregation. As she bandages the woman's wounds, Claxton's wife argues that women shouldn't preach because they are unclean. Hoskins disagrees and the wife retorts:

Wife: Have you had a child?

Hoskins: No but—

Wife: Then you don't know. We wouldn't be punished if it wasn't for something.

Hoskins: We're not—

Wife: And then they die. You don't know.

Hoskins: They die because how we live. My brothers did. Died of hunger more than fever. My mother kept boiling up the same bones. (11)

Claxton uses a metaphor to describe how different classes respond to hardship:

How we live is like the sea. We can't breathe. Our squire, he's like a fish. Looks like a fish too, if you saw him. And parson. Parson can breathe. He swims about, waggles his tail. Bitter water and he lives in it. Bailiff. Justices. Hangman. Lawyer. Mayor. All the gentry. Swimming about. We can't live in it. We drown. I'm a drowned man. (12)

We later see one of the Parliament men taking over a former royalist estate and reverting to the same exploitative behavior as the previous landlord. Churchill uses a monologue by a butcher, unrelated to any plot development, to set the moral tone during Cromwell's reign:

All of you that can buy meat. You've had your meat. You've had their meat. You've had their meat that can't buy any meat. You've stolen their meat. Are you going to give it back? Are you going to put your hand in your pocket and give them back the price of their meat? I said give them back their meat. You cram yourselves with their children's meat. You cram yourselves with their dead children. (29)

The very condition of having money for food implies collusion in an exploitative economic system.

Two left-wing plays produced in 1978 dealt with early nineteenth-century workers' strikes: *Taking Our Time* by the Red Ladder Theatre and Peter Whelan's *Captain Swing*. The Red Ladder Theatre, a Leeds-based socialist theatre company that works as a collective, performing in working-class industrial communities, began in 1968 as the Agit-Prop Theatre. *Taking Our Time*, which premiered at the East Hunslet Labour Club, Leeds, January 17, 1978, retains a few of the agitprop staging devices, including songs and dances and a Tinker Clown who acts as a master of ceremonies and narrator and becomes the only character on stage killed during industrial riots. The play otherwise presents a fairly straightforward domestic drama with a labor theme. The Chartist "Plug Riots" in 1842 hover in the background of a plot about the ill-fated romance between the daughter of a Chartist worker and a progressive mechanic who believes in reaching an accommodation with the new forces of industry. The climax occurs when he refuses her request to pull the plug on the factory boiler. James Akroyd, the relatively liberal self-made mill owner, was apparently based on a historical character, but the others are invented. The lyrics of a concluding song blatantly state the moral:

He's making multi millions from the modern factory line
Twentieth-century schemer. . . .

Will you wake and take this world and turn it upside down
Twentieth-century dreamer?[46]

Peter Whelan's *Captain Swing*, which opened at the RSC at the Other Place in Stratford on June 26, 1978, also dealt with a failed workers' revolution.[47] Influenced by E. J. Hobsbawm and George Rude's Marxist history of the same name, Whelan's play dramatized the agricultural uprisings in Sussex in the fall of 1830, seen principally from the perspective of the rioters. A threshing barn serves as a unit set for fairly realistic scenes periodically punctuated by the dreamlike appearance of "Corn-men," ritual figures dressed in corn stalks, with thrashers, who serve as imaginary figures of violence. Pressure from extremists threatens the moderate position of the protagonist, the idealist laborer Matthew Hardeness. On one side stands Michael O'Neil, a professional agitator who advocates violence in order to overthrow the establishment, and the whore Gemma. The most extreme revolutionary on stage, Gemma has rescued the title character, Farquarson, known as Captain Swing, who has been burned and remains in a semicoma. On the other side, the representatives of the ruling society are depicted with some sympathy. Matthew gains a kind of victory in that the rioters destroy only property, but they attain no reforms and are themselves subject to the violent punishment that they eschewed. At the play's end, Matthew becomes a late convert to the need for rebellion.

The Royal Shakespeare Company returned to a left-wing social history with David Edgar's *Maydays*, an imaginary "history" of the failure of left-wing movements from 1945 though the early 1980s, which opened at the Barbican on October 13, 1983. Though the context is specific as to time, the characters are imaginary. Edgar juxtaposes the affairs of a group of radical Brits against the rebellion of a Russian officer, Lermontov, who realizes that the Soviet state has betrayed the ideals of communism. We follow the central British character, Martin, from prep school through middle age disillusionment, but he functions as a vehicle for the broader social failure of radicals as a group. The style is realistic with a few rallies, blaring radios, and press conferences, but no narrative intrusions. With three acts, twenty-four scenes, and a large cast, the play generates a feel of epic scope. Recurring Maydays do provide chronological rhythm for the play but the metaphor does not obtrude.[48]

Barrie Keeffe's *Better Times* is one of the few plays about a successful civil protest. Written for the Theatre Royal, East Stratford, London, and produced there on January 31, 1985, this play dramatizes Poplarism, the 1920s tax revolt of the council of the London borough of Poplar. The Labour-controlled council, elected in 1919, attempted to enact progressive legislation providing for rent restrictions, public housing, and parks but was stymied by the inadequate tax base of the borough. Thirty members were led by George Lansbury into prison for refusing to levy a tax they considered unjust and unaffordable for their impoverished borough. Largely because of the vigil maintained outside the prison by thousands of sympathizers, the council members were released and a policy of unequal taxation among boroughs was initiated by the London City Council. The play ostensibly focuses on Lansbury, but actually develops the history of the entire group, many of whom were workers and housewives without political experience.

Characters, in a few minor instances, address the audience, but Keeffe's aim seems largely realistic. In the introduction to the play, he writes of the actor playing Lansbury:

wearing his false mutton chop whiskers and walrus moustache, Robert Keegan—complete with bowler hat and walking cane—looked so much like Lansbury some of the old uns cornered him, talking to him as though he was actually Lansbury. And in doing so solved some of the questions unanswered by all the newspaper clips, council minutes and dusty boxes of files and documents. ([4])

Although most of Keeffe's characters represent specific council members, he identifies others abstractly as "Constable," "Clerk," or "Judge." Both these and the named characters illustrate political types: a Constable represents the conservative police force; a Clerk, the sympathetic government bureaucracy; Herbert Morrison, the pragmatic head of the twelve London Labour mayors. Susan Lawrence is the tough suffragette; Nellie Cressall, the somewhat naive and pregnant councilwoman; Sam March, the self-effacing and blunt-spoken cockney mayor.

Keeffe used Noreen Branson's *Poplarism: George Lansbury and the Councillors' Revolt* as a source, but he also asked in the letters column of the local newspaper for information from anyone about Lansbury.[49] Although carefully researched, this is no documentary. The events depicted occurred, but Keeffe invents dialogue. Although the nineteen scenes show personal interactions, the play is more political than biographical, because Keeffe develops his characters largely through their political choices and shows them primarily when they are involved in political activities such as swearing-in ceremonies, speeches, votes, and arrests.

Keeffe's message is clearly presented. At the play's conclusion Lansbury stares at the audience and says, "When the law is wrong, break it. And in doing so, may you create a classless society" (43).

All of the Marxist history plays depict financial inequities that result from some form of class exploitation. All, including those plays that retain a biographical format, deal with strikes, revolution, or some form of civil protest, but with the exception of *Better Times* and *Fanshen*, all of these revolutions fail. None of these plays, however, leaves the audience with the sense that human efforts are futile or that history proceeds without individual effort and sacrifice. The majority of these plays are social histories with group protagonists, often reflecting collective methods for developing or producing scripts. With the exception of a handful of plays that deal with Marxist leaders, the majority of these plays dramatize events "from the bottom up," with major events occurring offstage and the primary personalities of traditional history either reduced to minor parts or not present. Even though there are exceptions, Brechtian staging devices are widely used, including the basic assumption of historification that the depiction of the past illuminates the present. This often leads to an overt call for social or political action at a play's end.

NOTES

1. Howard Falperin, " 'Cultural Poetics' versus 'Cultural Materialism': The Two New Historicisms in Renaissance studies," in *Uses of History: Marxism, Postmodernism and the Renaissance*, ed. Francis Barker, Peter Hulme, and Margaret Iversen (Manchester: Manchester University, 1991), pp. 76–100.

2. Harvey J. Kaye, *British Marxist Historians*, new ed. (New York: St. Martin's, 1995), p. 4.

3. Elizabeth Fox-Genovese and Eugene D. Genovese, "The Political Crisis of Social History: A Marxian Perspective," *Journal of Social History* 10, no. 2 (Winter 1976): 205–20. Cited in Gertrude Himmelfarb, *The New History and the Old* (Cambridge, MA: Harvard, 1987), pp. 24–25.

4. Kaye, *Marxist Historians*, p. 226.

5. John McGrath, *A Good Night Out, Popular Theatre: Audience, Class and Form* (London: Methuen, 1981), p. 90.

6. This work was continued in more detail by Paul Sweezy, Maurice Dobb, H. K. Takahashi, Rodney Hilton, and Christopher Hill, *The Transition from Feudalism to Capitalism* (New York: Science and Society, 1954).

7. D. Keith Peacock, *Radical Stages: Alternative History in Modern British Drama* (Westport, CT: Greenwood, 1991), pp. 13, 15.

8. Christopher Hill, *The World Turned Upside Down: Radical Ideas During the English Revolution* (New York: Viking, 1972).

9. "Kleines Organon für das Theater" [1948], *Versuche*, 12, trans. John Willett, ed. Eric Bentley (Frankfurt-am-Main: Suhrkamp, 1953), in *Playwrights on Playwriting*, ed. Toby Cole (New York: Hill & Wang, 1960), p. 86.

10. Steve Gooch, *All Together Now: An Alternative View of Theatre and Community* (London: Methuen, 1984), p. 36.

11. For example, see Eric Bentley's introduction to Bertolt Brecht, *Seven Plays* (New York: Grove, 1961), pp. xi–li.

12. Edward Bond, "Introduction," *Plays: Two* (London: Methuen, 1978), p. xiv.

13. The subject of the left-wing dramatization of history in Britain through 1986 has been competently explored in Peacock, *Radical Stages*.

14. For a detailed if somewhat partisan account of this see John McGrath, *The Bone Won't Break* (London: Methuen, 1990).

15. Guiseppe Fiori, *Vita di Antonio Gramsci*, 7th ed. (Bari: Editori Laterza, 1981).

16. Trevor Griffiths, *Occupations*, rev. ed. (London: Faber & Faber, 1980), p. 68. First published London: Calder and Boyars, 1972.

17. Nairn's article, quoted by Griffiths, *Occupations*, p. 7, appeared Nov. 3, 1971.

18. Richard Findlater, ed., *At the Royal Court: 25 Years of the English Stage Company* (New York: Grove, 1981), p. 155.

19. Edward Bond, "Introduction" to *Bingo: Scenes of Money and Death*, in *Plays: Three* (London: Methuen, 1987), p. 6.

20. Edward Bond, *The Fool* [1975], in *Plays: Three*, pp. 125–26.

21. *Sunday Telegraph*, Nov. 23, 1975.

22. Howard Brenton, *The Churchill Play* [1974, 1978], in *Plays: One* (London: Methuen, 1986), p. 114.

23. Angus Calder, *The People's War* (London: Jonathan Cape, 1969).

24. Howard Brenton, *Plays: One*, pp. xiii–xv.

25. Michael Billington, "Problem of 'Relevance' disappearing as Social Conditions Change: 'The Churchill Play,' " *Guardian*, Aug. 22, 1978.

26. Tariq Ali and Howard Brenton, *Moscow Gold* (London: Nick Hern, 1990), p. 47.

27. From *Marxism Today* in Ali and Brenton, *Moscow Gold*, p. 88.

28. John McGrath, *A Good Night Out* and *The Bone Won't Break: On Theatre and Hope in Hard Times* (London: Methuen, 1990), and Steve Gooch, *All Together Now*.

29. Alan Plater, *Close the Coalhouse Door* (London: Methuen, 1969), p. vii.

30. John Elson, "Alan Plater," in *Contemporary Dramatists*, 4th ed. (Chicago and London: St. James, 1988), p. 433.

31. Steve Gooch, *Will Wat? If Not, What Will?* (London: Pluto, 1972).

32. Steve Gooch, *Female Transport* (New York: Samuel French, 1974).

33. Gooch, *All Together Now*, p. 75.

34. Elizabeth MacLennan, *The Moon Belongs to Everyone: Making Theatre with 7:84* (London: Methuen, 1990), p. 10.

35. John McGrath, *The Cheviot, the Stag, and the Black, Black Oil* (London: Eyre Methuen, 1981).

36. John McGrath, *The Game's a Bogey* (Edinburgh: Edinburgh University Student Publications, 1975).

37. John McGrath, *Joe's Drum* (Aberdeen: Aberdeen People's Press, 1979).

38. Discussed in Janelle Reinelt, *After Brecht: British Epic Theatre* (Ann Arbor: University of Michigan, 1994), 197–203.

39. McGrath, *Cheviot*, xxvii.

40. David Hare, *Fanshen*, in *The Asian Plays* (London: Faber & Faber, 1986), p. 5.

41. "The Play Is in the Air," in *Writing Left Handed* (London: Faber & Faber, 1991), p. 32.

42. "Fringe Beneficiaries," *Time Out*, Sept. 24–30, 1976, pp. 10–11.

43. Norman Cohn, *The Pursuit of the Millennium: Revolutionary Millenarians and Mystical Anarchists of the Middle Ages* [1957], rev. ed. (London: Temple Smith, 1970), and Christopher Hill's *The World Turned Upside Down*.

44. Caryl Churchill, *Light Shining in Buckinghamshire* (London: Pluto, 1978), p. 6.

45. David Mairowitz, "God and the Devil," *Plays and Players* 24, no. 5 (Feb. 1977): 24.

46. The Red Ladder Theatre, *Taking Our Time* (London: Pluto, 1979), p. 51.

47. Peter Whelan, *Captain Swing* (London: Rex Collins, 1979).

48. David Edgar, *Maydays* (London: Methuen, 1983, 1984).

49. Barrie Keeffe, *Better Times* (London: Methuen, 1985), p. 3.

6

Feminist History Plays

Feminist playwrights have written history plays since the 1970s and these provide a clear example of the connection between a specific social agenda and the related treatment of historical material in a play. Feminism gains some portion of its legitimacy by validating the historical record of neglect, exclusion, and repression; so not surprisingly the revisitation of history offers an important way to demonstrate the legitimacy of feminist grievances. Monstrous Regiment, one of the leading feminist theatres in Britain, declared at its 1976 founding that among its aims was "reclaiming the history play from women's point of view"[1] (37). Their first production, *Scum: Death, Destruction and Dirty Washing* by C. G. Bond and Claire Luckham, was set in a laundry in Paris during 1870–71, when Parisians briefly declared self-government in the Paris Commune. That same year the company also did Caryl Churchill's *Vinegar Tom*, a play about the victimization of women during the witch hunts in England in the seventeenth century.

A history play about a woman is not necessarily a feminist history play. Since the time of Euripides, individual playwrights, including John Webster, Nicholas Rowe, Henrik Ibsen, and George Bernard Shaw, emphasized women's issues; however, from some modern feminist viewpoints, these writers still reflected the male, albeit liberal, values of their own times. As Michelene Wandor, the early chronicler of recent feminist theatre in Britain, has noted, "It is perfectly possible to have an all-female play which reinforces all the most negative things about female experience." She labeled such plays *feminine* rather than feminist.[2]

The fact that a playwright is a woman similarly offers no assurance that a play is feminist. To succeed commercially, women playwrights had to cater to the standards of audiences that were predominantly male until the twentieth century and thereafter still reflected the values of a male-oriented society. Elizabeth Mackintosh, for example, wrote commercially successful history plays in the 1930s, including *Queen of Scots* (1934) with its female protagonist, but she wrote under the male nom de plume Gordon Daviot, and her plays romanticized female political figures.

History plays written before the 1960s with female protagonists typically focused on "major players," women in history, often queens, who exercised some political power. Even so, these plays usually depicted women romantically rather than politically. Wandor notes that prior to Feminist Theatre, even the occasional play with a central heroine fit into a system of predominantly male concerns, sometimes highlighting the concerns by projecting them on women, "but rarely shifting the ground to the territory of female experience as such. Women are thus either ciphers for men's concerns or adjuncts to the male protagonists."[3]

The definition of feminism both in the theatre and as an approach to history has been a changing one, reflecting developments in feminist consciousness as well as differences in sociopolitical focus in different intellectual climates in different countries. Feminist history developed through four overlapping phases that reflect the increasing deemphasis of the masculine context of history: compensatory, contributory, social, and gender-focused.[4] The development of feminist themes in historical drama lags behind their development among historians; so history plays manifest these four approaches without regard to the order of their emergence in historical studies.

The first stage, compensatory feminist history, developed from biographical histories and focused on notable women whose lives had been distorted by masculine-biased histories or had been given less than deserved notice in traditional historical accounts. Writers now recounted "her-stories" rather than "his-stories." The feminist historian Joan Scott asked, "By what processes have men's actions come to be considered a norm, representative of human history generally, and women's actions either overlooked, subsumed, or consigned to a less important, particularized arena?"[5] Scott noted that in the 1960s, "feminist activists called for a history that would provide heroines, proof of women's agency, and explanations of oppression and inspiration for action."[6] Feminist historians answered the call, focusing particularly on early figures in the women's rights struggles, but these personalities failed to attract dramatists, and compensatory histories of women emerged in the theatre only in the late sixties. Most biographical plays in the sixties and seventies that focused on historically important women, such as William Francis's *Portrait of a Queen* (1965), Robert Bolt's *Vivat! Vivat Regina!* (1970), John Bowen's *Florence*

Nightingale (1975), and Hugh Whitemore's *Stevie* (1977), demonstrated little in the way of feminist consciousness. All were written by men, and, perhaps understandably, the chief examples of feminist compensatory dramatic biography are Pam Gems's *Queen Christina* (1977) and *Piaf* (1978).

The second phase of feminist history, what the historian Gerda Lerner calls contribution history, describes "women's contributions to, their status in, and their oppression by male-defined society."[7] Lerner observed in *The Majority Finds Its Past: Placing Women in History* that the "history of 'notable women' does not tell us much about the activities in which most women engaged"[8] However, "woman centered" narratives, according to Lerner "reveal what women themselves were doing, saying, and thinking, the factors that affected their lives, and the motivations that lay behind their actions."[9] This phase differs from the first largely in terms of the prominence of the subjects. The women are less likely to be famous, more likely to be dominated by males, and more traditionally defined as being in "supporting roles." History plays reflecting this phase include Ann Jellicoe's *Shelley, or The Idealist* (1965) and Steve Gooch's *The Women Pirates Ann Bonney and Mary Read* (1978).

This second phase also represents a shift away from political history to personal history, or, as Michelene Wandor suggests, a rejection of the dissociation of the personal and the political. Wandor notes that the slogan "The personal is political . . . is peculiarly apt for the situation of women, since the 'personal' has always been identified with the female, the emotional, the home and family, and women's presence in other spheres of life has either been ignored or undervalued." Wandor, writing in 1981, commented that this focus on the personal caused most women playwrights to eschew the epic-scaled history play. As Timberlake Wertenbaker stated, "Women don't write 'State of England Plays.' They have a more encompassing view of history perhaps because they have been so long outside of history."[10] In contrast, many male socialist writers in the 1970s reacted against the bourgeois 'indoor' plays that detached individuals from political responsibility, but the danger in this, according to Wandor, was that emphasis on a person's social and political environment could exclude individual and emotional life from a definition of "politics."[11]

The third phase in the growth of feminist history took its impulse from social history that granted groups like peasants, workers, teachers, and slaves status as historical subjects. This category differs from the previous one by emphasizing group behavior rather than individual women. Historians explored women's activities in political organizations, in the workplace, and within the family. The plays in this group includes Steve Gooch's *Female*

Transport (1973) and Caryl Churchill's early plays *Light Shining in Bucking-hamshire* (1976) and *Vinegar Tom* (1976).

Finally women's history focused attention on the wider issue of gender, not on biologically defined issues of sex, but on the ways that society assigns roles to men and women. Gender studies borrow techniques from the deconstructionists, searching for what cultural historians call the " 'mechanics of representation': how actions acquired significance, how symbols were created and used, how words not only 'reflected social and political reality' but also 'were instruments for transforming reality.' "[12] Lerner insists, "Women's history must contain not only the activities and events in which women participated, but the record of changes and shifts in their perception of themselves and their roles."[13] She explains, "The central question raised by women's history is: what would history be like if it were seen through the eyes of women and ordered by values they define?"[14] Michelene Wandor wrote in 1981:

The area of historical reclamation (in both new subject matter and in its new possibilities of language and form) is also wide open; at one level the whole of received history is available for re-interpretation, and at another, levels of the submerged history of women and sexuality wait to be dramatised. . . . Perhaps the most exciting challenge is to see what we, as women theatre workers today, make of the history and experience of women in the past, bringing our own interpretive perspective from today's feminism.[15]

The plays in this group are more explicitly feminist; they include Caryl Churchill's *Top Girls* and *Cloud Nine* (1980), Timberlake Wertenbaker's *New Anatomies* (1984) and *The Grace of Mary Traverse* (1985), Shirley Gee's *Warrior* (1989), and Claire Tomalin's *The Winter Wife* (1991).

The depiction of women as victims of a male-dominated society is nascent in the first phase and emerges increasingly with each category. Women who are proven shakers and movers are less likely to be seen as victims than those hidden in the fabric of society, but a historical perspective delimited by gender emphasizes differences that must by feminist definition reveal patriarchal oppression in any situation.

History plays that develop a feminist perspective reflect these four overlapping stages in the development of feminism as well as other changes in historiography that we have already discussed. Compensatory feminist history, for example, largely uses a biographical approach, differing from other biographical drama only to the extent that the condition of being female, per se, principally determines the protagonist's actions. The later phases share with other social histories a focus on the group rather than the individual.

What characteristics define the feminist historical drama that emerged in Britain during the last twenty years? Michelene Wandor identifies three major features:

1. A challenge to the assumption that "history consists of a series of great men master-minding great events"
2. The breaking of sexual and "body" taboos with a particular concern with female sexual independence
3. A validation of female friendship and solidarity[16]

Wandor also notes, as do others, that in Britain, feminism tends to be socialist rather than radical, relating sexism to issues of class and economic oppression.[17]

BIOGRAPHICAL HISTORIES OF WOMEN

Several history plays that dealt with prominent women were written by men in the sixties and seventies, but the plays express the traditional representation of women rather than any new feminine consciousness. A brief examination of several of these will clarify this difference.

Romance or sexual appetite remains a persistent component of "she drama" into the seventies. For example, Robert Bolt's *Vivat! Vivat Regina!*, produced in 1970, reduces the political conflict between Mary Queen of Scots and Elizabeth I to a drama of repressed sexuality. Although Bolt's women have an outspoken toughness that reflects the 1960s, the fundamental characterization of Mary remains essentially the same as that in Gordon Daviot's play thirty-five years earlier that showed a fickle, irresponsible Mary who sacrificed her duty to Scotland in order to pursue her personal passions.[18]

Bolt reveals his two protagonists largely through their interaction with male lovers and counselors, but the women do not seem particularly victimized by men. Mary emphatically accepts responsibility for her own actions. After the murder of her secretary and lover David Rizzio, she laments, "He was my friend," and Morton replies, "He was more than that." Mary answers, "The fault of that was mine. And I ought to have paid for it."[19] To serve Bolt's existentialist theme, Mary must control her own actions. As she approaches the headsman, Bolt has her assert the value of her hedonism in contrast to Elizabeth's love denying *realpolitik*, "There is more living in a death that is embraced than in a life that is avoided across three score years and ten. And I embrace it thus! *She throws off the black revealing scarlet head to foot*" (95). This conflict in historical drama between political responsibility and personal passion is certainly as old as *Antony and Cleopatra*, striking male as well as female protagonists, and Bolt's treatment of history here looks more backward to these love/honor conflicts than forward to feminist sensibilities.

John Bowen's *Florence Nightingale*[20] shares with Bolt's play an overlay of Freudianism that disparages women, but Bowen takes more pains to show the extent to which male prejudice victimizes his central character. Bowen deromanticizes his protagonist, but the resulting portrait retains much of the patronizing attitude of the traditional "she dramas" and could hardly be considered a feminist history. Bowen's play premiered at the Marlowe Theatre, Canterbury, in November of 1975 and like James Saunders's *Next Time I'll Sing to You*, discussed earlier, uses a play-in-rehearsal format to allow the actors to raise questions concerning the motives of the characters they depict.

Bowen's staging is intentionally Brechtian. The introduction, for example, suggests an "all-over Brechtian lighting." The Director and occasionally an actor provide narrative surrounding scenes depicting sixty-five of Nightingale's ninety years. Actors play multiple roles by drawing costumes and hats from a basket; men occasionally play women. The idea of actors rehearsing allows for the alienating effect that the audience is aware of the actor behind the character and allows for commentary, albeit scripted, by the fictionalized "actor." Although more Brechtian than Bolt's *A Man for All Seasons*, Bowen's play, like Bolt's, lacks the social consciousness that justifies Brecht's epic staging.

The Director and leading actress debate the causes of Nightingale's sometimes idiosyncratic and compulsive behavior. The Director's perception of her is ambivalent. He acknowledges that she was "forever battling against male short-sightedness" (6), and he notes that by Victorian standards, even as a thirty-two year-old woman, Florence needed her parents' permission to become a nurse (9), and that "given the prejudices of the time, *had* to work—through men" (47). However, he is also uneasy about Nightingale's use of psychosomatic ill health to manipulate others and particularly her tendency to consume with overwork the men devoted to her. Bowen's Nightingale, largely because of her parents' repressive influence, emerges as an obsessive neurotic, whose "Lady with a Lamp" image is chiefly a romantic invention. This characterization uncomfortably resembles the Victorian view of "female hysterics." Although the actress playing Florence, early in the play, accuses the Director of being "bloody pig-ignorant about women" (3), Bowen's iconoclastic characterization of Florence supports the idea that she was manipulative and obsessive. The Director's discomfort with Florence's behavior seems less an ironic comment on his masculine bias than Bowen's final word on Nightingale. At the play's conclusion, the actress playing Nightingale insists on giving Florence an opportunity to defend herself, but by this time the actress has been absorbed into the personality of her character, and the defense is not in feminist terms. As the Director observes early in the play, "Miss Nightingale wasn't a twentieth-century lady. She was a Victorian" (6). Bowen's staging note that the Director, with just a few line changes, could be played by a woman, also suggests that he did not intend his characterization to be an ironic comment on the masculine biases in Bowen's own play. A female Director would present a less obviously masculine slant on Florence's behavior. Another way to regard the play is that Bowen raised issues of gender that he perhaps did not fully understand. Certainly a feminist would have called this characterization of Nightingale into question. In final analysis the actors' ruminations focus on issues of characterization and motive but largely ignore the social and gender issues latent in Nightingale's struggles against Victorian sensibilities.

Biographical dramas with female protagonists periodically appear as vehicles for prominent British actresses. *Stevie*, by that inveterate writer of biographical drama Hugh Whitemore, opened at the Vaudeville Theatre, London, March 1977, with Glenda Jackson playing the poet Stevie Smith. Essentially a star turn for Jackson, the play has two additional characters: Stevie's Aunt, and a "Man" who serves as interlocutor, a narrator, and finally a personification of death. Rather than being organized around a dramatic conflict, the play consists of discussions on a series of topics each amplified with selections from Smith's poetry. Overriding themes are Stevie's fascination with death and unsuccessful attempts to escape life. In one episode she reflects on the extent to which marriage defines women's identities in her suburban world, and she rejects a marriage proposal because "If we get married, I won't be Stevie any more. I'll be Mrs Freddy,"[21] but this one passing acknowledgment of male-dominated social values does not constitute a feminist perspective.

COMPENSATORY FEMINIST HISTORY

In contrast, another biographical history play that appeared in 1977, Pam Gems's *Queen Christina*,[22] which the Royal Shakespeare Company presented at The Other Place in Stratford, shows a clearer feminist view of history. This play had been commissioned earlier by Ann Jellicoe, who was literary manager at the Royal Court, but by the time it was completed, Jellicoe had left, and the script was turned down because "it would appeal more to women than to men."[23]

Gems, who says she was motivated to write principally to create big roles for women,[24] used the conventional form of a historical chronicle to dramatize the life of the seventeenth-century Swedish monarch from childhood to her death at fifty-nine, but Gems selected historical incidents that emphasized the particular problems of a female ruler in a male-dominated society. From the opening screams of childbirth as Christina's mother bears yet another stillborn male heir, issues of gender more than politics define the play's conflicts. Gems described this as a "uterine play,"[25] and the reviewer Irving Wardle observed, "Political history features only where it casts light on [Christina's] quest for identity."[26] Raised as a man, and in many respects more independent and masculine than many of her subsequent male suitors, Christina has ambivalent attitudes about her own sex. Having to play the role of progenitor of kings offends her, and she finds childbirth repulsive, but later in life, she regrets not having children. Attracted sexually to both men and women, Christina in her sexual practices reflects both the masculine appetites to which she has been trained and her inherent preferences as a woman.

The refocusing of attention from the political to the domestic, a shift that characterizes much of feminist drama, offended one male critic, B. A. Young of *Financial Times*, who wrote, "When the abdication is reduced from a grand public ceremony to a bad tempered domestic quarrel, when the political assassination of Monaldescho becomes a squalid scuffle with the Queen herself striking the fatal blow, these are the inward content of great events as Miss Gems chooses to see them."[27]

Eventually forced to abdicate, Christina converts to Catholicism and retires to Rome. The RSC production emphasized the continuity of masculine oppression by doubling roles so that the same actors play different characters who hold similar power relations with Christina in Sweden and in Rome: the actor playing the Swedish chancellor Oxenstierna reappeared as the pope and Prince Karl as Cardinal Azzolino.[28] The players change but the game is the same.

Reviewing the play's opening in 1977, John Barber wrote that Gems "is the only English playwright concerned with the role of women in society,"[29] but in her history of British feminist theatre, Michelene Wandor stated that Gems was suspicious of organized politics and rejected the feminist label. Wandor thought, however, that the play's action, though "centering on the existential choices facing Christina, faces us with the same question that political feminism has explored in theory and political analysis; what is it to be 'male'? What is it to be 'female'?" Wandor concluded, "Gems's work is strongly woman-centered, in that men come and go in the plays, and none of her major female characters are seen working through relationships with men."[30] Gems herself, in a program note to the 1993 London revival of *Piaf,* attributed her turn to playwriting when she was in her early forties to neofeminism's personal impact in the 1970s.

The success of *Queen Christina* and more so of *Dusa, Fish, Stas and Vi* led to the production in 1978 at the Other Place of a play that Gems had originally written in 1973 as a vehicle for a Romanian actress who performed songs of the French chansonnière Edith Piaf. *Piaf* appeared subsequently at Wyndhams and on Broadway, where Jane Lapotaire won a Tony for her performance. Peter Hall directed a successful 1993 revival at the Piccadilly Theatre in London.[31] Piaf's eventual empowerment results from success as a performer rather than political status, but as in Christina's case, abuse early in her life leads Piaf to self-destructive misuse of power. As her costar and lover Eddie Constantine commented, "Men had done her so much harm when she was young I think she was taking her revenge by seducing all possible men. . . . The best looking and most important . . . for her this compensated for all her suffering."[32]

Gems's play, with short episodes and songs bridging almost thirty years, shows a hardened character raised in the gutters of Paris who is thrust into stardom but never able to shake behavior conditioned by her youth. While following the traditional rise and fall pattern of the morality play, Gems focuses largely on incidents that show Piaf's interactions with men, either lovers or "managers." Early scenes show her as a victim of men; later scenes show her manipulating men; but Gems dwells more on Piaf's dependence on than exploitation by men. Piaf seems self-destructive, driven less by external events than psychological compulsions: guilt for the death of her daughter and self-hatred for her own appearance and behavior. A program note for the 1993 production quotes the 1984 autobiography of Piaf's friend Marlene Dietrich, who wrote, "She was a fragile bird, but also the Jezebel whose insatiable thirst was made to compensate her insecurity and her self-confessed ugliness." The beauty of Piaf's songs throughout the play emphasizes the extent to which the emotionality of her art resulted from the pain of her own life and leaves the audience with a strong sense of waste.

Michelene Wandor saw the play as affirming basic tenets of the feminist agenda, resilience, friendship, and sexuality:

Piaf is so far the clearest expression of faith in women's basic resilience. . . . Piaf and her friend Toine are tough street-women . . . and the women's friendship survives the succession of men who pass through their lives. . . . Piaf is a woman for whom female independence means an active and vigorous sexuality, which at its most intense parallels the orgasmic satisfaction she gets from singing, and a bristly individualistic identification with being working-class which enables her to resist all the flannel and hypocrisy of showbiz.[33]

Tim Rice and Andrew Lloyd Webber dramatized a similar up-from-the-streets-woman in their popular 1978 musical, *Evita*, about the Argentinian populist Evita Peron. Although Rice and Lloyd Webber show the male exploitation of Evita, who, like Piaf, reverses control when she becomes empowered, class rather than gender issues take center stage here.

Virginia, a biographical drama about a figure with clearer feminist credentials, Virginia Woolf, was written by the Anglo-Irish novelist and short story writer Edna O'Brien. This star vehicle for Maggie Smith premiered at the Stratford Festival, Ontario, June 1980, and was later moved to London, where it opened at the Haymarket Theatre on January 29, 1981.[34] An extra man and woman play several roles in the cast of three. Although the play is not a monodrama, Virginia, who only once leaves stage, intersperses narrative, stream of consciousness thought, and imitation of the voices of others, a real showcase for Maggie Smith. With material taken from diaries and letters of Virginia and Leonard Woolf, the nine scenes in two acts range from the death of Virginia's mother to her own suicide. O'Brien's focus is on Virginia's fear of recurring insanity and on the extent to which her relationships with her father, sister Nessa, Leonard, and Vita Sackville-West shape her personality. Virginia's passion is for Vita, but she really does love Leonard, who is extremely rational, respectful of her talent, and tolerant of her peculiarities.

Although not strongly feminist in tone, the play clearly shows how reactions to her as a woman shape Virginia's sensibilities. After being raped by her half brother, she observes, "Make no mistake the Greeks are for men, the Treasury is for men, Whitehall is for men, the world belongs to men" (15). At another point she comments, "Women are hard to women. Women dislike women" (18). As she loses her sanity, her monologue reveals the extent to which sexual abuse and anxiety contribute to her dementia: "Yes, one must meet one's apparitions. . . . Those books are stained, they're breeding, they're breeding mushrooms. And spiders are under my skirt. They're crawling up there, great long black . . . bestial" (27).

FEMINIST CONTRIBUTION HISTORIES

All of these plays focus on women whose prominence was to some extent granted by traditional historical measures. A feminist view of history requires that we focus on women whose importance has been neglected or relegated to a contributing role in a male-dominated society. The American feminist writer Janelle Reinelt, for example, sees a feminist consciousness in Edward Bond because of his "treatment of women as serious agents of history, responsible for internalizing and teaching the dominant discourse of the patriarchy." [35] Plays in this second category focus on figures normally seen as secondary in a male-dominated context. An example is one of the earliest history plays to show a clear feminist perspective, Ann Jellicoe's *Shelley, or the Idealist*, which opened at the Royal Court on October 18, 1965. In spite of the biographical focus on Shelley, Jellicoe in the preface emphasized that her interests were on controlling social forces rather than biography: "I wanted to build a story which would proceed step by step, each action drawing upon itself inevitable social consequences which would dictate the next action."[36] The play, using a cast of twelve with doubling, presents a chronological dramatization in seventeen scenes of Shelley's life, beginning in 1810 when he was an eighteen-year-old Oxford student and ending with his death in 1822.

Although Shelley is unquestionably the central character, Jellicoe develops him largely through his relationships with the women in his life: his sister Hellen; his first wife, Harriet; his mistress and later his second wife, Mary; and Jane Williams. Mary Shelley is the most fully developed of these women, and although she qualifies as a prominent literary figure in her own right, her importance in this play depends on her position in a group: "Shelley's Women." After two initial scenes revealing how Shelley's unconventional values lead to his expulsion from Oxford, the remainder of the play shows the destructiveness of Shelley's consistent application of his own liberal principles, particularly regarding the separation of marriage from love outside marriage. Jellicoe dramatizes effects rather than causes. She shows little of the influences that shape Shelley's values, but we see how his hedonism and rebellion against social convention destroy the women around him, who are unwilling to relinquish him to his next infatuation. His first wife, Harriet, is bound by convention; his second wife, Mary Godwin, is not, but both suffer. Harriet drowns herself in the Serpentine after being abandoned by Shelley for Mary, and although Mary outlives Shelley, Jellicoe depicts her as broken by the apparent transfer of Shelley's affections to Jane Williams and by the death of her children as a result of Shelley's exile and wanderings.

Shelley's passions beguile because he appears to be motivated by a naive presumption that people can live without the constraints of social convention. Jellicoe develops the central conflict in the play as a clash between a free new order espoused by Shelley and rigid older society represented by a variety of disapproving minor characters in the play. The women are caught in the middle, seduced by Shelley's cry of freedom but inescapably tied to the order of marriage and child rearing.

Even though Shelley sounds like an early advocate for women's rights, Jellicoe presents his liberalism ironically. Early in the play Shelley gives Harriet a copy of *The Rights of Woman* written by Mary Shelley's mother, Mary Wollstonecraft, whom he calls "calm, clear-headed, dignified, daring, oh a magical woman."[37] Shelley's ideal woman, however, behaves as he does: "a woman of consummate courage, nobility and strength, and above all, education. That is the key. The power to reason, to understand, that makes her free to act. Educated as a man, to think as clearly and boldly as the best of men" (72). Mary, who seems to embody these values, is ultimately defeated by the demands on her as a mother. "You thought you could change the world," she tells Shelley. "Look at the misery you've dragged me into, sitting here at the end of the world, waiting to miscarry" (106). The other spokesman for liberalism in the play, the radical philosopher William Godwin, Mary Wollstonecraft's husband and Mary Shelley's father, emerges as an economically exploitive opportunist who overlooks his daughter's misery in return for payments from Shelley. The play becomes a comment on the professed liberalism of the sixties radical male, who largely ignored women's issues. D. Keith Peacock, in his study of left-wing history plays, notes that even in the radical theatre of the sixties, women were depicted stereotypically by male dramatists.[38]

Two other plays deal with Shelley and his circle, *Blood and Ice* by Liz Lochhead and *Bloody Poetry* by Howard Brenton, which is not particularly feminist and has been examined in the framework of biographical drama. *Blood and Ice* focuses principally on Mary Shelley, with four other characters: Byron, Bysshe, Claire, and a maid, Elise. An earlier version under the title *Mary and the Monster* was presented at the studio of the Belgrade Theatre in March 1981, a second revision at the Traverse Theatre in Edinburgh in August 1982; the final published version opened at New Merlin's Cave, London, February 27, 1984. The play begins and ends with Mary's reaction to Shelley's drowning and death. The dialogue in the nine scenes is treated realistically, but Mary and her sister Claire occasionally revert to role playing games that provide brief flashbacks, and Mary's monologues punctuate the play. Byron is a more central character than Shelley, forcing Mary to confront her responsibility for her own acts and to some extent even embodying Mary's own worse impulses. Near the play's end, Byron challenges Mary's assertion that she has examined herself and found herself guiltless:

Byron: Infants do benefit from travel, don't they? Florence, Venice, Padua, a bit of culture and cholera does broaden the mind.

Mary: You are a twisted person.

Byron: Oh yes, Mary, there is something in us which is very ugly. Do you not think we are somewhat alike? We are put together all wrong.

Mary: Loathesome.

Byron: Well if I am the monster, who or what are you? Mary Shelley.[39]

Frankenstein becomes a central image as Mary quotes and paraphrases the book throughout the play. In a final monologue she ponders the book's meaning for herself:

I am Frankenstein, the creator who loves creation and hates its results. Then I thought: no, I am the monster, poor misunderstood creature feared and hated by all mankind. And then I thought: it is worse, worse than that, I am the female monster, gross, gashed, ten times more hideous than my male counterpart, denied life, tied to the monster bed for ever. . . . But now I see who I am, in my book. I am Captain Walton, explorer. Survivor. My own cool narrator. The one who once dreamed of that land of wonder, where, way beyond the pole, sailing over a calm sea, further than the flickering Northern Lights—Men and Woman Might Live in Freedom. (115)

This Mary Shelley is less a victim than either Jellicoe or Brenton's Mary. The maid, Elise, whom Mary discharges for having a child out of wedlock, fires back that having been taught to read by Mary and having read *The Rights of Woman* by Mary's mother, Mary Wollstonecraft, she knows about freedom: "At least freedom for the Woman with six hundred a year and a mill-owning husband to support her—and a bevy of maid-servants sweeping and starching and giving suck to her squalling infants—not to speak of her rutting husband." In response, Mary slaps her (107). When Mary argues with Byron that she was only sixteen when she ran off with Shelley, Byron reminds her that Shelley's wife, whom Mary has effectively destroyed, was also sixteen when she married Shelley: "Did her little dripping wet sixteen year old ghost visit you on your wedding night?" (109). Lochhead's Mary Shelley has moved beyond being merely a victim in a male world and has become a victim of the incongruity between her own idealism and the reality of her own needs as a person and as a woman. This is not to deny the importance of gender. As she says in her final speech: "My heart sickened at the workings of my loins" (116).

The appeal of Shelley and his circle to playwrights rests largely on being an early model of an alternative life-style, which Stephen Gooch found in pirate society in *The Women Pirates Ann Bonney and Mary Read*, produced by the Royal Shakespeare Company at the Aldwych Theatre on July 31, 1978. A play with feminist overtones written by a man, this pleasant, seemingly entertaining drama, although not stridently didactic, does have a clear message: "alternative" pirate society restricts unconventional women as much as established society. This production was removed from the RSC schedule because of its failure to attract an audience after receiving almost universally bad reviews. The reviewers, who were overwhelmingly male, seemed mostly offended by what Milton Shulman of the *Guardian* described as "lesbian, sexually sleazy and totally irrelevant characteristics."[40] Irving Wardle, writing for the *Times* and applying the standards of traditional positivist history, complained about the "confusion between the desire to recreate past events objectively, and the desire to shape them into a historical reflection of the female gay movement."[41]

The thrust of the play is more socialist than feminist, what Shulman called "a touch of infantile Marxism."[42] With a line of self-justification reminiscent of Peachum in *The Threepenny Opera*, the pirates present themselves as social protesters. One exclaims, "Damn ye, sir, ye're a sneaking puppy! And so are all men who submit to laws made by rich men for their own security. There is only this difference between us: they rob the poor under cover of the law, while we plunder the rich under the protection of nothing but our own courage."[43]

In act I, the chronologically organized scenes switch back and forth between the stories of the two women. The first three scenes of act II take place aboard the pirate ship, and the final scene shifts to a courtroom. Gooch presents individual episodes with a fair degree of realism but bridges scenes with "singers" who narrate and comment in rhythmic, occasionally rhymed verse.

Bonney and Read are not important because they influence events but because they are women serving effectively in a male-dominated arena. The two women come to piracy by different routes. Mary was raised as a boy and maintained her masculine persona except for a few years when she was married to a Flemish tapster who served with her in the army. Both were illegitimate, but Ann was the relatively affluent daughter of an Irish lawyer turned planter. Stronger than any of her suitors, she finally rebels against courtship conventions that she finds constricting by eloping with a pirate. The play is mildly scatalogical and sexual freedom is one sign of the women's enfranchisement into pirate society. They ultimately avoid the gallows because they are pregnant, but as Ann laments even after their release, "there still won't be a place for us, and there'll still be some man telling us he knows better." The chorus concludes, "All around the world / Sugar and spice and all things nice, / But not for little girls" (73).

Pam Gems, who established a reputation largely on her dramatization of the lives of prominent women, turned to a male protagonist in *Stanley*, produced at the National Theatre in 1996, but her focus on the modern British painter Stanley Spencer distracted in no way from her abiding interest in the way that women accommodate to standards set by men, no matter how bizarre. Spencer's paintings mixed religious and erotic imagery, often with very realistic depictions of ordinary people, including him and both of his wives, in the nude. The plot centers on the self-indulgent Stanley's efforts to maintain simultaneous relations with two women: first, his long-suffering model and first wife, Hilda; second, his predatory second wife, the minor artist Patricia Preece. Stanley, smitten with Patricia's apparent elegance, justifies his infidelity to Hilda first with "I believe it's perfectly possible for me to have a strong spiritual closeness to more than one woman," and later with, "I could manage twenty wives—why not?"[44] He divorces the devoted Hilda only to discover

Patricia's inseparable attachment to her lesbian companion. Stanley renews his sexual relations with Hilda but cannot persuade her to remarry him. Patricia bankrupts Stanley, who by the end of the play realizes that he intensely loved the now-deceased Hilda, with whom he still converses. Like that of Shelley in Jellicoe's play, Stanley's liberal-mindedness seems to gratify only his own sexual desires and ignores a woman's need for some degree of loyalty. Gems essentially writes a love story, but Stanley's articulate libertinism accentuates the behavior that Gems questions.

FEMINIST SOCIAL HISTORY

Steve Gooch's self-proclaimed venue is community theatre, and the RSC production of *The Women Pirates* was an isolated encounter with establishment theatre. His first dramatization of women's issues occurred five years earlier and was the first clear example of feminist social history, a play dealing with a group rather than historically prominent individuals. In November 1973, *Female Transport* premiered at the Half Moon Theatre, described by Gooch as a "scruffy" hundred-seat community theatre in London, which a year earlier had presented another of his history plays, *Will Wat? If Not, What Will?*.[45] Set in a cell in the hold of a female prison ship during its six-month voyage to Australia in the late eighteenth century, the play was staged fairly realistically except for the insertion of a few folk songs.

In the best tradition of feminist drama, Gooch develops the friendship among the women, which in this case compensates somewhat for the terrible exploitation that they suffer on the voyage, but this concentration on the group rather than the individual caused mixed critical reaction. John Barber, reviewing the play for the *Daily Telegraph*, complained that the production "awakens interest in its characters but never allows us to get to know them."[46] In contrast, Michael Billington praised "each of the six sharply characterized" female prisoners, but he acknowledged that "Gooch's prime concern is with the inequity of a system that simply dumped its criminals in another country like so much social refuse and allowed the ship's crew to make a handsome profit out of their labours during the voyage."[47] Even though Gooch individualized his characters for dramatic purposes, he focused on the lower-class prisoners, not on the personalities who shaped penal policy or guided the Prison Fleet. Rather than sharply defined individuals, a group portrait emerges, for which he was commended by the *Observer* critic, Irving Wardle: "He has written a believable historical play (not a documentary) and he has convincingly evoked an enclosed community of women."[48] Wardle presumably differentiates this play that deals with a historical situation from a documentary that builds upon specific historical documents. The characters, identified only by their first names, are fictional, unlike Timberlake Wertenbaker's 1988 play, *Our Country's Good,* which expanded on actual personalities from Australia's first penal colony. However, even Wertenbaker had very little detailed information on the prisoners and fleshed out her characters with invented personalities.

The absence in historical records of personal data about individuals outside the male power structures frustrates feminist historians trying to compensate for the depersonalization of marginalized female participants in past events. Although the social historian may use census data or domestic archaeology, the impersonality of this material works at cross-purposes with the theatrical impulse to build specific characters. The shift away from the major players of traditional political history and the consequent loss of documentary evidence from which a playwright can reconstruct character force the imaginative recreation of missing details.

Caryl Churchill, the most prolific and influential feminist playwright in Britain, also deemphasizes ruling-class characters in her history plays. In her first historical drama, *Light Shining in Buckinghamshire,* a Joint Stock production that premiered at the Edinburgh Theatre Festival in September of 1976 and played that same month at Royal Court Theatre Upstairs, she dramatized the English Revolution without showing any of the traditional textbook characters. She depicted the usually ignored disenfranchised participants such as the Levellers, Diggers, and Ranters and minimalized the importance of individual characters even further by having different actors play one character. The script contains segments that deal specifically with gender issues, but the play is not principally feminist, as discussed earlier.

Churchill's focus on social groups rather than prominent individuals is also consistent with her neo-Marxist stress on the impact that historical events have on working-class characters. In England a number of feminist Marxist histories appeared in the 1970s: Sheila Rowbotham's *Woman, Resistance, and Revolution: A History of Women and Revolution in the Modern World* (1972) and *Woman's Consciousness, Man's World* (1973), and Juliet Mitchell's *Woman's Estate* (1973).[49]

Churchill's next history play, *Vinegar Tom,* written for Monstrous Regiment, appeared in November of 1976 at Humberside Theatre, Hull, and then toured to the Institute of Contemporary Arts (ICA) and Half Moon theatres, London. Churchill dramatized the witch hunts in seventeenth-century England straightforwardly, presenting each of the twenty-one scenes with a fair degree of realism, but between many of the scenes, actors in modern dress sing songs that reflect on the conditions of modern women. Churchill was influenced by Barbara Ehrenreich and Deidre English's feminist history of women healers, *Witches, Midwives and Nurses,*[50] but *Vinegar Tom* also resonates inevitably of

The Crucible, one of the most popular American plays in Britain. Unlike Miller, Churchill has no prominent central figure, no redeeming humanistic insight by a protagonist to compensate for the oppressive social environment. The drama is situational; the characters, minor. Churchill's play is not driven by reactions like Miller's to McCarthy era oppression but by her own sense of the economic bases for misogyny. As she states in the preface, "I wanted to write a play about witches with no witches in it; a play not about evil, hysteria and possession by the devil but about poverty, humiliation and prejudice, and how the women accused of witchcraft saw themselves."[51] Churchill links the oppression of women to declining economic conditions that result in the persecution of all subordinate groups. The chorus makes this point in the song "Something to Burn":

> What can we do, there's nothing to do,
> about sickness and hunger and dying.
> What can we do, there's nothing to do,
> nothing but cursing and crying.
> > Find something to burn.
> > Let it go up in smoke.
> > Burn your troubles away.
>
> Sometimes it's witches, or what will you choose?
> Sometimes it's lunatics, shut them away.
> It's blacks and it's women and often it's Jews.
> We'd all be quite happy if they'd go away. (154)

The characters and specific incidents are invented except the final scene, which dramatizes Kramer and Spenger's *Malleus Maleficarum, The Hammer of Witches* (1487), which Churchill uses as a thematic epilogue. Witchcraft is a sustained metaphor for being female. Churchill, in the preface, states, "I discovered for the first time the extent of Christian teaching against women and saw the connections between medieval attitudes to witches and continuing attitudes to women in general" (129). These biases are so pervasive that even the women accused of witchcraft hold the values of the society that persecutes them:

Susan: I must think on how woman tempts man, and how she pays God with her pain having the baby. So if we try to get round the pain, we're going against God.

Alice: I hate my body.

Susan: You mustn't say that. God sent his son . . .

Alice: Blood every month, and no way out of that but to be sick and swell up, and no
    way out of that but pain. No way out of all that till we're old and that's worse. I
    can't bear to see my mother if she changes her clothes. (146)

As frequently occurs in feminist drama, women who represent the dominant
male society betray those who rebel against that patriarchy. The witch hunters
succeed partly because they coerce the women into testifying against one
another.

Churchill emphasizes her message for a modern audience when near the
play's end, the chorus sings "Lament for Witches," admonishing the women
in the audience, "Look in the mirror tonight. / Would they have hanged you
then? / Ask how they're stopping you now" (176).

Stephen Lowe's *Touched* also deals with the responses of imagined characters
to real historic events. Focusing on the contrasting responses to World War II
by three working-class sisters in England during the one hundred days between
VE Day and VJ Day, the play illustrates a subgenre as old as Aeschylus: dramas
depicting women without men during a war. *Touched* premiered at the Nottingham Playhouse, June 9, 1977, and was performed at the Royal Court
Theatre in August of 1977, and revived by RCT on January 20, 1981.[52]
Periodically played recorded broadcasts establish the wider historical background, but the realistic internal plot develops around the false pregnancy of
the middle sister, Sandra, who has lost an earlier child to an automobile
accident during a blackout, and the decision of Betty, the younger sister, to
stop mourning the death of a young soldier with whom she had only a fleeting
relationship. The forward movement of the play occurs largely through unfolding exposition. In a note before the play, Lowe indicated that under the
influence of his mother and Angus Calder's social history, *The People's War*, he
set out to dramatize a group largely neglected in histories of the war: those who
stayed at home.

In an encounter with her assembly line boss, the older sister Joan states the
contrasting roles of men and women in the war:

You men are dirty boggers. All supposed to be out there, fighting for King and Country,
instead of which, they're sweating away doubling the population of Germany in nine
months. And we gals have to stand on our feet all day, kidded on by the likes of you,
making these tubes to be jabbed in our lads' arms so they can safely have another couple
of rounds with some Deutschland tart. (34)

The women develop strategies for coping, but they depend ultimately on
the real or imagined men in their lives. When, on VJ day, Joan voices hope for
resurrecting her failed marriage with her returning husband by emigrating,

Sandra comments, "You'll not go anywhere. You'll end up changing his pants for him twice a day, bathing him, turning him over. You both deserve better than that" (68).

Juxtaposed against recordings of Attlee and MacArthur's VJ Day pronouncements is Sandra's suicide, an ironic deflation of the heroic and masculine image of war. Lowe has not simply refocused history on the home front; he has attempted to use the public pronouncements as touchstones for the private victories and defeats. His success was debated among his reviewers. Paul Allen, in a *Plays and Players* review of the 1977 production, complained that if Lowe "has made a connection between the public and private worlds he doesn't pass them on."[53] Michael Billington, however, in a *Guardian* review praised the 1981 revival as "a beautifully written piece effortlessly linking the private and public worlds."[54]

As was discussed in an earlier chapter, plays based on community history represent the most successful dramatization of social history. The promenade dramatizations of local histories, to the extent that they depict everyday life in a community with a proportionately greater emphasis on women's activities, would seem to offer an ideal form for feminist social history, but although women figure prominently, these productions tend to reinforce community values rather than highlight feminist issues. Dewhurst's adaptation of Flora Thompson's trilogy for the National Theatre, *Lark Rise* (1978) and *Candleford* (1979), are thinly veiled autobiographical portraits of Thompson, but she was no feminist. David Edgar's *Entertaining Strangers* (1985) has a female co-protagonist, but the play's consciousness is not feminist. Because these plays celebrate the values of the communities they dramatize, their use as vehicles for feminist consciousness must probably await changes in community attitudes.

GENDER BASED FEMINIST HISTORIES

The most blatantly feminist histories are those that deal directly with gender issues, and as a group, they present the most unconventional treatments of historical material.

Caryl Churchill's *Top Girls* is a play *about* history, not a history play in any accepted use of the term. The first half of the play presents an imaginary dinner party between a modern businesswoman, Marlene, and five quasi-historical figures from periods spanning a thousand years. The women narrate their personal histories, all of which involve victimization because they are women, and engage in free ranging discussions of women's issues. This symposium helps to establish and give historical significance to problems raised in the last half of the play, where Churchill presents a more realistically staged domestic conflict between the businesswoman and her working-class sister, who has raised Marlene's child. Churchill shows that Marlene, like her predecessors in the first act, adopts masculine standards of success that corrupt her relations with other people, including her own daughter.

Churchill's *Cloud Nine*, first produced by the Joint Stock Theatre Group at Dartington College of Arts February 14, 1979, and subsequently opening at the Royal Court, August 30, 1980, is also not a true history play but, as Churchill explains, uses a historical setting as a metaphor: "colonialism as a parallel to sexual oppression."[55] Like *Top Girls*, the first half of *Cloud Nine* uses historical material, and the last half is contemporary. The first act, set in Victorian Africa, presents, in the broadly simplified style of parody, a series of domestic entanglements in the household of a patriarchal colonial administrator. To accentuate the gender-defined role playing, Churchill uses cross dressing. Because the wife, Betty, emulates the male image of the ideal man so much, a man performs her role; and the son, Edward, who upsets his father by preferring to play with dolls, is acted by a woman. Victoria, the daughter, is literally a dummy (puppet), and to extend the role playing to racial issues, a white man plays Joshua, the black servant who aspires to the affluence and power of the whites he serves. Act II shows the "next generation," in which the varied sexual combinations and entanglements introduced in the Victorian period now play out in a contemporary setting. The act I children are twenty-five years older but the second act takes place over a hundred years later. To discourage the audience from taking the characters in any literal sense, the same actors appear in act II, but not playing the same characters. As with *Top Girls*, the historical perspective introduced in the play's first half sensitizes the audience to gender issues developed more subtly in the contemporary second half.

Timberlake Wertenbaker also uses Victorian colonialism as a metaphor for sexual oppression, in *New Anatomies*. Produced in 1984 by ICA, this biographical drama deals with the Russian Arabist Isabelle Eberhardt, who toured French Morocco dressed as a young Arab male. Like *'H'* and *Translations*, *New Anatomies* is a colonial history that uses the contact between an empowered and an oppressed culture to call into question the European hegemony. Wertenbaker expands from this central idea to the more general issue of freedom from the constraints of convention, and to the more specific issue of gender. The audience's first exposure to Isabelle is designed to offend conventional ideas of appropriate feminine behavior as she stands on stage calling out, "I need a fuck." Her behavior contrasts with that of her half sister and of her sister-in-law, who advocate and follow Victorian norms.

Isabelle's Arab friends, unlike the Europeans, accept her for her perceived wisdom without regard for her gender. When Isabelle spurns the offer of a

French captain to "protect" her, he attempts to expose her disguise to Saleh, her Qadria companion:

Captain: This Si Mahmoud is a woman. (*Silence. BOU SAADI laughs stupidly. SALEH doesn't react at all.*) Look under her clothes if you don't believe me.

Saleh: (*slowly*). Si Mahmoud has a very good knowledge of medicine. He's helped people with their eyes and cured children.

Captain: Probaby told them to wash. It's a woman I tell you. You must be stupider than I thought not to have noticed or at least asked a few questions.

Saleh: It is a courtesy in our country not to be curious about the stranger. We accept whatever name Si Mahmoud wishes to give us.

Isabelle: You knew.

Saleh: We heard. We chose not to believe it.[56]

Not all of the Arabs are so enlightened, and Isabelle also suffers from Muslim conservatism when, late in the play, a Muslim assassin attacks her because he believes that she violates Islamic law.

Like Churchill, Wertenbaker uses doubling and cross dressing to call attention to gender role playing. The play is performed by five actresses, each of whom, except the actress playing Isabelle, plays a Western woman, an Arab man, and a Western man. Several of the female characters other than Isabelle also assume masculine dress. Having a woman play a male role quickly creates an alienation effect and gives an ironic twist to any speeches by the male character that contain underlying gender biases.

The central story advances in a series of flashbacks framed by scenes that occur shortly before Isabelle's death, with the French lesbian journalist Severine serving as Isabelle's chronicler. The core of the play shows a series of encounters that shape and define Isabelle, encounters initially with her family and later with representatives of society, soldiers and judges, who manipulate her for their own purposes. Isabelle initially gravitates to the Arabs because of romantic fantasies that she shared as a child with her brother. She possesses no particular feminist sensibility, but simply wants the freedom to pursue her obsession. The situation, however, exposes the gender biases of the Europeans she encounters, and Wertenbaker develops the issue of gender by using Isabelle's return to France further to expose gender biases in European culture. The second act begins with a scene set in a salon in Paris that seems almost a symposium on women's roles, with four of the five female characters dressed as men. Isabelle, who frequently speaks from an alcohol- or drug-induced stupor, has relatively little to say, but the other women discuss why they have been forced to assume men's roles in order to lead what they consider to be full lives. For example,

Severine, who dresses as a man principally in order to take her girlfriends to coffee bars without being pestered by men, laments that as a lesbian, she is always an outsider:

Normality, the golden cage. And we poor banished species trail around, looking through the bars, wishing we were in there. But we're destined for the curiosity shops, labelled as the weird mistakes of nature, the moment of God's hesitation between Adam and Eve, anatomical convolutions, our souls inside out and alone, always alone, outside those bars. (37)

Wertenbaker uses a historical setting for two of her subsequent plays, *The Grace of Mary Traverse* produced in 1985 at the Royal Court Theatre and *The Love of the Nightingale*, produced by RSC at the Other Place, Stratford-upon-Avon, October 28, 1988. In an introductory note to *The Grace of Mary Traverse*, she states that this is not a historical play: "All the characters are my own invention and whenever I have used historical events such as the Gordon Riots I have taken great freedom with reported fact. I found the eighteenth century a valid metaphor, and I was concerned to free the people of the play from contemporary preconceptions."[57]

Feminist playwrights frequently use this Brechtian strategy of historicizing material to encourage the audience to take a detached view of contemporary issues. The American feminist Janelle Reinelt, in *After Brecht: British Epic Theatre*, states that the usefulness of this epic theatre device to the feminist agenda arises from another characteristic: "Historicizing gender relations . . . explicitly challenges the notion of transhistorical male and female modes of being and recovers a marginalized alternative narrative of women as active subjects determining the concrete course of human events."[58]

In a manner similar to Churchill's use of Victorian colonialism in *Cloud Nine*, *The Grace of Mary Traverse* uses eighteenth-century plays and novels as a nonspecific context, particularly exploiting the female Quixote stereotype. Eighteenth-century literary traditions are more important here than literal history. The "plot" is the education of Mary Traverse under the tutelage of Mrs. Temptwell, a housekeeper trying to corrupt Mary in order to avenge the execution of Temptwell's mother by Mary's uncle. Mary "traverses" from upper middle-class respectability to life on the street. The first scene establishes the male-centered social context by showing Mary being taught by her father how to carry on a social conversation. Mary's sexual education and awareness of the perfidity of men culminate when, in a gender inversion of an episode reminiscent of *Tom Jones*, she nearly has a sexual liaison with her own father. Rape, sexual intercourse, and lesbian intercourse are enacted on stage. Characters' names, in eighteenth-century fashion, identify their *function* in the play: Lord

Exrake, Mr. Manners, the oversexed Mr. Hardlong, and so forth. In the eighteenth-century fashion, characters on occasion directly address the audience. Mary Traverse is accompanied by Sophie, a traditional passive female victim whom Lord Gordon rapes. Sophie finds her voice near the play's end and becomes a spokeswoman for life affirmation in opposition to Mary's more cynical view of the world. The plot broadens to issues of class conflict and political manipulation of the populace, and the play moves from a domestic melodrama to a social parable, leaving the the issue of women's roles behind. Wertenbaker's agenda here is broader than the issue of feminism. She uses the suppression and exploitation of women as indicators of wider social malignancy.

Wertenbaker has frequently translated and adapted Greek drama, and she turns to Greek mythology for *The Love of the Nightingale*.[59] Like *The Grace of Mary Traverse* this play reflects a historic literary style more than a treatment of history per se. The plot develops the story of Tereus, king of Thrace, who rapes his sister-in-law, Philomele, and then cuts out her tongue in an unsuccessful attempt to prevent her telling about the rape. His wife, Procne, kills their son, Itys, in revenge. Fragments exist of Sophocles's lost *Tereus*, and Wertenbaker crafts her play in the manner of a classical Greek drama. The members of two choruses, male and female, speak in individual voices but serve the traditional functions of a Greek chorus. The marriage of Tereus and Procne is arranged in a few lines with a comment from the Male Chorus: "It didn't happen that quickly. It took months and much indirect discourse. But that is the gist of it. The end was known from the beginning" (5). Wertenbaker enriches the Greek conventions with modern theatricalism. A condensed version of a Hippolytus play is enacted within the framing play, and the killing of Itys, after being depicted from outside the room where the action occurs in the traditional fashion of Greek drama, is then replayed to show the actual event.

The play advances a clear feminist perspective. Tereus is war-loving, unreflective, brutal, exploitive. The women are passionate, life-loving, rational, and victimized. One of the Female Chorus comments, "The first meaning of danger is the power of a lord or master" (20). Wertenbaker uses the chorus to press home the modern application of the plot when one of the Female Chorus members asks, "Why are little girls raped and murdered in the car parks of dark cities?" (45).

Wertenbaker's most popular play, *Our Country's Good*, staged at the Royal Court Theatre in 1988 and subsequently produced in the West End, dramatizes the convict production in 1789 of *The Recruiting Officer*, the first play staged in Australia, and even though it contains some discussion of the low status of women prisoners, the primary thrust is not feminist.

Plays that incorporate a feminist perspective do not have to advance an exclusively feminist agenda. Shirley Gee's *Warrior*, produced at the Chichester Festival Theatre, Minerva Studio, on June 23, 1989, takes an anti-war, antiviolence position that is stronger than its feminism. Based on a book, *The Female Soldier*, published in 1750, the play develops the story of Hannah Snell, who served as a marine from 1745 to 1750. After her discovery and discharge, she made her way for a time as a stage attraction and ultimately wound up in an institution for the mentally deranged. However, as Gee says in a brief introduction, "I have pressed Hannah into my service, made her sail my troubled seas."[60] Gee invents a series of "visions," including an atomic explosion, based on Hannah's ability to foresee the future, a premonition that finally deranges her. Gee also changes events to allow Hannah to escape to France rather than die in an asylum as she actually did.

Gee describes the play's style as "tuppence coloured,"[61] but the main fabric is fairly realistic. The structure interweaves scenes of Hannah's treatment in the lunatic asylum with flashbacks to her earlier life. The flashbacks catch up with the present action in the middle of the second act. The asylum scenes introduce the acts and reappear a couple of times but remain fairly unobtrusive. Gee handles transitions rapidly with costumes or props. The emotional climax is marked by a "swing treatment" for Hannah, "a large, heavy contraption rather like a see-saw with a chair in which the patient is strapped at one end, a weight at the other" (1). This and a mast are permanent scenic elements. A few ballads are introduced but are justified by context.

Even though Hannah's situation points to obvious forms of sexual discrimination in her society, she successfully synthesizes her masculine action-oriented persona with her fundamental impulse to nurture. Gee also emphasizes the way in which gender shapes behavior through a number of sympathetically characterized men. Hannah has a devotée in Billy Cuttle, a guileless soldier who becomes her follower after she protects him from harassment by other soldiers. Billy discovers her disguise when shrapnel strikes her in the groin during battle, and, assuming the more traditional female role, he nurses her back to health. Two other men represent more traditional authority figures but remain sympathetic to her: Godbolt, her sergeant, who subsequently becomes something of a manager, and Cumberland, a nobleman, who obtains a pension for her. Even Scully, the operator of the sanatorium, seems basically well intentioned, and the equal involvement of his cohort and wife matches any barbarity of his. The only significant other female, Hannah's sister-in-law, Susan, is trapped in the web of eighteenth-century values and appears more rigidly unsympathetic than many of the male characters.

Claire Tomalin's play about the New Zealand writer Katherine Mansfield, *The Winter Wife*,[62] shows the extent to which a sharper focus on gender issues changes the thrust of what is basically a biographical history. First produced at the Nuffield Theatre, Southampton, February 12, 1991, and then at the Lyric Theatre, Hammersmith, March 5, 1991, the play takes place in a French villa to which the consumptive Mansfield has retreated in 1920, three years before her death. Examinations by a French doctor provide the chief means of exposition. Focusing principally on her domestic relations rather than her life as a writer, the play gradually reveals the exploitation of Mansfield by her absent husband, John Middleton Murry; her choice to break away from him; and, with the guidance of the sympathetic doctor, her acceptance of her dependence upon her devoted female companion, Ida Constance Baker, whom Katherine had initially tyrannized. The play offers this relationship between women as an alternative to Katherine's overdependence on men.

In summary, what characterizes the dramatization of feminist history?

1. History is depicted from a woman's point of view, which usually means that the protagonist is a woman victimized by or opposing a male-dominated culture. Of the plays examined, only *Shelley* has a male protagonist, and Jellicoe developed him largely through his negative impact on the women in his life. In the absence of a major female player in a historical event, playwrights create fictionalized groups of women and relegate the "textbook" shakers and movers to offstage actions.

2. Incidents depicted are more likely to be personal or domestic than public or political. Of the feminist history plays, only *Queen Christina* deals with a political figure, but Gems depicts her largely in term of her domestic relations. Feminist writers reject any division between a woman's personal life and her political role. Most of the women dramatized were artists—Mary Shelley, Edith Piaf, Virginia Woolf, Flora Thompson, and Katherine Mansfield—but even here, the plays center on their personal lives, not their artistic activities.

3. A woman's reliance on a man is usually self-destructive, and minor female characters oppose the protagonist in proportion to their dependence on the patriarchal hegenomy. Even though a few of the plays like *Virginia* and *Warrior* present friendships between men and women in a positive light, in all of the plays discussed, women are significantly defined by their sexual relationships with men, always to the detriment of the women. Even in *Top Girls* with its all-female cast and focus on relationships among women, male reactions largely shape the self-characterizations of the historic women presented in the first half of the play.

4. The plays value women's learning to rely upon one another. This is increasingly true the more the subject matter leans toward social history, but it also figures as a major theme in *Piaf, Top Girls*, and *The Winter Wife*.

5. In opposition to the female bonding theme, most feminist histories show women who represent the dominant male society betraying those who rebel against that patriarchy. This highlights the contrast between the free and the dominated woman, but this conflict also represents a major obstacle in the way of feminist goals.

6. Gender differentiates character traits, with men often decisive and action oriented; women, frequently more sensitive to conflicting emotional demands. Even when women successfully assume male roles, as in *Queen Christina, The Women Pirates Ann Bonney and Mary Read, Top Girls, New Anatomies*, and *Warrior*, the need to emulate masculine behavior places the women in conflict with their essential selves.

7. Female protagonists often flout conventional sexual conventions, usually by seizing the initiative with multiple heterosexual liaisons, rarely by seeking lesbian ties. Playwrights use liberated attitudes toward sex and the female body for shock value. None of the plays discussed centers on characters with traditional marriages.

8. Women, both characters and performers, often dress in men's clothing, a common device in the plays of Churchill and Wertenbaker, but also used in Gems's *Queen Christina*, Gooch's *The Women Pirates Ann Bonney and Mary Read*, and Gee's *Warrior*. This seems less a concession to occasional all-female performing groups than a device to emphasize how gender influences the meaning of speech. The alienation device of a woman playing a man calls attention to any disparity between the gender of the performer and any male sexism or chauvinism, either latent or overt, in the performer's speeches.

Some features that might be expected do not seem to occur:

1. Structurally the feminist histories are not significantly different from nonfeminist historical drama. Although Caryl Churchill is among the most experimental of dramatists, the history plays of John Arden, Edward Bond, or Howard Brenton are equally innovative. Feminist history plays are no more likely to be episodic, to be nonlinear, or to have small casts.

2. Relations with children do not play a significant thematic role, with the exception of *Queen Christina* and *Top Girls*.

Feminist histories have been written principally for production organizations devoted to women's issues or for performances on the "second stages" of state-supported theatres. In England, Pam Gems is the only writer of history plays treating women's issues who has enjoyed any significant commercial success. Caryl Churchill's plays have been performed extensively by college and regional theatres in America. Feminist history, however, is a relative newcomer, and as feminist values become more widely accepted, feminist history plays should appear more frequently.

NOTES

1. Michelene Wandor, *Understudies: Theatre and Sexual Politics* (London: Methuen, 1981), p. 37.

2. Ibid., p. 70.

3. Ibid., p. 21.

4. Gerda Lerner develops the first two categories in *The Majority Finds Its Past: Placing Women in History* (Oxford: Oxford University, 1979), pp. 145–146.

5. Joan Scott, "Women's History," in *New Perspectives on Historical Writing*, ed. Peter Burke (University Park, PA: Pennsylvania State University, 1993), p. 51.

6. Ibid., p. 42.

7. Lerner, *The Majority*, p. 146.

8. Ibid., p. 145.

9. Judith P. Zinsser, *History and Feminism: A Glass Half Full* (New York: Twayne, 1993), p. 444.

10. Panel discussion at a symposium, "Shouting in the Evening: British Theater, 1956–1996," University of Texas, Austin, Nov. 9, 1996.

11. Wandor, *Understudies*, p. 87.

12. Zinsser, *History and Feminism*, p. 55.

13. Lerner, *The Majority*, p. 161.

14. Ibid., p. 162.

15. Wandor, *Understudies*, p. 87.

16. Ibid., p. 71.

17. Ibid., p. 16.

18. Gordon Daviot [Elizabeth Mackintosh], *Queen of Scots* (London: Victor Gollancz, 1934).

19. Robert Bolt, *Vivat! Vivat Regina!* (London: Heinemann, 1971), p. 54.

20. John Bowen, *Florence Nightingale* (London: Samuel French, 1976).

21. Hugh Whitemore, *Stevie* (London: Samuel French, 1977), p. 36.

22. Pam Gems, *Queen Christina* (London: St. Luke's, 1982).

23. Playbill for *Piaf*, Picadilly Theatre, 1993.

24. Ibid.

25. Wandor, *Understudies*, p. 65.

26. "Queen Christina," *Times*, Sept. 12, 1977.

27. *Financial Times*, Sept. 12, 1977.

28. Richard Allen Cave, *New British Drama in Performance on the London Stage: 1970 to 1985* (New York: St. Martin's, 1988), p. 257.

29. *Daily Telegram*, Sept. 12, 1977.

30. Wandor, *Understudies*, p. 65.

31. Pam Gems, *Piaf*, in *Three Plays* (Harmondsworth: Penguin, 1985).

32. Constantine, 1969, quoted in *Piaf* program note, 1993.

33. Wandor, *Understudies*, p. 64.

34. Edna O'Brien, *Virginia* (London: Hogarth, 1981).

35. Janelle Reinelt, *After Brecht: British Epic Theatre* (Ann Arbor: University of Michigan, 1994), p. 67.

36. Ann Jellicoe, *Shelley, or the Idealist* (New York: Grove Press, 1966), p. 17.

37. Ibid., p. 49.

38. D. Keith Peacock, *Radical Stages: Alternative History in Modern British Drama* (Westport, CT: Greenwood, 1991), p. 180.

39. Liz Lochhead, *Blood and Ice*, in *Plays by Women*, vol. 4, ed. Michelene Wandor (London: Methuen, 1985), p. 110.

40. *Guardian*, Aug. 1, 1978.

41. *Times*, Aug. 1, 1978.

42. *Guardian*, Aug. 1, 1978.

43. Steve Gooch, *The Women Pirates Ann Bonney and Mary Read* (London: Pluto, 1978), p. 37.

44. Pam Gems, *Stanley* (London: Nick Hern Books, 1996), pp. 38, 41.

45. Steve Gooch, *Female Transport* (New York: Samuel French, 1974), p. 6.

46. *Daily Telegraph*, Nov. 16, 1973.

47. *Guardian*, Nov. 16, 1973.

48. *Observer*, Nov. 25, 1973.

49. Sheila Rowbotham *Woman, Resistance, and Revolution: A History of Women and Revolution in the Modern World* (New York: Pantheon, 1972), and *Woman's Consciousness, Man's World* (Harmondsworth: Penguin, 1973); and Juliet Mitchell's *Woman's Estate* (New York: Pantheon, 1973).

50. Barbara Ehrenreich and Deidre English, *Witches, Midwives, and Nurses* (Old Westbury, NY: The Feminist Press, 1973).

51. Caryl Churchill, *Vinegar Tom*, in *Plays: One* (London: Methuen, 1985), 130.

52. Steven Lowe, *Touched*, rev. ed. (London: Methuen, 1981), First published Todmorden: Woodhouse, 1979.

53. *Plays and Players*, 24 (Aug. 1977), p. 19.

54. *Guardian*, Jan. 21, 1981.

55. Caryl Churchill, *Cloud Nine*, rev. American ed. (New York: Methuen, 1984), p. viii. First published London: Pluto, 1979.

56. Timberlake Wertenbaker, *New Anatomies* (Woodstock, IL: Dramatic Publishing, 1984), p. 30.

57. In Timberlake Wertenbaker, *The Love of the Nightingale* and *The Grace of Mary Traverse* (London: Faber & Faber, 1989), p. 57.

58. Reinelt, *After Brecht* (Ann Arbor: University of Michigan, 1994), p. 83.

59. In Wertenbaker, *The Nightingale*.

60. Shirley Gee, *Warrior* (London: Samuel French, 1991).

61. Ibid., p. xii.

62. Claire Tomalin, *The Winter Wife* (New York: Samuel French, 1991).

7

Deconstructionist and Postmodern History Plays and Satire

Deconstructionism, or as known in some fields, poststructuralism, developed hand in hand with postmodernism, augmenting the postmodern worldview that emerged in the 1960s. Adopted by almost every discipline, this nomenclature continues to search for definition, as meaning expands and changes contextually with varying use, a demonstration of indeterminacy consistent with the principles of deconstruction. These terms also describe a popularly perceived cultural fragmentation and skepticism that extend beyond their original application in fields such as linguistics, literary criticism, and architecture. The technical jargon of deconstructionism may befuddle the general public, but audiences understand the self-reflectiveness, the underlying mistrust of tradition, and the consequent pluralism and relativism.

Founded by the French philosopher Jacques Derrida (1930–) deconstruction is fundamentally a method of criticism rooted in linguistic analysis. Derrida, building on work of the Oxford linguistic philosopher J. L. Austin, among others, pointed out that all meaning in a text relates to a context of assumed meanings. The writer and the reader both operate within webs of understood meaning that change with time, place, culture, and situation. The greater the disparity among any of these factors, the more likely it is that the reader will misunderstand the writer, a particular problem with historical data. In two books published in 1967, *De la Grammatologie* (*Of Grammatology*) and *L'écriture et la différence* (*Writing and Difference*), Derrida developed a model for analyzing a text by tracking a chain of *différence* that underlies systems of signification whereby "presences" are defined by differentiating "absences" that a text omits but assumes. A logocentric tradition seeks to legitimize certain concepts by establishing a set of "violent hierarchies" that privilege a central term over a marginal one: male over female, nature over culture, and so on. Concepts do not take meaning from some objective reality but from this web of created significance; so presences can only be understood by analyzing their relationship to other texts. Critics of deconstructionism claim that this torturous process of analysis leads nihilistically to the diminishing reliability of the meaning of any concept.

Though resembling structuralism by arguing that meaning exists in the relation of parts rather than as an inherent feature of any one element, deconstruction rejects the possibility of any objectively perceived, self-contained structure and is therefore "poststructural." It also repudiates any theoretical system held to be universally valid.

Applied to history, deconstructionism calls into question all overriding ideas. For example, any developmental approach to history, when deconstructed, reveals an agenda, often hidden, that the present retroactively imposes on the past. All histories are constructed, a perception that blurs the difference between fact and fiction. Derrida's methods do not destroy history; they only remind us that we always experience history through texts written in the context of one set of assumptions but selected and interpreted, in turn, on the basis of different assumptions.

For New Historians already questioning the Eurocentric, masculine, politically oriented, nation building model of old history, deconstruction offers a philosophically articulated methodology for isolating and discrediting old ideas, though not a clear notion of what to use as a replacement. Derrida provides a model for deconstructing, not for constructing alternatives, although his relativistic, highly qualified intertextual analysis, in itself, suggests something of a paradigm. Deconstructionist history emphasizes short-term politics, individuals, and isolated events rather than long-term historical patterns of structuralist history. The deconstructionist historian Theodore Zeldin advocates using *pointillisme*, a methodological analogue to the impressionist painters' technique, "breaking down the phenomena of history into the smallest, most elementary units—the individual actors in history—and then connecting those units by means of 'juxtapositions' rather than causes. The reader would then be free to make 'what links he thinks fit for himself.' "[1] This closely resembles postmodernism, which presents an already deconstructed view of experience.

Postmodernism describes an even more vaguely defined attitude that emerged in the sixties and seventies, characterized by skepticism regarding any unifying tradition, a loss of clear identity, stylistic eclecticism, a breakdown in genres and other boundaries, and the use of disconnected images.

The historian most strongly associated with postmodernism, Michel Foucalt (1926–84), approached any conventional historical idea as a product of the cultural power of the tradition that legitimizes it. He thus saw history as a form of imaginary discourse with rhetorical force, a view that became a signature of postmodern historiography. Postmodern historians also reject chronology as a course of narrative order and remain skeptical of any form of "metanarrative," any supposition of an overriding view of truth.

The tactics of postmodernism coincide with those of a variety of contemporary ideologies. Janelle Reinelt in *After Brecht: British Epic Theatre* notes that Brechtian theory, materialist feminism, and postmodernist criticism seem to share tasks:

(1) to rupture the seamless narrative wherever a tightly knit, closed system of causal connections implies the inevitability of events; (2) to expose ideological assumptions carried in the terms or system of representation, whether this is the property system or the gender system; and (3) to deconstruct the integrity of "character" in order to show the subject as a site of contradictions, a position within an ideological field of social practices, neither unified nor stable and certainly not eternal.[2]

We have seen how feminist history plays, particularly those of Caryl Churchill, employ postmodern discontinuities. Marxist playwrights like Bond and Brenton similarly used deconstruction in order to attack the social establishment. That Brecht's alienation devices anticipate the use of disjuncture in postmodernism shows the difficulty of trying to isolate any one contributory factor on the form of the modern history play.

In theatre, the absurdist movement, which emerged in the 1950s, also foreshadowed many of the elements of deconstructionist and postmodern drama: the use of farce to upset pretensions of purposeful action, disrupted causality, juxtaposition of disparate styles, lack of linear form, inconsistent characterization, anachronisms, and self-consciously undercut conventions. The major absurdist playwrights showed little interest in the history play, but writers of postmodern historical drama, particularly with satiric overtones, drew from the absurdist tradition.

SATIRICAL HISTORY PLAY

Many of the characteristics of deconstructionist and postmodern history resemble the comic techniques for satirical history plays. This transformation from serious philosophical to comic concerns has a precursor in absurdism, which derived from Albert Camus's depiction of a grave state of human despair in the face of a meaningless universe, but absurdism also kept its roots in the traditionally comic definition of absurdity as a form of the ridiculous. The use of discontinuity and surprise, the juxtaposition of unlike categories—what Henri Bergson, the early twentieth century French philosopher, called the "reciprocal interference of series"[3]—the deflation of pretentiousness, the exposure of mechanical behavior, the undermining of the established order by a more flexible opportunistic new order—all comic devices—also resemble deconstruction and postmodern strategies. The postmodern device of fabulation, taking delight in self-conscious verbal artifice as a means of rejecting realism, also describes the exuberance of comic language. The use by postmodern writers of pastiche, a self-conscious imitation of styles borrowed from earlier writers or periods, resembles parody but without mockery as a necessary goal. This is not to suggest that deconstructionist or postmodern theorists saw their enterprise as comic, but that their techniques, deprived of their serious pretensions, can become comic. Just as the nineteenth-century playwright Ludwig Tieck saw comedy as the consequence of the metaphysical despair of German romanticism, some contemporary playwrights transform a postmodern into a comic worldview.

The idea that English music hall entertainment anticipates deconstructionism sounds like an opportunity for a music hall parody, but even though live music hall entertainment has largely vanished in Great Britain, replaced principally by television comedy, its influence lingers on in historical drama. The 1957 success of John Osborne's *The Entertainer*, in which Laurence Olivier performed the "turns" of an old music hall performer, sparked interest in the dramatic possibilities of music hall conventions. Joan Littlewood linked this with historical subjects in *Oh What a Lovely War*, a parody of romantic histories of World War I, developed and first staged by the Theatre Workshop at the Theatre Royal, in the working-class neighborhood of Stratford in London on March 19, 1963, and subsequently presented at Wyndham's Theatre in London's West End for a successful run. A running band of lights upstage spelled out casualty figures: "SEPT 20 . . . MENIN ROAD . . . BRITISH LOSS 22,000 MEN GAIN 800 YARDS."[4] The cast dressed in Pierrot and Pierrette costumes. Charles Marowitz, reviewing for *Encore*, remarked, "Stylistically, the show is an astounding achievement, for it creates a context which accommodates—naturally and without strain—a number of different and often antithetical styles."[5] Critics objected to the one-sided stereotyping of the officer set, but otherwise the general critical response was positive and the production was a great commercial success.

As we have seen, political dramas were particularly attracted to the use of music hall satire to undercut establishment histories, a technique used in such plays as Charles Wood's *Dingo* (1967), Tariq Ali and Howard Brenton's *Moscow*

Gold (1990), and community-based political drama such as Peter Cheeseman's "Documentaries" at Stoke-on-Trent, and the plays of John McGrath, Red Ladder, and Steve Gooch, particularly *The Motor Show* (1975).

A long tradition of Footlights Revues and "smoking concerts" at Cambridge University spawned, in the late fifties and sixties, a string of satirical writers and performers who created the popular stage revue *Beyond the Fringe* and subsequent television programs such as *That Was the Week that Was* and *Monty Python's Flying Circus.*[6] One of the authors and performers in *Beyond the Fringe*, which appeared at the Edinburgh Theatre Festival in 1960 and at the Lyceum Theatre in London beginning May 1961, was Alan Bennett, who in later years made much use of historical material in both comic and serious veins. Bennett's first staged drama was *Forty Years On*, which premiered at the Apollo Theatre in London on October 31, 1968. By Bennett's own admission, still as much a revue as a play, *Forty Years On* uses the form of a school play within a play. The inner play, set during World War II years, contains, in turn, parodies of events from the early decades of the twentieth century. According to Bennett's own description, "the time-scale of the first play gradually catches up with the time scale of the second, one cog the years 1900–39, the other 1939–45, and both within the third wheel of the present day."[7] Students and faculty, including Bennett, who appeared as Tempest, a junior master, present the school play to honor the retirement of the Headmaster, played by John Gielgud. The Headmaster, somewhat whimsically, voices his longing for the England of the past, and his school, named Albion House, in the midst of a fundamental change of order, serves as a loose metaphor for England.

Bennett's roots in *Beyond the Fringe* show in the loosely justified parodies of historical figures contained in the inner play, presented by adult members of the school. Parodied, among others, are Oscar Wilde, Max Beerbohm, Bertrand Russell, and Lady Ottoline Morrell, the latter played by two ill-coordinated boys, one on the shoulders of the other. The school play format allows a variety of self-conscious artifices such as dates posted on a hymn board, interruptions by the actors to correct misbehaving school boys, and disapproving commentary by the Headmaster. Other alienation devices include the arrival of a rowdy rugby team and the periodic chiming in of a boys' chorus.

In a piece of dialogue between the Headmaster and his successor, Franklin, the author of the inner play, Bennett reveals his agenda for history:

Headmaster: Would it be impossibly naive and old-fashioned of me to ask what it is you are trying to accomplish in this impudent charade?

Franklin: You could say that we are trying to shed the burden of the past.

Headmaster: Shed it? Why must we shed it? Why not shoulder it? Memories are not shackles, Franklin, they are garlands.

Franklin: We're too tied to the past. We want to be free to look to the future. The future comes before the past.

Headmaster: Nonsense. The future comes after the past. Otherwise it couldn't be the future. Mind you, I liked that last bit, the bit that I read. Was it true?

Franklin: Truth is a matter of opinion, really, isn't it, Headmaster? (69)

This is a debate between Old History and New History.

Monty Python's Flying Circus, begun in 1969 as a BBC Television series, provided one of the most vivid examples of comic deconstruction of history and a highly influential model for later parodists. Michael Palin and Terry Jones, two of the founders, explored the idea of parodying history in *The Complete and Utter History of Britain,* a short-lived series that they developed that covered history from the caveman to Oliver Cromwell and appeared on five Sundays in early 1969 for the independent London Weekend Television. The methods of Monty Python looked back to absurdist as well as forward to deconstructionist strategies in its iconoclastic debunking of virtually everything in sight, frequently including historical figures and events. These techniques culminated in two films on quasi-historical subjects: *Monty Python and the Holy Grail* (1974) and *The Life of Brian* (1979), which juxtaposed different time periods, presented historical events in the context of modern stereotypes, disrupted the narrative sequence with commentary or surrealist cartoons, and parodied both romantic and realist conventions for depicting history. The influence was not lost to reviewers. In his review of Howard Barker's *Victory,* which was set in the early Restoration period, Nicholas de Jongh credited the play with the "Pythonesque idea that this class are congenital nit-wits and cretins."[8]

During the 1981–82 season, a group known as the National Theatre of Brent toured England with two- or three-person history plays including *Light Brigade, Zulu,* and *The Black Hole of Calcutta,* the last two written by the feminist playwright Bryony Lavery. *The Black Hole of Calcutta* uses a faint narrative to connect sketches including a spoof of *The Jungle Book* and a contortionist representing the map of England. The audience is recruited to represent the Sepoy army. The net effect is a comic ridicule of all that's English.

The mock heroic provided a way in modern history plays to satirize the power figures of traditional history. John Arden, after *Serjeant Musgrave's Dance* in 1959, experimented with a variety of approaches to historical material, including satire. Arden and his collaborator wife, Margaretta D'Arcy, drew on yet another form of Victorian popular entertainment, the nautical drama, for their comic dramatization of the life of Horatio Nelson, *The Hero Rises Up.* In the published preface to the play, they explained that they intended for the play to demonstrate the opposition between the "rectilinear" principles of government and the "asymmetrical curvilinear" temperament of Nelson.[9] England manages to subvert Nelson into a killing machine for which it finally repays him by ignoring his request for a government bequest to his mistress, Emma Hamilton, after his death.

The prologue raises the issue of whether the individual or social forces make the historic moment. Although the playwrights with their Marxist materialist interpretation of history could be expected to side with the latter position, the play has it both ways. Rather than a fully developed character, Nelson is more of a two-dimensional cutout, even something of a buffoon, manipulated by the establishment, but his idiosyncratic choices do determine the course of action. At the same time, the playwrights sully the heroic image of Nelson by including incidents that show him at his worst, such as the Caracciolo affair, in which he killed the republican defender of Naples.

Premiering at the Institute of Contemporary Arts at the Round House, Chalk Farm, on November 6, 1968, the writers "meant to write a play which need not be done properly" (5); in other words, the play itself could be curvilinear. As they explained, "The public, by and large, like Lord Nelson, is inherently 'curvilinear' but under compulsion 'rectilinear': they will respect official art, but never love it" (8). The plot, however, develops in a fairly straightforward chronological order, developing Nelson's love affair with Emma Hamilton, Lord Hamilton and Fanny Nelson providing the complications. The play employs a variety of epic devices, many of which have precedent in the nineteenth-century nautical drama. Scenes are titled, and Nelson's sailor–servant, Allen, functions as a chorus figure. Nelson occasionally steps out of the nineteenth-century time frame and speaks to the audience as a contemporary. Emma narrates her own seduction (p. 46). Some sections are rendered into rhyming verse, and songs are set to eighteenth- and nineteenth-century aires. Dramatic conflicts are resolved theatrically rather than psychologically. For example, when the king of Naples at first resists the bombardment of his rebellious city, Emma sways him with a song that culminates in the possessed king's doing a dervish dance and calling for the blood of his subjects (28).

The deconstruction of Nelson's heroic image serves Arden and D'Arcy's thematic intent but also creates a comic effect. In a tableau with Hamilton studying ancient bronze statues, the king and queen of Naples sitting formally, and Emma languidly singing a song about the weary heart of the exile so far from his native land, Nelson and "A Dolly" "commence to roll and tumble together" (22). An automated mechanical plume on Nelson's hat produces some Gilbert and Sullivan–inspired silliness. The play ends with Nelson's rising from his bier to be borne off in a chariot with his wife on one side and Emma Hamilton on the other, complete with mermaids and the rest of the characters grouped in "a baroque composition around the chariot." The chariot rises to the accompaniment of a bosun's whistle, the rhythmical cries of seamen, and the cast singing, "Fa lal lal la la la la la la" (101–2). Captain Nisbet comments, "This is not to be construed as an historical reconstruction: and even as an act of poetic justice, I am afraid it will fall rather short" (100).

Adrian Mitchell's *Tyger*, an Aristophanic caper pitting a 1960s William Blake against the artistic establishment, also owes much to popular entertainment, in this case pantomime and the music hall. The National Theatre staged this exuberant production at the New Theatre, London, opening on July 20, 1971, under the direction of Michael Blakemore and John Dexter. Mitchell takes a free hand with his historical material as shown in a scene in which Blake and his wife appear with a baby. Sir Joshua Rat, a parody of the establishment artist Joshua Reynolds, comes rushing on stage:

Sir Joshua.   This is outrageous. Beyond everything.
                 Everyone knows Blake had no offspring.
                 This is no mere anachronism.
                 No children were born to William Blake—

Kate.   It takes a fake to spot a fake.
                 But you're wrong, Sir Joshua—

Sir Joshua.   —and history's wrong?

Kate.   Yes, history is very wrong.
                 Ask all the murdered people and see what answer you get.
                 But history hasn't finished yet.[10]

Rather than being organized chronologically, each of this musical's eight vignettes develops a situation conceived with an Aristophanic sense of the bizarre: An MI5 agent and the home secretary, who are investigating Blake's sanity, are pursued by a six-foot version of Blake's engraving *Ghost of a Flea*. Kate routs Three Randy Women delivered in a box in answer to Blake's newspaper ad to find "the lineaments of gratified desire." The British Cultural Committee denies Blake a grant. A "private property" robot is auctioned at a supermarket. Act II begins with Blake at a party, one hundred years after his death, attended by poets ranging in time from Chaucer to Ginsberg. After scenes in which Blake is acquitted of sedition charges and in which Mad King George the Fifty complains to Sir Joshua Rat about the world being taken over by millions of William Blakes, the play ends with Blake sent to the moon.

Mitchell uses anachronisms, catchphrases, and slangy verse couplets inter-mixed with song and dance. At one point during the poets' party, "The CHORUS OF CRITICS come charging on. They are all girls wearing erotic variations on military uniforms and wielding various weapons. They emerge as a ferocious, high-disciplined chorus line, high kicks and all." After repeating the chorus several times, the line is broken up by Coleridge staggering through the ranks, looking for opium. After a slapstick fight, "every poet except WHITMAN and GINSBERG has lifted a CRITIC off the stage and carried her off with howls of lust." Whitman then carries off Ginsberg (69).

Mitchell uses rapidly juxtaposed incongruities to depict with theatrical economy what would take a more realistic play much longer to establish. For example, Blake was tried on charges of treason in 1804, apparently the result of a personal vendetta by a soldier whom Blake expelled as a trespasser. The soldier, in Mitchell's hands, becomes an undercover provocateur for the British Cultural Committee. When the soldier finally gets Blake to cry out, "Damn the Queen of England. All her soldiers are slaves," and Kate to add, "And so are all her poor people," a judge and lawyer immediately appear to try Blake on sedition charges. On trial, however, Blake declares, "God bless the Queen of England. All her soldiers are free," and Kate chimes in, "And so are all her poor people." Blake explains to the judge, "To put it bluntly, I shall lie to you, and I will tell good lies, and you will believe me," at which point the judge acquits him (71). The nontraditional treatment of the historical material in the play deconstructs the image of Blake as an idealized Romantic poet, and the travesty communicates Blake's own lack of conformity as an unconventional artist, leading to Mitchell's broader theme of the strategies required by a highly idiosyncratic artist to survive in a repressive society.

Another form of popular entertainment, the pantomime, was the basis for *Poppy*, Peter Nichols's 1982 satire on Victorian involvement in the Chinese Opium Wars, which we discussed in Chapter 3. Nichols deconstructs the Victorian "panto" to expose its underlying jingoism.

Tom Stoppard's plays provide the clearest connection between absurdism and deconstructionism. The targets for Stoppard's deconstruction have been largely literary or philosophical rather than historical, but *Rosencrantz and Guildenstern Are Dead* (1966), like Edward Bond's *Lear*, revises a piece of historical fiction that has virtually attained the status of history. Stoppard's strategy of revisiting *Hamlet* from the point of view of two minor characters is an analogue to the approach of revisionist historians who shift the focus away from major shakers and movers.

Travesties (1974) has a clearer historical point of reference, but Stoppard builds his imaginative construct on the almost incidental coincidence that

Lenin, James Joyce, and the dadaist Tristan Tzara were in Zurich at the same time. As he did with *Rosencrantz and Guildenstern Are Dead*, Stoppard keeps the emphasis on out-of-focus characters by having events seen through the eyes of a senile minor character, Henry Carr, a factotum at the British Consulate, and maintains the literary parody by having the action and some of the dialogue mimic the plot of *The Importance of Being Earnest*.

DECONSTRUCTIONIST HISTORY PLAYS

Deconstruction is a method of philosophical, historical, or literary criticism that needs no political basis, but the deconstructionist history play is rooted in political radicalism. D. Keith Peacock in *Radical Stages* described a strategy followed by radical playwrights known as situationalism, a belief that

any revolutionary activity must not only attack economic or social structures but must also subvert all manifestations of establishment culture. . . . History was viewed by the Situationalists as but another spectacular official fiction which it was necessary to *disrupt* in order to provoke that radically new perception of reality necessary for life to be fundamentally changed.

Peacock observed that Howard Brenton and Howard Barker followed the example of Arden and particularly of Bond's *Early Morning* to use the structure of the play itself as "a means of disrupting and subverting the audience's perception of authoritarian social structures."[11]

Deconstruction provides a methodology for accomplishing these political purposes, but its presence in these plays may result less from self-conscious use by playwrights than from the fact that deconstruction grows out of the same radical political climate. Political, historical, and theatrical forms share a common iconoclastic intent.

Edward Bond's *Early Morning*, the last play to be forbidden performance in its entirety by the Lord Chamberlain's Office, was given a single private performance by the English Stage Society at the Royal Court on March 31, 1968, and was restaged there in 1969.[12] Described by Keith Peacock as an assault on history more than a history play,[13] this travesty of Victorian history shows Albert and Disraeli plotting Victoria's death, only to be foiled when the queen first kills Albert with poisoned champagne drunk from Florence Nightingale's slipper. The princes Arthur and George are Siamese twins, and when George dies, Arthur is burdened with an increasingly disintegrating corpse. Florence is betrothed to George but seduced by Victoria, who forces Florence to disguise herself as John Brown, historically the man-in-waiting on whom Victoria became increasingly dependent after Albert's death. The last six of twenty-one scenes are set in Heaven, where all of the resurrected characters cannibalize one another. Arthur develops into a martyr who refuses to eat and is finally eaten by others. The play is episodic, but individual scenes develop in a fairly straightforward dramatic fashion. The content creates the surreal feeling rather than style or structure.

Bond's intent is not comic; the tone of this depiction of bizarre incidents seems deadly serious. Niloufer Harben spends a chapter in *Twentieth-Century English History Plays* analyzing the factual basis for these events in an attempt to make the play fit into his naive definition of a history play as one that "evinces a serious concern for historical truth or historical issues."[14] He argues that although Bond's "fidelity to history is often obscured by the extraordinary nature of his treatment," he based the play on historical values and in some instances on documented personal views or idiosyncrasies of his subjects.[15] In fact, Bond calls into question the very concept of historical truth. He deconstructs the Victorian view of history in order to expose its mythical encumbrances and to reveal its underlying predatory assumptions. For instance, Bond makes us aware of the violence inherent in Victorian values by exaggerating it to grotesque proportions. Using the comic technique of literalization, treating something figurative as if it were actual, the Marxist Bond sees the commercially competitive Victorians as actual cannibals. Victorian aggressiveness becomes an aggressive Queen Victoria.

Howard Brenton, the most consistent user of deconstructionist strategies in playwriting, first applies them to historical materials in a play that deals with the Rillington Place murderer who was hanged in 1953. *Christie in Love* was first performed by the Portable Theatre on November 23, 1969, under the direction of David Hare. Brenton organized this short three-character play around the investigation of Christie; the question is "Why did he murder the women?" but the scenes offer a series of surrealistic explorations of the topic more than a coherently developed plot. The opening scene, for instance, shows the Constable digging for bodies while reciting a series of obscene limericks. Christie reenacts one of his murders using an inflatable doll whose voice is provided by the falsetto speaking Constable. In an introductory production note, Brenton explained his strategies: he wanted Christie to be acted very naturalistically and the policemen like "stage coppers": "But they have 'sudden lights', unpredictable speeches beyond the confines of pastiche. As if a cardboard black and white cut-out suddenly reaches out a fully fleshed real hand." Brenton aimed, he said, for "a kind of dislocation, tearing up one style for another, so the proceedings lurch and all interpretations are blocked, and the spectator hunting for an easy meaning wearies."[16]

Brenton's next history play, *Wesley* (1970), has been discussed as a biographical history, but the next year, he wrote *Scott of the Antarctic or What God Didn't See*, a largely comic debunking of another establishment hero, the Antarctic explorer Robert Scott. The play was first performed on ice at the 1971 Bradford Festival by the Bradford University Drama Group, headed by Albert Hunt. Hunt, who had worked with Peter Brook's 1966 *US* production, developed at Bradford, through a series of productions, an approach for satirizing world rulers by reinterpreting their actions as those of film stars acting out parts. Brenton's short play depicts Scott as a self-deluded victim of Victorian ideals. The beginning of the play establishes the style as travesty. George Five has a nightmare that "the half of the world that's English went (Claps his hands. 'Bom' on a drum) Foreign";[17] so he goes to Westminster Abbey to pray and is answered by God, an old man in a wheelchair, and Jesus, who is cheerfully pulling a cross. When God asks how Jesus's hands are, the two break into a commercial for Valderma, for cuts and sores. They decide that George needs a new English hero. What ensues is a reenactment of the Antarctic expedition with the explorers doggedly plodding toward the pole in the midst of an ice extravaganza with skaters whizzing around the struggling polar party. The acting is very presentational with many lines of the polar party repeated in megaphones to audience on both sides of the playing area. An announcer frequently sets the scene and provides commentary: "Ladies and gentlemen, men make their own history but they do not make it just as they please. The traditions of the dead generations weigh like a nightmare on the brains of the living" (79). God and Jesus look on and intervene at times:

God: I think I'll drop the temperature.

Jesus: Poor sods.

God: Nonsense! They like it! (p. 81)

The Devil, who enters riding pillion on a motorcycle driven by his Hell's Angel henchman Snodgrass, behaves like a panto villain, but decides not to let Snodgrass "do 'em" since Scott and his party will "do themselves."

Brenton principally tries to undermine the heroic image of Scott. The lighting designer, Roland Miller, in collusion with Brenton, developed a character who provided a clownlike ironic counterpoint to the main action. Even before the performance Miller sat outside in an explorer's costume torn to the flesh, exposing him to the cold. On the rink he hovered around the edge of the action, clutching a teddy bear to signify Scott's protective attitude toward the expedition's animals. Brenton described him as "a kind of anti-Scott" (9).

Brenton avoids making any special matter of the death of Scott himself and dispatches him in a final orgy of macabre ridiculousness:

Figures of great explorers appear and approach the tent, Armstrong, Drake, Livingstone. They converge and tear the tent apart, fall on the Polar Party's bodies and eat them. Spots on GOD and JESUS come up at a great distance blessing the spectacle. And on the tape the blizzard turns to gobbling noises. (103)

The final scene in the play parodies the death of Captain Lawrence Oates and demonstrates how Brenton deconstructs historical myths. A sound tape that has projected a variety of background sounds, including sections of Vaughan Williams's *Sinfonia Antarctica,* now plays a blizzard effect:

Devil: And now we give you, the famous death of Captain Oates.

　(Drumroll)

　Wait for the famous phrase folks.

　(The tent bulges.)

　Is it coming now, is it?

　(Tent bulges violently. Tape gathers momentum.)

　Get your hankies out! Really moving bit. Tears, the lot.

　Brave Englishman giving his life for his friends. Even

　I, ladies and gents, have a salty trickle.

　(Tent bulges more violently.)

　Yes! Here comes the famous phrase . . . Now.

　(Nothing)

　Oh. Snodders!

Snodgrass: Hello.

Devil: Get the famous phrase song sheet out.

　(Two lackeys come on with a banner. It reads "I am just going outside and may be some time.")

　Maestro, please.

　(Very bad ugly chord from the band.

　SNODGRASS sings horribly walking along the banner.)

Devil and Snodgrass: I . . . Am . . . Just . . . Going . . . Outside . . . And . . . May . . . Be . . . Some . . . Time . . .

　(OATES's head appears out of the tent with megaphone.)

　Devil: Here it is! Here it is!

Oates: I am just going . . .

    (Tape getting loud.

    SCOTT's head and megaphone pokes out.

    Interrupts.)

Scott: What?

Oates: I am just . . .

Scott: What?

Oates: I . . .

Scott: What? (102–3)

Oates never completes the phrase, but collapses on the ice with a football chant, "England, England," playing over the loud speaker.

    Brenton confronted the question of how we fabricate history even more directly in *H.I.D. (Hess is Dead)*, staged by the Royal Shakespeare Company at the Almedia Theatre on September 26, 1989. The play's premise is that a reporter (Palmer) has been called by the widow (Charity) of one of the three persons, all now dead, commissioned by the Allies to attest that the Nazi leader Rudolf Hess committed suicide in September of 1987. Charity attempts to persuade Palmer that her husband and the two other members of the commission were murdered in order to conceal the fact that the imprisoned "Hess" was an imposter, and the real Hess had been shot down by Himmler, an idea that Brenton credits in the play's introduction to Hugh Thomas's *Hess: A Tale of Two Murders.*[18]

    The form of the play itself demonstrates one of its principal themes—that the media control our view of events. Audio- and videotape presentations interwoven into the plot provide the primary evidence for reconstructing past events. In spite of its unconventional staging, the play remains fundamentally a retrospective investigation of a mystery much like *Equus* or, for that matter, *Oedipus Rex*.

    The play borrows techniques from performance art. Charity dances out the old age and death of Hess as she comments for Palmer on an earlier videotape showing the same performance. Brenton explains in a stage direction, "The idea of the dance is that from the pitiful, sordid state of HESS's old age that she mimes, she is choreographing something that is, unacceptably, beautiful" (15). This provides another example and a strong image of how the telling of a story transforms our perception of the event. Brenton makes heavy use of asides to allow characters to express the disparity between the exterior appearance and the inner reality of an event. For example, we see a videotape of the initial meeting between the other two members of the commission, Nicole and

Raymond, then the scene is replayed live, with Palmer looking on, but with new asides in which the characters reveal private thoughts that undercut the dialogue.

Brenton used a variety of devices to make the audience aware of his own contrivance as a storyteller. The asides are in highly structured verse. A taped argument between Charity and the cameraman interrupts Charity's dance of Hess's death. The tapes contain extraneous material from old television commercials or earlier uses, including snatches of Charity in bed with her husband, what Brenton describes as a palimpsest of old tapings, like the faint tracing of earlier texts erased from old manuscripts. At one point a figure in a seventeenth-century costume falling backward through a door appears briefly in the midst of the tape, presumably made by secret cameras, of Nicole and Raymond's meeting on the day of Hess's death. Palmer replays the tape twice more, and the figure becomes a little more distinct each time, but this has no impact on the plot.

The three members of the commission are academic historians, and Brenton sees the media and historians as coconspirators with the same intent to deceive. Palmer tells Charity,

In my trade, facts are all. They are stones. Stones are real. That was said, that was done. But hard facts can, I find, go . . . mushy. The stones turn to marshmallow. The . . . assassination of John Kennedy? Was there a second gunman? The death of Mozart, poisoned by Salieri? The world has seen *Amadeus*, the movie. Actually, Salieri was a good friend to Mozart. Who was not a pauper, but a man with a carriage and servants. Not poisoned, he just caught the flu. But once the world has seen the movie. . . . Hard facts become "beliefs". Puffs of smoke. Phantoms. (13)

Charity says that her husband, Istvan Luber, feared that the photographs of Hitler and Company would change: "Slowly. That even the negatives, in the archives, would become lies." He believed that "all history decays" (16). When, near the play's end, Luber appears on a tape addressed to the other two commission members, he asks:

What is it: This thing, this state of mind . . . History? That we bend, that we distort? From which we want . . . *The truth?* . . . Ours is the new treason of the clerks . . . we have become specialists, technicians of acceptable truths . . . this is a new age, that only has use for our expertise . . . it has seduced us. . . . We are morticians, we deliver history with an acceptable face . . . acceptable facts, which may or may not be true. (59)

Nicole realizes that the "official report" issued by their commission has been a gross media manipulation: "It is an encoding of the truth. No more no less. Our statement is a construct. Like any sentence or photograph" (46–47).

Raymond asks, "Who will write the history of the rewriters of history?" (50). And he and Nicole agree that they "market history . . . to remove impurities. To add artificial sweeteners" (51).

The reviewers understood Brenton's message. Michael Billington, reviewing the play for the *Guardian*, wrote, "What he is really writing about is the way we doctor history and launder the past. He suggests that if we demolish the walls of Spandau to make way for a supermarket, we pulverize the memory of horror."[19] Alan Radnor wrote in the *Jewish Chronicle*, "*H.I.D.* is a disturbing play in that it questions what we accept as truth. We tend to believe reports in newspapers, television and radio particularly if they agree about the basic facts. But can we be entirely sure?"[20] Catherine Wearing told her readers in *What's On* that the play is about "how we remember and who we trust to represent the past."[21]

A comment that he puts in the mouth of Raymond suggests that Brenton understood the deconstructionist thrust of his play: "How Goebbels would have loved modern literary theory" (47).

Tom Stoppard's *Arcadia*, which opened at the Lyttelton Theatre on April 13, 1993, and later in the West End, deconstructs the idea of history.[22] Stoppard's invented incidents interleaf two time lines occurring in the same room on a country estate, one between 1809 and 1812, the other in the present. Two of the present-day characters, Bernard Nightingale and Hannah Jarvis, are literary historians, trying to reconstruct 180 years later the events that the audience witnesses, sometimes before and sometimes after the modern scenes in which they are discussed. Stoppard shows the historians' misconstructions, based on surviving documents, of events that the audience has observed. He also baits the audience into incorrectly anticipating what will happen when early nineteenth-century scenes follow scenes showing the historians' speculations about what occurred. For example, the first act sets up an expectation of an early morning duel between the tutor Septimus Hodge and a minor poet, Ezra Chater. After a twentieth-century scene speculating about the causes of Chater's apparent sudden death, the act ends with a lighting change to early morning and an offstage pistol shot, leading the audience to think that Chater has been killed. The next act opens with another modern scene and speculation that Hodge's school chum, Lord Byron, who was a guest at the estate, was the one who killed Chater in a duel. The next scene, "a reprise," repeats the lighting cue and pistol shot, but Hodge enters with a rabbit that he has shot. We learn that there has been no duel and that Chater has left in the middle of the night to become a botanist for a West Indies voyage of exploration.

Near the play's end, Stoppard has characters from the two periods on stage at the same time and one actor plays a character in each time frame, but this appears more a theatrical tour de force than a postmodern device. The two time frames remain clearly separated in the minds of the audience members.

Stoppard returned to interwoven time lines in *Indian Ink*, which opened at the Aldwych Theatre in London on February 27, 1995, after a tryout at the Yvonne Arnaud Theatre in Guildford. Here, as in *Arcadia*, time periods function like a chemical mixture in which the parts are separable, where in postmodernism, different time periods compound so that the parts are insepa- rable from the whole. The research of a literary historian and biographer, Eldon Pike, in the 1980s provides a matrix in which we see played the events surrounding the visit of the English poet Flora Crewe to India in the 1930s. As in *Arcadia*, the audience confronts the disparity between the reconstructed history and the observed event. Pike attempts to discover whether an Indian painter, Anish Das, has made a nude portrait of Flora. At one point Pike's Indian colleague accuses him: "You are constructing an edifice of speculation on a smudge of paint on paper, which no longer exists."[23] Pike's "footnotes" from his edited edition of Crewe's letters periodically punctuate the play with a litany of "facts," but Flora's sister and Das's son, working from a more personal and emotionally based understanding, come closer to reconstructing events. The play gently exposes the unattractive side of British colonialism, but it is fundamentally a romance about the love of Das for Crewe.

POSTMODERN HISTORY PLAYS

On a fundamental level, postmodernism responds to the deconstruction of traditional forms of thought including the idea of factual history. After exposing the lack of externally verifiable truths, what remains? The idea of a postmodern Weltangschauung may seem oxymoronic, but clear features emerge: the juxtaposition of disparate styles, periods, or genres; the use of fabulation and pastiche; the disruption of any clear narrative progression, even to the extent of disrupting causation (aleatory disconnection); the appearance of *bricolage*, an improvised assembly of found materials; an emphasis on disconnected images, often drawn from television, commercials, or other forms of pop entertainment. Each work does not have to show all of these features but only enough to present a picture of dislocation. When Charles Marowitz, in a review for *Village Voice*, complained that Edward Bond's *Early Morning* was "style-muddled," he was reacting to a postmodern aspect of the play.[24]

Anachronisms, which frequently appear in postmodern plays, can empha- size either continuity or disjointedness. In medieval drama with its sense of timelessness, anachronisms demonstrate unchangableness; in postmodern his- tory, they upset chronological order and the possibility of causation. John

Arden's one-act Christmas play, *The Business of Good Government*, transforms the conventional use of anachronisms in medieval drama into a form that anticipates postmodernism. Originally written for an amateur production at Brent Knoll in Somerset in 1960, the play intentionally nurtures its sense of improvisation. The staging conventions mimic those of a medieval mystery play, but the characters' voices are thoroughly modern. Herod thus addresses the audience like a modern politician and the angel functions as a talking sidebar. Arden describes it as "a straightforward narration of the events given in the Gospels, with incidental references backwards to ancient Judaea and forwards to the twentieth century." Arden calls for the costumes to reflect this dual sense of time: "I do not think that true historical costume or straightforward modern dress would be entirely satisfactory: what is required is that each individual character should appear to be the *essence* of that person, from whatever period the details of his costume be drawn."[25] The play makes its satiric point about the oppressive tendencies of any established government without sounding at all strident.

Postmodern tendencies cannot be separated neatly from deconstruction in Howard Brenton's work, but Brenton has several history plays that disrupt chronology by juxtaposing disparate time frames, particularly *Hitler Dances*, *Weapons of Happiness*, and *The Romans in Britain*. *Hitler Dances* was built partially from actor improvisation, a rehearsal method used by Edinburgh's Traverse Theatre Club, which initially staged the play in January 1972. Based on an imagined incident, this is not a true history play, but a Poor Theatre exploration of a historical theme. A group of children resurrect a World War II German soldier, who proceeds to "tell" a story of a female British spy dropped behind enemy lines, a parody of the 1958 Rank film *Carve Her Name With Pride*. Brenton describes the resurrection as "a horror holy piece," a suggestion of influence by the American company the Living Theatre, which in 1965 had similarly used a company of actors to "build" Frankenstein's monster on stage. Brenton, however, undercuts his ritual with a commentary by two watching characters who treat the resurrection as a TV event. The soldier is a "A Dirty Old Man," and according to Richard Boon's introduction to the published version of the play, this relationship between children and an old man, also explored by Brenton in *Gum and Goo*, is a metaphor for the relation between history and the present.[26] In *New British Political Dramatists*, John Bull observed that the children conjure the dead soldier "with the meaningless names of 'great men' of history as they would with those of their comic book heroes. . . . Their absurd mythologizing is a simplistic version of the essentially comic-book view of history through which most of their grown-up counterparts attempt to view the modern world."[27]

Providing a revisionist view of World War II, emphasizing violence and aggression, the play, structured like a loosely assembled music hall piece, uses a matrix of children's games and songs, particularly those with violent undertones. Some scenes use more than one actor to play a single character.

In *The Churchill Play* (1974), which we have already discussed as a Marxist historical drama, Brenton uses a play within a play to present a resurrected character without violating a more realistic treatment of time, but with *The Weapons of Happiness*, which opened at the Lyttleton Theatre on July 14, 1976, Brenton returned to overlapping time frames. This first new play commissioned by the National Theatre in its new facilities intermixes the story of the takeover of a factory by a group of young radicals with the imprisonment and execution of Joseph Frank and Vladimir Clementis, Czech Communists who were purged by Stalin in 1952. Brenton resurrects Frank, like the German soldier in *Hitler Dances*, and makes him an unwilling participant in the 1977 strike. Janice, a young radical who has become Frank's lover, berates him for always slipping into the past:

Frank. They died.

Janice. Good.

Frank. Suffered.

Janice. Don't care.

Frank. They hold my hands when I eat. They tie my shoes when I dress. When I speak they hold my tongue. They turn my head to see a dead bird in the garden. They pull open the lids of my eyes when I wake.

Janice. Oh what you carry around. Wads a rotting stuff. All in your pockets, all stuffed down your shirt, urrgh.

Frank. History . . .

Janice. Don't care about history.[28]

These reenacted scenes from the past overlap the present action, and Frank occasionally must interact simultaneously in two time frames. Frank serves as both participant and narrator for the flashbacks. The transitions from past to present often create jarring theatrical effects. For example, Frank replays his final meeting with Clementis before he is hanged. As the guards place a noose around his neck, Clementis reads a letter declaring his innocence to the head of the Czech Communist party:

Clementis. Long live the Communist Party of Czechoslovakia.

Capital Radio. Hello all you nightriders out there. *A snatch of music. Mini Ripperton sings "Loving You".* CLEMENTIS *begins to sink through the stage.*

Janice (*Off*). Joseph?

Ken (*Off*). Oy Joey! Where you got to?

Clementis. I tried to keep my trousers up in court! I did not show my bum in disrespect!

Capital Radio. Insomniacs all, cold out there? Here comes California sun!
  The radio plays the Beach Boys singing "Good Vibrations".

  CLEMENTIS *has sunk to his chest.* JOSEF FRANK *kneels beside him.*

Clementis. I've got a handful of raisins. In a matchbox. I'd give them to you if I were
  alive.
  CLEMENTIS *disappears.* JOSEF FRANK *looks upstage as* STALIN *comes out of the
  dark smoking his pipe.* KEN *comes out of the dark carrying a transistor radio.* (p. 55)

Brenton uses the disrupted time sequence to convey Frank's mental torment
and to contrast the suffering of the old Communists with the undisciplined
self-indulgence of the young radicals.

Brenton also juxtaposed the past and the present in *The Romans in Britain*,
which opened at the National Theatre on October 16, 1980. The first part of
the play recreates a conflict between invading Romans and resident Celts in
54 B.C., but at the very end of the first act, Caesar reappears in a jeep with
Roman soldiers costumed in British military uniforms of the 1970s. The
second half of the play intermixes a modern with a period plot, the first
involving a British spy waiting to assassinate an Irish Republican Army (IRA)
figure and the second, the breakup in 515 of a Celtic family in the face of the
threat of a Saxon invasion. Less than disrupting the narrative, the juxtaposition
here serves more the time honored purpose of establishing a parallel between
a historical and a modern situation, between Caesar's invasion and the British
in Northern Ireland. In the introduction, Brenton stresses that "the scenes of
the past are haunted by the 1980s with another army, the British, blundering
around in another foreign country, Ireland."[29]

A high percentage of the scenes end with murder and Brenton dwells on
offputting business—human sacrifice, nudity, buggery, hemorrhoids, Caesar
pulling out a rotten tooth, and patricide—for which the play was widely
attacked by critics and moralists.[30] The director, Michael Bogdanov, was
unsuccessfully sued for violating the Sexual Offences Act of 1956, a highly
publicized case that took a year to resolve and probably contributed to the
packed houses enjoyed by the production. Brenton presents distasteful incidents to demythologize the historical material he dramatizes. He also has a
scene at the play's end in which two cooks who have been stretcher bearers
decide to pass the time by making up the story of King Arthur, inventing, as
it were, a historical myth before our very eyes.

Brenton also developed a contrast similar to Arden's idea of the conflict between rectilinear and curvilinear forces discussed earlier. According to Brenton, the Romans "built straight roads and 'brought law,' " but as shown by the "off-centre, curled, triangular" motif in their decorations, the Celts had an "asymmetrical view of the world" (vii–ix). In the collision between these tendencies, the asymmetrical may initially appear disadvantaged but has power of adaptation that suggests long-range survival. Brenton's method for organizing his plot also seems curvilinear with incidents developed in a tag progression rather than following individual characters. One of two Irish characters introduced in the first scene is killed in the second scene by three Celts, two of whom are killed by Romans in the third scene. In the second act, the twentieth-century plot is interlaced by events involving two separate refugee groups, the survivors of which join in the final scene. In spite of the episodic structure, Brenton clearly defined the dramatic conflicts.

Howard Barker's treatment of history is even more shocking and disorienting to his audience than Brenton's. One of his characters in *The Europeans* expresses what appears to be Barker's attitude toward history: "To know who we are, we must know who we were."[31] However, as much as deconstructing traditional history, Barker seems bent on constructing his own very idiosyncratic histories. In an interview in the theatre magazine *Gambit*, he discussed his unusual use of historical materials:

My history plays are imagined history. I don't do research, they are an amalgam of intuitions, and the absence or misuse of facts does not make them any less historical. . . . I use history not for nostalgia, but to hack away at comforting images of the past in order to evoke, or unlock, feelings about the present. I don't do this for a political purpose, I do it to subvert conventions of thought.[32]

Sheridan Morley, in a review of Barker's *Victory*, which was set in 1660, observed that the play was "no more a flight into the past than was Brecht's *Caucasian Chalk Circle*—instead it's an attempt to put the present into a different context."[33]

After a tryout in Brighton, the Joint Stock Company opened *Victory* at the Royal Court on March 25, 1983, with a cast of ten doing thirty roles.[34] The play has a fairly cohesive plot centering around the efforts by the widow of John Bradshaw, the judge who pronounced the death sentence of Charles I, to gather the remains of Bradshaw's dismembered body, which Charles II has placed on display after his ascension to the throne. Nicholas de Jongh, in his *Mail on Sunday* review, described the play as "a guerrilla-like assault upon the 17th-century Restoration period."[35] Barker deconstructs the Restoration with heavy emphasis on scatological dialogue, sexuality, and grotesquerie. One of

King Charles's mistresses masturbates him in public as members of the court throw things at the impaled head of John Bradshaw. Later, Nell Gwynn plants a passionate kiss on Bradshaw's rotting skull, which the king carries around in a sack. Bradshaw's widow, who among other indignities becomes a pickpocket and maid to one of the king's mistresses, marries a cavalier bully who has raped her. After he has been tortured for murdering the king's banker, she leads him around at the end of a rope. Barker invents a poet laureate, Samuel Clegg, who recites heroic quatrains against this background of debauchery. Neil Chaillet, reviewing for the *Wall Street Journal*, observed that Barker "brusquely translates the flowery appeal of cavalier poetry into its unspoken components of rape and brutality."[36] Barker does the same for both the court and Puritan values of the period.

Barker repeatedly sets his plays in the past. *Scenes from an Execution*, a 1984 radio play, occurs in sixteenth-century Venice. *The Castle*, produced in 1985 at the Royal Shakespeare Company's Pit Theatre at the Barbican, is set after the Crusades. *Pity in History*, written for television in 1985 and staged at Edinburgh in 1986, takes place in a battered church during the Civil War.

The Bite of the Night, produced at Barbican's Pit on August 31, 1988, shows even more overtly the postmodern disregard for chronology.[37] John Connor, reviewing for *City Lights*, noted that "the narrative is deconstructed; there is no crucial stanza, merely a collage of scenes which builds to a whole."[38] The play, which ran over four and a half hours in performance, and its characters move through time with aplomb. Modern and period references mix indiscriminately. Savage, a university classics professor, and his one student visit eleven lost Troys, all populated by a continuing set of characters including Helen, the embodiment of erotic love; Creusa, the frustrated and spurned woman; Homer; Fladder, Helen's husband; Gummery, Epsom, and Slade, soldiers; and Gay, Helen's fanatical daughter. Scenes are built around metaphorical actions rather than a developing plot. For example, "The Political Fuck," the marriage of Macluby and Creusa, occurs on a bed with surrounding crowd noises. Except for verse prologues to each of the three acts and an interlude involving Schliemann, the style is fairly straightforward; only the content is strange. In a piece of business reminiscent of *Monty Python and the Holy Grail*, Helen loses legs and arms (subsequently provided by Savage's student) and ages progressively as the play goes on. Items of discussion seem to shift by free association.

Barker, in a *Guardian* interview just before the play's opening, discussed its unconventional style. He called for a theatre of "Catastrophism":

The abolition of routine distinctions between good and bad actions, the sense that good and evil co-exist within the same psyche, that freedom and kindness may not be compatible, that pity is both a poison and an erotic stimulant, that laughter might be as often oppressive as it is rarely liberating, all these constitute the territory of a new theatre practice, which lends its audience the potential as a personal re-assessment in the light of dramatic action. . . . These moments of loss involve the breaking of the narrative thread, the sudden suspension of the story, the interruption of the obliquely related interlude, and a number of devices designed to complicate and to overwhelm the audience's habitual method of seeing.[39]

Even though he does not discuss the disruption of historical expectation, that obviously fits into this pattern and was clearly seen by the reviewers as the principal theme of this play. Lydia Conway writes for *What's On*, "History teaches us, so Barker would have it, that we never learn from the past because we never understand it. The play promises to reach down beyond the known for once and gives us, the audience, the right of interpretation."[40]

Michael Billington complained in the *Guardian* that the play "offered too little reward for the effort involved," but

what emerged for me was the idea that what we call History is a series of convenient myths: that just as we are led to believe that Sarajevo caused the First World War so we glibly assume that the rape of Helen inspired the Trojan War. . . . Barker shows us that history is confused, barbaric, non-sequential. . . . Literature, Barker intimates, also creates History. . . . Barker is obsessed by the unknowability of the past.[41]

Barker returned to a pseudohistorical setting for his 1990 play *The Europeans*, which he placed in Vienna in 1683 after the defeat of Islam by the Poles and Austrians. Even though the setting is historical, most of the minor characters and the incidents are imaginary. The play's subtitle, *Struggles to Love*, indicates its thematic interest in the power of individuals to love in spite of or because of suffering. A hint of a plot involves Katrin, who has been raped by Turkish soldiers and is attempting to purge her feelings of violation and to sustain a loving relationship with Starhemberg, the disillusioned hero of the Allied forces. Her sister Susannah unsuccessfully tries to establish an alliance with the priest Orphuls, who cannot reconcile himself with either passions of the flesh or his own ambitions. The relations of these two pairs are set in contrast; each of the men, for example, struggles with his mother. Some plot issues reach a resolution: Orphuls is executed for killing his mother; Katrin gives birth to a child named Concilia. Starhemberg gives the child to the Turks and the play ends with him and Katrin embracing.

The play's unconventionality rests less in its style of presentation or structure than in characterization and dialogue. Barker places about 10 percent of his text in boldface, indicating passages that he wants the actor to stress. These phrases sometimes grow out of dialogue, but they are often emphatic expressions of a character's inner dialogue or an important theme. The Emperor Leopold opens the play on a plain, where a battle has taken place:

I laugh
I laugh (He walks toward some squatting PRISONERS.)
I laugh
I laugh
Where's the painter? (A FIGURE enters with an easel and board.)
I laugh
I laugh (The PAINTER sketches.)
The pain which soddens every turf
This bowel which droops from every bush
The crop of widows and orphans
I laugh[42]

Leopold wanders throughout the play intoning, "I laugh; I laugh," interspersed with fairly rational dialogue as he tries to rebuild Europe after the Turkish invasion. The play is expressionistic in tone without a solipsistic point of view. Characters are abstracted metaphors of Barker's ideas, often with abstract names. Barker tends to write a series of images more than a coherent plot. Some of these images are obtuse, others vivid and poetic. For instance, the Painter complains that the war has distracted him from beauty, but he is irresistibly drawn to a beheading in the midst of doing a portrait of Katrin. Many scenes reveal themes or characters but further the plot in no way, for example; Katrin exposes herself to physicians at the Institute of Science (I,4); Orphuls encounters his mother; Starhemberg slums it with the beggars; Leopold debates the principles of new art with art critics. History plays rarely forward a subjective view of events, but Barker comes close to expressionism.

Part of the initial appeal of postmodernism was shock effect, its ability to challenge audiences' expectations of a unified period and style, a coherent plot, developed characterization, and themes based on established values. This disorientation should, theoretically, allow old standards to be questioned and replaced by new. The danger, of course, is that the audience will simply reject the new history. Barker, in 1984, noted that his plays rarely fill even a small theatre like the Court.

If the rewriting of history failed to attract a large following, postmodern staging, particularly for Shakespeare, became commonplace in Britain by the late 1980s. During the summer of 1990, I saw seven Shakespeare productions, including those at the National Theatre and the Royal Shakespeare Theatre both at Stratford and at the Barbican Theatre in London, all using, within a single production, eclectic costumes and staging conventions from various periods, none with a very clear justification for doing so. In these instances postmodern staging provided a convenient means for allowing costumes particularly to make a strong comment on character without regard for period authenticity and did not necessarily imply a radical deconstruction of history itself. However, as happened with absurdist theatre, familiarity begins to lessen the shock of unconventionality. A postmodern view of history has clearly entered the cultural mainstream when a critic like Michael Billington, reviewing *The Bite of the Night*, can write, "Barker seems to me to be beating at an open door. Does anyone, outside the writer of text-books, still see History as a series of ordered events with clear cause-and-effect?"[43]

NOTES

1. Theodore Zeldin, "Social History and Total History," *Journal of Social History* 10, no. 2 (Winter 1976): 242–43.

2. Janelle Reinelt, *After Brecht: British Epic Theatre* (Ann Arbor: University of Michigan, 1994), pp. 83–84.

3. Henri Bergson, "Laughter" [1900], in *Comedy*, ed. Wylie Sypher (Garden City, NY: Doubleday, 1956), p. 123.

4. Theatre Workshop, Charles Chilton and members of the original cast, *Oh What a Lovely War* (London: Methuen, 1965), p. 102.

5. Charles Marowitz, *Confessions of a Counterfeit Critic: A London Theatre Notebook 1958–71* (London: Eyre Methuen, 1973), reprints an *Encore* review, p. 66.

6. Roger Wilmut documents this comic tradition in *From Fringe to Flying Circus* (London: Eyre Methuen, 1980).

7. Alan Bennett, *Forty Years On* [1969] in *Forty Years On, Getting On, Habeas Corpus and Enjoy* (London: Faber & Faber, 1992), pp. 9–10.

8. *Mail on Sunday*, March 27, 1983.

9. John Arden and Margaretta D'Arcy, *The Hero Rises Up* (London: Methuen, 1969), p. 5.

10. Adrian Mitchell, *Tyger: A Celebration Based on the Life and Work of William Blake* (London: Jonathan Cape, 1971), p. 34.

11. D. Keith Peacock, *Radical Stages: Alternative History in Modern British Drama* (Westport, CT: Greenwood, 1991), pp. 65–66.

12. Edward Bond, *Early Morning* [1968], in *Plays: One* (London: Metheun, 1977), pp. 137–223.

13. Peacock, *Radical Stages*, p. 140.

14. Niloufer Harben, *Twentieth-Century English History Plays* (Totowa, NJ: Barnes & Noble, 1988), p. 18.

15. Harben, *Twentieth-Century English History Plays*, p. 216.

16. Howard Brenton, *Plays: One*, pp. 2–3.

17. Howard Brenton, *Scott of the Antarctic or What God Didn't See*, in *Plays for Public Places* (London: Eyre Methueun, 1972), p. 75.

18. Hugh Thomas, *Hess: A Tale of Two Murders* (London: Hodder and Stoughton), cited in Howard Brenton, "Author's Note," *H.I.D. (Hess is Dead)* (London: Nick Hern, 1989).

19. *Guardian*, Sept. 30, 1989.

20. *Jewish Chronicle*, Oct. 13, 1989.

21. *What's On*, Oct. 4, 1989.

22. Tom Stoppard, *Arcadia* (London: Faber & Faber, 1993).

23. Tom Stoppard, *Indian Ink* (London: Faber & Faber, 1995), p. 59.

24. Marowitz, *Confessions*, reprints a *Village Voice* review, p. 142.

25. John Arden, *The Business of Good Government* (New York: Grove, 1963), p. 10.

26. Howard Brenton, *Hitler Dances* (London: Methuen, 1982), p. ix.

27. John Bull, *New British Political Dramatists* (New York: Grove, 1984), p. 33.

28. Howard Brenton, *Weapons of Happiness* (London: Eyre Methuen, 1976), p. 57.

29. Howard Brenton, *The Romans in Britain* [1980, 1989], in *Plays: Two* (London: Methuen, 1989), p. viii.

30. Philip Roberts, "Howard Brenton's *Romans*," *Critical Quarterly* 23 no. 3 (1981): 5–23, defended the historical accuracy of the play.

31. Howard Barker, *The Europeans*, in *The Europeans and Judith* (London: John Calder, 1990), p. 29.

32. "Interview with Howard Barker," *Gambit*, 11, no. 4 (1984): 34–35.

33. *Punch*, March 26, 1983.

34. Howard Barker, *Victory* (London: John Calder, 1983).

35. *Mail on Sunday*, March 27, 1983.

36. *Wall Street Journal* [European ed.], Mar. 25, 1983.

37. Howard Barker, *The Bite of the Night* (London: John Calder, 1988).

38. *City Lights*, Sept. 15, 1988.

39. Howard Barker, "The Triumph in Defeat," *Guardian*, Aug. 22, 1988.

40. Lydia Conway, *What's On*, Sept. 9, 1988.

41. Michael Billington, *Guardian*, Sept. 7, 1988.

42. Barker, *The Europeans*, p. 1.

43. Billington, *Guardian*, Sept. 7, 1988.

8

The Search for a Theatrical Form

Has the structure, language, or staging of the history play changed in response to new ideas about history? We saw how many plays reflect the various approaches of New History in their selection and presentation of historical material. The most defining feature of the plays based on New History has been the point of view from which they present material. Rather than depicting events as objective fact, but from the assumed vantage of the hegemony, many contemporary history plays offer alternative viewpoints. Caryl Churchill or David Storey's decision to describe the English Civil War from the perspective of common soldiers and citizens rather than from the standpoint of Charles I and Cromwell sets their approach off from traditional history. The dramatization of the Reformation in terms of Luther's rebellion against his father, the depiction of Shakespeare's final years as an economic betrayal of the citizens of Stratford, or the representation of piracy as an alternative subculture with a regressive view of women implies new perceptions of the appropriate subject matter of history. How do these changes in content influence the form of contemporary history plays? Do the plays reveal the influence of New History or merely show the influence of new trends in theatre that have nothing to do with changing historiography?

NARRATIVE

Controversially, some New Historians tried to abandon the narrative form of traditional history. Even at the beginning of the twentieth century, positivists had attacked narration as a source of distortion in historical studies, which, they argued, should objectively present facts without trying to shape them into a story. In defense of narration, the English popular historian George Macaulay Trevelyan, in 1913, criticized what he perceived as a German-influenced aspiration to make history scientific, a misplaced effort that neglected "what is after all the principal craft of the historian—the art of narrative."[1] Trevelyan saw scientific investigation as only the first of three steps taken by the historian, followed by imaginative or speculative development and, finally, the literary process of writing the history.[2]

From the 1930s the *Annales* school advocated abandoning chronological narrative in favor of a way of describing the past by "asking questions" and "formulating hypotheses," emphasizing structures rather than chronology.[3] The contemporary English historiographer John Tosh points out the *Annales* historians belief that narrative was unsuitable for the "silent changes" in history—"those gradual transformations in mental and social experience which were reflected on the surface of events in only the most oblique manner."[4] However, doing without narrative proved easier in theory than practice. In response to the British historian Lawrence Stone's 1979 declaration that the *Annales* historians had returned to narrative, Philippe Carrard, in his critique of the French New Historians, argues that they had never forsaken it.[5]

Carrard suggests that the animosity toward narrative was really guilt by association: linking narrative with "metanarrative," any presupposition of a single overriding view of truth.[6] Jean-François Lyotard defined postmodernism in terms of its "incredulity toward meta-narrative,"[7] a position shared by virtually all New Historians. One way the *Annales* historians could avoid an overarching view without abandoning narrative itself was to use "mininarratives," stories that presumably avoided overarching social judgment and focused rather on local or specific instances such as Natalie Davis's *The Return of Martin Guerre*, a historical study of life in a sixteenth-century French village, which was made into a film and a popular musical.[8]

The deconstructionists observed that any approach to history that posited development from formative beginnings retrospectively imposed present values onto the past. However, in arguing for the inescapable intrusion of the historian's values, even in data-based historical studies, they called into question any significant distinction between narrative literature and history, thus relegitimizing the place of narrative in history.

The New Historians also associated narrative with dependence on a chronological structure. The English economic historian R. H. Tawney wrote, "Time, and the order of occurrences in time, is a clue, but no more; part of the historian's business is to substitute more significant connections for those of chronology."[9] John Tosh contends that narrative creates the false impression that sequentiality is causality: "because B came after A does not mean that A *caused* B, but the flow of the narrative may easily convey the impression that it did."[10]

Chronological order is obviously not the only way to structure a story, and the Cambridge historian Peter Burke appealed for the use of a "modern narrative" to replace traditional chronologically structured narratives:

Many scholars now think that historical writing has also been impoverished by the abandonment of narrative, and a search is under way for new forms of narrative which will be appropriate to the new stories historians would like to tell. These new forms include micro-narrative, backward narrative, and stories which move back and forth between public and private worlds or present the same events from multiple points of view.[11]

Burke observed that Natalie Davis had worked simultaneously on the published and film versions of her history *The Return of Martin Guerre*, and as a consequence the historical study incorporated film techniques such as flashbacks and crosscutting.[12]

Narration is even more difficult to escape in the theatre than in history books. Performance theory in recent years has made us more aware of alternatives to narrative theatre, but a plotted story remains the major device for holding audience interest. In addition to the question of point of view, narration in drama and in history plays entails the narrative structure of the "story" or plot and may include an overt use of a narrator.

Narrative Structure

The question as to what incidents a playwright chooses to dramatize, whose point of view to forward, and what cause and effect relationships to imply has occupied much of our earlier discussion. Neocolonial and feminist history plays, for example, develop characters and events ignored by establishment histories. Marxist history plays presuppose a degree of economic causality usually missing in other histories. These are issues more of content than of structure.

To "tell a story," a playwright may organize events in a variety of ways: follow a sequential time progression with incidents proceeding in a causal fashion; observe chronology but abandon causality; retain an overriding sense of chronology but present events out of linear order; mix episodes from disparate time periods; or minimize chronology for the sake of topical development.

Chronological Order. Because a play uses a chronological arrangement, the order of events need not imply a cause-and-effect progression. Such lack of causality identifies episodic structure, a trait of the early English chronicle play that recreated major events in the life of a ruler without necessarily advancing explanations of cause. Biographical focus provided the major source of unity in these early chronicles, but biography in the New History plays tends to emphasize domestic, or in a few cases psychological causes, narrowing the scope of the action and emphasizing causality by finding personal motives for public behavior. Modern episodic plays more likely derive their unity from an overarching event or theme: the Civil War, the failure of radical politics, the exploitation of the Scottish people.

Charles Wood's 1969 play *'H'*, about the Indian Mutiny, or as Indian historians sometimes refer to it, the Anglo-Indian War, shows the shift away from biographical unity in favor of diffused episodes that attempt to capture varied aspects of a historical event to illustrate a political theme. The title would lead us to expect the play to center on General Havelock, and it does back-handedly, but Havelock emerges largely as a symbol for and victim of broader forces of Victorian imperialism that he himself never fully comprehends. The focus on Havelock determines the duration of time that the play covers: from his assumption of command at the end of June 1857 until his death in November. We first see Havelock in the third scene, and he appears in slightly more than half the play's thirty-two scenes, but many of these do nothing to advance the plot and function less to reveal the influence of Havelock's personality on events than to expose the extent to which he represents Victorian values. For example, a Bible reading class that Havelock conducts in act I, scene 5 exposes the Victorian notion that the military serves a divine mission in India. Except for rare instances such as when he leads a shirking regiment back into battle, Havelock seems less to advance the action than to move forward at the mercy of nationalist forces beyond his control. His principal action is to die of dysentery, which occupies the entire last act and serves as an ironic counterpoint to the British military victory.

The play begins with a prologue narration by an Indian artilleryman, The Bombardier, a sycophant who serves as one of the two chief spokesmen for the Indian viewpoint and also explains Indian terminology for the audience. We immediately see a new young ensign trying to take Indian troops through an order of arms without being able to speak their language. This drill also establishes the use of chupatties, flat cakes of unleavened bread used to signal the beginning of the mutiny, and the Muslim soldiers' anger at having to break open in their mouths cartridges treated with pork fat, the supposed catalyst for the Mutiny. The script alone does not make the significance of these details clear, but they are part of the national history traditionally taught to British schoolchildren, and a program note explains for others. As the prologue ends, the sepoys stab the young ensign in the head, and he only reappears to punctuate the end of the play. He briefly encounters the old Havildar, who acted as a sergeant for the native troops seen in the prologue.

Havildar. I am sorry.
   You should not have stopped speaking
   to us sahib.
Ensign Mullet. I never knew what to say.[13]

These episodes emblematically show the relationship between the Indians and their British overlords.

The first scene after the prologue introduces three characters who spend as much time on stage as Havelock: Captain Jones Parry, who serves as a Victorian Everyman; his wife, whom the mutineers seize and who gives birth to a child fathered by the Bombardier; and Surgeon Sooter, who acts as the traditionally cynical physician commentator. The Jones Parrys arrive at his post in this first scene. Although Jones Parry appears in most scenes, we see his wife intermittently in her own subplot. At the end of scene 4 she comes on stage just in time to see her husband depart for the battle of Futtahpore. In scene 6 she refuses to leave for the safety of Calcutta, and after her husband's departure at the end of the scene, she exits pursued by a naked sepoy and the Bombardier. Scene 12 shows her refusal to commit suicide after her capture, as instructed by her husband, and her consequent rape. In the fourth scene of act II, we see a naked but irrepressible Mrs. Jones Parry forced to carry the Bombardier's kit. In scene 5 of the third act, she reunites with her husband, and in the epilogue, which takes place eleven years later, the Jones Parrys return with her son to Lucknow to pay homage at Havelock's tomb.

Except for Mrs. Jones Parry's scenes, the first two acts are organized as a march from Allahabad to Lucknow with intervening battles. Each scene does less to prepare for the scene following than to provide a snapshot of events. Act I, scene 2, shows Havelock taking over command from Colonel James Neill, but its purpose is to contrast Neill's draconian treatment of prisoners with Havelock's concern for just punishment. These sepoy captives, condemned to hang, go wandering through several scenes as Harry Havelock, the general's son and aide-de-camp, tries to find someone to hang them because he lacks stomach for the task. The third scene undercuts Victorian images of heroism by showing Havelock trying to deliver an inspirational speech to soldiers more interested in playing a game of Housey Housey. In the next scene a minor character narrates the Battle of Futtahpore, but the main business is Captain Jones Parry's refusal to hang the captive sepoys. The play wanders on its way in the style of epic cinema and succeeds in conveying a feeling for the war partly because of its disrupted order. Shakespeare used the same technique for battle scenes, but here the entire play has this episodic structure.

Wood further disturbs the narrative line by having scenes within scenes. In act II, scene 5, within a larger scene that shows the officers at dinner after the Battle of Cawnpore, Wood places five "inscenes" between a captive Indian officer, known as a *jemadar*, and his corporal guard. The final inscene becomes as large as the framing scene and leads into scenes 6 and 7, which focus on the jemadar's condemnation of the British invasion of his country and his subsequent death by being fired from a cannon, a punishment designed by the "Christian" Havelock. Wood abandons chronology for the entire third act, which shows Havelock dying, but within which Wood places five scenes taking place earlier in time that he labels "Scene Two within Scene One," and so on. At points other characters help Havelock from his death bed to participate shakily in these flashbacks.

Nonlinear Chronology. Although the vast majority of history plays observe a chronological progression, experiments with alternate structures began as early as Elizabethan drama. *Henry IV, Part I*, for example, developed parallel actions, showing scenes in sequence that occur simultaneously in time. *Henry V* used a narrator contemporaneous with the audience, who makes the audience aware of the extent to which their imagination figures as an ingredient in the reconstruction of historical incident. The principal variation on chronological narrative is the use of the flashback. Plays like Shaffer's *Royal Hunt of the Sun* (1964) and *Amadeus* (1979) use a narrator to recount past action in which that narrator participated. Tim Rice and Andrew Lloyd Webber's *Evita* (1976) begins with the announcement of Evita's death and uses Che Guevara as a narrator to introduce scenes that develop Evita's life in chronological sequence. These narrators set the scene and occasionally intrude from the present into the past to make a comment, but most of the action stays in the past.

John Spurling's *The British Empire, Part One* (1980) uses an even more complex chronological structure, intertwining five instances of colonial exploitation spanning the thirty years between 1820 and 1850 and three continents. Although each of the plot lines observes its own chronology, they overlap without regard for their relative timing. Isabella and Richard Burton provide a narrative frame from yet another time perspective, but theme provides the principal source of unity: all of the episodes show natives betraying their colonial masters and suffering consequent vengeance.

Other plays manage the flashback without a narrator. Terence Rattigan's *Ross* (1960), for example, uses events from T. E. Lawrence's experiences as a disguised airman in 1922 to frame flashbacks to his adventures in Arabia five years earlier. The first three and the last two of the play's sixteen scenes are set in

1922; the central portion, earlier. Although the narration moves backward in time, the play and the audience preserve a clear sense of chronology and of the effect that earlier events have on later ones. Michael Hasting's *Lee Harvey Oswald: A Far Mean Streak of Independence Brought on by Negleck* (1966) uses a more complex intermingling of present action and flashbacks, switching back and forth between the Warren Commission investigation of John F. Kennedy's assassination, film clips of earlier events, and reenactments of Oswald's life, but the two chronologies are clearly distinguishable. John McGrath's *The Game's a Bogey* (1974) ironically juxtaposes the life of an early twentieth-century social reformer against the present, switching from 1907 to 1973 and back to 1913.

Hugh Whitemore's *Breaking the Code* (1986) uses a police inquiry as a framework for the gradual discovery and reenactment of events leading up to the incident being investigated. Two unfolding time lines interweave with the inquiry: one showing major events in Alan Turing's life, beginning with his school days and continuing through his work at the British decoding center at Bletchley Park; the second, the more recent events leading to his arrest as a homosexual. Each section of the story develops chronologically until the end when Whitemore disrupts the time sequence of the present action for dramatic effect. In the penultimate scene, we see his mother's reaction to Turing's death, but the actual suicide occurs in the final scene. To a large extent this is a play in search of causes, and even scenes set in the present often look backward. Act II, scene 4 employs a police interrogation to frame a reenactment of the events that lead to Turing's arrest. Act II, scene 7, uses his encounter with a Greek boy who does not speak English as an excuse for him to explain for the audience's benefit how the Enigma code had been broken a decade earlier.

A similar search for psychological sources of behavior shapes Diane Samuel's intermixing of past and present action in *Kindertransport* (1993). Characters from the World War II years occupy the stage at the same time as characters from the nineties, and the two plot lines overlap seamlessly. Present relations between a mother and daughter precipitate the discovery of the mother's feelings of betrayal by her own Jewish mother, who sent her for safety to England from Germany in 1939.

Shirley Gee's *Warrior* (1989) adds another twist to the chronological ordering of narrative by using "flashes forward" to give her eighteenth-century heroine, Hannah Snell, visions of nuclear war. Gee describes her play about a woman committed to an asylum after serving in the English army disguised as a man as "one giant flashback, bracketted [*sic*] by the madhouse scenes, until . . . the play catches up with itself and continues in a straight line until the end."[14] Gees cleverly segues from the flashbacks into the asylum scenes by building on moments of stress during Hannah's "remembered" actions.

The frequently used play-within-a-play convention, which we will examine in more detail later, provides another device for mixing different periods without challenging the audience's sense of "real time." Howard Brenton may trap his audience into confusion at the beginning of *The Churchill Play* (1974) by not letting them know that they are watching a play within a play, but he quickly exploits the surprise discovery, and the remainder of the play adheres to its imaginary chronology.

Playwrights, like Howard Brenton, Caryl Churchill, and Howard Barker, who construct postmodern histories take the greatest liberties with traditional chronology. Brenton moves resurrected characters from the past into a later time in *Hitler Dances* (1972) and in *Weapons of Happiness* (1976). He reverses the process in *Romans in Britain* (1980), placing modern characters in the middle of a past action. Brenton experiments with a variety of devices to justify his deconstruction of chronology. In *Hitler Dances*, actors play children who play games, acting out roles and scenes from the past and the present. This device emphasizes the interpretive aspects of the performance and makes the audience aware that the performers manipulate time. On the surface, *Weapons of Happiness* appears much more realistic, and the audience only gradually becomes aware that Josef Frank is a refugee from a place and time twenty-five years earlier. Frank does not flash back to the earlier time until half an hour into the play, and then it seems a conventional memory device for probing the influence of the past on a mentally unstable character. Not until late in the play do we realize that Frank had been executed earlier. His appearance in the present is explicable only in theatrical terms or in a view of history less interested in reconstructing a chronology than in making a political point.

In *The Romans in Britain*, Brenton develops the play's first half in strict chronological order, even specifying in the program that events occur on August 27, 54 B.C., and on the following dawn, the date of Julius Caesar's occupation of Britain. However, at the end of the first part of the play, "From the back the Roman Army advances in British Army uniforms and with the equipment of the late 1970's." Automatic weapons fire kills stone-throwing characters from 54 B.C.[15] The second part of the play alternates between modern scenes set in Ireland and scenes set in England in 515 A.D. Characters from each period stay on stage while the others perform, but otherwise they interact in no way. The juxtaposition, however, emphasizes the thematic connection stated by the central modern character, a reluctant English assassin, just before the Irish Republican army officer that he was sent to assassinate kills him instead:

> I keep on seeing the dead. A field in Ireland, a field in England. And faces like wood. Charred wood, set in the ground. Staring at me.
>
> The faces of our forefathers.

Their eyes are sockets of rain-water, flickering with gnats.
They stare at me in terror.

Because in my hand there's a Roman spear. A Saxon axe. A British Army machine-gun.

The weapons of Rome, invaders, Empire. (89)

Brenton employs analogous action, a convention as old as the Tudor history plays, but he draws his sources from three widely separated periods.

Brenton carried his experiments with narrative order further in *H.I.D. (Hess is Dead)* (1989), which uses multimedia devices and performance art techniques to intermix past and present actions. The play uses the format of a mystery with the central characters trying to reconstruct the past in an effort to understand events surrounding the death of Rudolf Hess at Spandau Prison. The audience has no difficulty separating past and present actions, but the play moves freely back and forth, using the two actors from the present time frame to interpret the events from the past. For example, early in the play, the audience sees a tape of Charity, the widow of a commissioner sent to investigate the Hess death, reenacting Hess's death. Charity, now a resident in an expensive sanatorium, also provides live commentary on the tape for the benefit of Palmer, an investigative reporter and the principal character in the framing action. While the tape plays, Charity periodically performs an interpretive dance based on Hess's death. This is as close as the audience comes to seeing the death.

Brenton repeats actions. At one point Palmer plays a tape, presumably made by hidden cameras, of the arrival of two of the investigating commissioners shortly after Hess's death. The tape contains traces of earlier uses as well as an inexplicable glimpse of a seventeenth-century character falling through a hidden door. Palmer replays the tape several times in an attempt to understand the mysterious figure, who appears to change slightly with each replaying. We then move directly to live actors performing the scene we have just witnessed on tape, only now the actors have verse asides expressing their thoughts. As the scene progresses, the asides ride over the dialogue:

Nicole: (To the OFFICER.) Lieutenant. The meetings of the
UNESCO International Standing Committee . . .
(Aside.) Blah blah I go
No need to listen
to myself[16]

After returning briefly to the dialogue, the officer begins to mouth his lines mutely so we can hear Nicole's aside. The scene then continues past the point that we had viewed earlier on the tape. The live scene from the past melds into the framing scene when the Officer uses the same video player to show a tape to the investigators, a tape that the watching reporter interrupts. After some tape switching and a monologue by the reporter, the action cuts back to the investigative committee, but to a later point where they announce their findings. The play continues this mixture of frame, tape, and reenactment when we see a video recording of Charity's husband developing his theory that the Spandau Hess was an imposter planted by the Allies. At the end, the reporter leaves us with his theory that Charity, a former television producer, concocted all that we have witnessed, using production resources available in the upscale sanatorium.

Brenton's theme is the fabrication and exploitation of history by the media and by political forces. The play both demonstrates and exposes this manipulation. The fusion of past and present illustrates the traditional idea that the past influences the present, and also Brenton's message that the present creates the past.

Caryl Churchill also implodes time in two 1980 plays, *Top Girls* and *Cloud Nine*, both of which use historical materials without reconstructing a historical event. The first half of *Top Girls* abandons altogether the convention of dramatic action to depict a symposium of characters, both imaginary and historical, from times ranging from the ninth century to the present. Each narrates her personal history, and monologues or dialogues often overlap one another. The second half of the play presents a conventionally structured domestic melodrama, set in the present and involving only the modern character from the symposium, but using the same actors to play different characters. Partly because of the doubling, partly because of the unusualness of the first part, the audience searches for connections, which exist on a thematic but not on a chronological level.

Cloud Nine similarly juxtaposes two actions separated in time, the first in Victorian Africa, the second in London a hundred years later. Three characters from the first half of the play are central to the second half, and a fourth undergoes only a thinly veiled transformation, but over the century, all have aged only twenty-five years. The first part of the play uses cross dressing, one character played by a dummy, an African servant played by a white actor, and a variety of farce devices, which create a suspension of disbelief that encourages the audience to accept the incongruities in the time progression. The second half seems less to develop a plot than to explore through conversation a variety of sexual and gender relations. These relations change and develop as the act moves on, but the characters appear to report on the changes rather than act to bring them about. Near the end of the play, characters from the first act begin making brief appearances. The final stage direction is "BETTY from Act

One comes. BETTY and BETTY embrace."[17] Earlier two characters enter in the middle of conversation, and one states, "As I said to the professor, I don't think this is an occasion for invoking the concept of structural causality" (320), a comment left unpursued, but which aptly describes Churchill's approach to her material.

Howard Barker's *Bite of the Night* (1988) has a prologue that declares,

> Clarity
> Meaning
> Logic
> And Consistency
>
> None of it
> None.[18]

Later in the play, a character states, "Why shouldn't dates be flexible! What's wisdom if it can't burst calendars? What's a system if it can't call this the New Year One and abolish stacks of squalid centuries?" (70). Barker sets out, by his own admission, to "break the narrative thread," as he does with a vengeance, to force the audience to reassess its habitual way of viewing history.[19]

The play invites the audience to see the action as a temporal progression—some characters seem to age; Helen of Troy becomes a grandmother; a succession of Troys rise and fall; Homer appears early and Schliemann late in the play—but this sense of the passage of time bears no close scrutiny. Anachronisms abound. References to tanks, pistols, razor blades, and dictionaries appear in the speech of ancient Trojans. Barker takes liberties with traditional history, making a character named Fladder the husband of Helen and king of the Greeks and marrying Creusa to a university professor named Savage. Some characters age, but not in proportion to the apparent passage of time, and other characters seem timeless. More fundamentally, no one scene causes the next; each begins *in medias res* and characters undergo inexplicable reversals. For instance, Fladder, who rules the victorious Greeks during the First Troy and becomes governor of Paper Troy, the second of the eleven Troys presented by Barker, declares suddenly in the fourth scene that he wants to be tried and executed, and by the end of the scene torturers have beaten him and ripped out his tongue. Barker seems to say that if history is a cultural construct, he is as entitled as anyone to fabricate a history of his own. However, in the absence of "Clarity, Meaning, Logic, and Consistency," the audience searches for an underlying key that will decode the bizarre incidents to reveal a hidden order.

Topical Order. Although history plays never totally abandon their story-telling dimension, a few embrace alternative structures that deemphasize narration. While embracing the idea that history should be descriptive without "telling a story" and forswearing narrative history based on major events, the New Historians were less clear about what to use as a replacement. When they tried to deal with macrohistory, the broader issues that transcended specific events, the problem remained of how to organize material. In theory they emphasized topicality and "stage" narratives. The question and answer approach that the *Annalistes* proposed was inherently topical, with a broad question subdividing into specifics. Barbara A. Hanawalt's *The Ties That Bound: Peasant Families in Medieval England*, for example, uses the medieval coroner's inquest to develop such topics as the household economy, patterns of child rearing, and stages of the life cycle.[20] Adding a temporal dimension produced what the historiographer Philippe Carrard described as "stage narratives": "They slice up the long term into a certain number of phases, which they characterize successively and piece together to constitute a narrative. This narrative, then, is not made up of events, but rather of situations or stages."[21] A few of the history plays attempt these methods of organization.

Charles Wood's *Dingo* (1967) presents an example of topical organization. The play centers on World War II and on a pair of common soldiers who remain on stage through most of the play, but no real plot drives the action forward. The war progresses without the aid of our characters. Each of the six scenes deals with a phase of the war, selected to explore items on Wood's agenda for revising jingoistic attitudes toward it. Act I, set in the middle of an early desert battle, develops apparent bureaucratic indifference to violence and suffering. Later, a prisoner of war camp shows the transformation of British prisoners into coopted martinets. "The Beaches of Normandy" provides a context for parodying the naive platitudes of patriotism "at home." In "Planning for the Battle of Arnhem," Wood uses a comic ventriloquist to emphasize Churchill's warmongering and Eisenhower's malleability. A postwar victory celebration turns on the common soldiers' embracing socialism and rejecting Churchill.

John McGrath's *The Cheviot, the Stag, and the Black, Black Oil* (1973) provides an example of a "stage" narrative. McGrath's play develops the theme of economic exploitation of the Scottish working class by showing instances widely separated in time: the Clearances in 1813, mid-nineteenth-century reversion of land for recreational purposes, and the oil exploitation of the 1970s. The company plays out episodes without an overarching set of characters or a single unifying action. Because of the highly theatrical style of presentation, the play can flick from an encounter in Canada between Scottish settlers and Indians to the Isle of Skye sixty years later. Actors serving as narrators interject statistical data and read sections of documents from each period. The documentary plays of Peter Cheeseman, McGrath's 7:84, Red Ladder, and others follow this same general structural pattern.

Caryl Churchill also uses documentary material in *Light Shining in Buckinghamshire* (1976), but with even less effort to impose a narrative structure. Churchill provides no narrator to describe a context for the episodes; so the elements seem particularly disconnected. She mixes sermons, dialogue, a debate, excerpts from a pamphlet, monologues, and articles read from a newspaper, all of which contribute to our awareness of the period without developing a story. Though we can recognize specific dramatized topics—questions of religious freedom, women's rights, and property distribution, for example—they are not sequentially developed. Seven characters, involved in a variety of overlapping issues, appear in more than one scene. Four of these meet in the final episode as a group of disgruntled religious reformers. However, by having more than one actor play a single character, Churchill disrupts any impulse to look to characterization for unity. Characters who never reappear are involved in half a dozen other brief episodes. For example, two women react to a mirror looted from a mansion, and later in the play, a starving woman decides to abandon her baby. Both incidents reveal conditions during the English Civil War but have no bearing on a developing plot. Although the incidents create a vague sense of the emergence and failure of alternative religious and political views during the war, no one episode prepares for the next; so we have no clear view of a developing plot. The subject matter and Churchill's point of view provide what unity there is, not characterization or plot.

The Use of Narrators in History Plays

Peter Burke suggested that rather than disavow narrative to prevent any distortion consequent to a narrative point of view, New History might emphasize the voice of the narrator to remind the reader of the inevitable presence of a point of view: "Historical narrators need to find a way of making themselves visible in their narrative, not out of self-indulgence but as a warning to the reader that they are not omniscient or impartial and that other interpretations are possible."[22] This resembles one of Brecht's justifications for epic style: that the narrator increases the audience's detachment, reminding us that what we see is subject to interpretation and, indeed, inviting us to make our own interpretation. In his analysis of French New Historians, Philippe Carrard noted their tendencies to invade the text with commentary, to emphasize the subjectivity of commentary rather than playing the part of self-effacing authors, to take sides by expressing strong personal beliefs, and to use first-person pronouns.[23] Carrard observed that historians and critics alike "have moved away from the convoluted maneuvers used in the 1960s to confer 'scientific' impersonality upon their texts, opting instead, in their most recent works . . . for an open approbation of the first person and its most visible signs."[24]

Some of the New Historians also diffuse the distortions of a metanarrative by democratizing the narrative voice, using interviews, anecdotes, and documents echoing numerous voices. Reflecting the technique of fiction that uses multiple points of view, these histories, such as Paul Thompson's *The Edwardians*, cobble together a view of a subject from many perspectives.[25]

The presence of a narrator in a play was also one of the hallmarks of Brecht's epic style, taken to indicate his influence on British theatre. For Brecht, a narrator assured that the audience not fall into the trap of empathizing with a character and thereby lose the capacity to assess the social significance of an action. A narrator placed emphasis on the story or parable rather than the character's psyche.

In spite of the common use of the phrase "Brechtian narrator," stage narrators are part of a long tradition in England. Shakespeare's *Henry V* used a narrator and the device never completely disappeared from the British history play. Approximately a third of the historical drama written in Britain during the last four decades makes some use of a narrator, but in varied ways: as a storyteller, a protagonist, a device to emphasize artifice, a source for documentary background, or a commentator.

Narrator as Storyteller. With more traditional approaches, the narrator principally serves as a storyteller without calling undue attention to his or her point of view. These narrators may speak contemporaneously with the action or look back from a later date. The narrator may stand outside the action or participate, usually in a minor role. Minor characters acting as narrators usually have a higher degree of detachment than major figures.

The narrator in *A Man for All Seasons* (1960) was often cited as a Brechtian device, but Bolt's Common Man serves less as a Brechtian commentator and narrator than as an expediter, like the chairman of some very old English music hall entertainment. He occasionally establishes locale and serves as a protean utility actor. His character expresses a point of view, but he exercises no control over an unfolding action that he influences in only a minor way in one of the small roles that he plays.

Portrait of a Queen (1963) by William Francis made one of the more innovative uses of narrative. Brief episodes in Queen Victoria's life were connected by a "Balladmonger" who provided sometimes scurrilous narrative and commentary. He occasionally furnished accompanying dialogue for the actors who mimed the action. Different minor characters frequently serve as a chorus, narrating the "public" response to events. Milton Shulman, reviewing for the *Evening Standard,* thought that the Balladmonger functioned "to provide an illusion of historical objectivity."[26]

A number of plays use a minor character for occasional narration, more as a device to set a scene quickly than for any substantive commentary. David Pinner in *The Drums of Snow* (1968) uses John Lilburne, "the first English Socialist," to narrate and to point out that the English revolution failed to create a democracy or benefit the commoners. In Brian Oulton's *Mr Sydney Smith Coming Upstairs* (1972), Smith's son, Wyndham, acts as a narrator. In their Arthurian trilogy, *The Island of the Mighty,* which the RSC produced at the Aldwych Theatre in December of 1972, John Arden and Margaretta D'Arcy use the magician Merlin as both a storyteller and a participant in the action. As Merlin becomes a more active participant in the second part and the protagonist in the third, the younger poet Aneurin takes over his narrative functions. The Red Ladder play *Taking Our Time* (1978) effectively uses a Tinker Clown to introduce characters and scenes, establish comic rapport with the audience, sing songs that reflect on events, and provide some commentary. He introduces the main plot as a "story" for the audience but projects little sense that he controls the telling. He flits around the edge of the action until he becomes caught up in a worker's strike and dies from a trooper's bullet, only to rise at the play's end to announce the moral of the production.

An Englishman Abroad (1988), by Alan Bennett, also uses a minor character as a retrospective narrator. The actress Coral Browne recounts and recreates her one meeting with Guy Burgess and also reenacts and comments on her buying expedition back in England on his behalf, which provides an opportunity to show contrasting reactions in England to the exiled spy. Burgess appears on stage, but Bennett's decision to use Coral as an intermediary keeps the spy at one remove from our view, increasing the feeling of his alienation. Reviewers unanimously agreed that Bennett had thus preserved the enigmatic character of Burgess.

The character of the Director in John Bowen's *Florence Nightingale* (1975) plays a central role in the framing action but stands outside the play-within-a-play and narrates Florence's story from his own point of view. Because he presents the play as an "exploration" into history devised by the company, the Director/storyteller also serves as surrogate playwright. The actors illustrate with snatches of dialogue what is essentially the director's narrative.

Narrator as Protagonist. Making the protagonist an introspective narrator conveniently exposes the inner workings of the character in plays with strong biographical or psychological interests. Peter Shaffer's *Royal Hunt of the Sun* (1964) used a retrospective storyteller, Old Martin, who also appeared as a minor character, Young Martin, in the main action. Even though Young

Martin's developing disillusionment with Pizarro marked a thematic progression in the play, Martin's point of view remained largely secondary to his storytelling role. His presence justified the artifice of a theatrical style of staging that relies on mime and emblematic action to convey panoramic events with modest resources. Shaffer promoted his retrospective narrator to the role of protagonist in the nonhistorical *Equus* (1973), a technique he used again with the biographical history play *Amadeus* (1979). Both plays develop plot, characterization, and theme around the viewpoints that the narrators articulate for the audience. This introspective narration provides an excellent vehicle for the psychological focus of Shaffer's histories. Criticism about the unflattering depiction of Mozart in *Amadeus* ignores the fact that we see Mozart through Salieri's eyes, a technique that owes much to expressionism.

In biographical drama, the narrative voice of the central character may move the story through time and place, reveal personal reactions, and maintain a strong connection between the subject and the audience. These plays usually serve as star vehicles and either have a very small cast that maintains the focus on the dominant personality of both the subject and the star or are one-person shows that rely heavily on narration as a substitute for dramatic development. With *Stevie* (1977), a vehicle for Glenda Jackson, Hugh Whitemore wrote more of a narrative discourse than a play. *Stevie*'s dialogue with her aunt and a mysterious man add variety, but little in the way of dramatic action. The aunt intersperses small talk in the midst of Stevie's monologues and picks up some of the storytelling responsibilities later in the play. The man recites passages from Stevie's poetry, acts as her interlocutor, occasionally comments on her life, and plays several minor characters, but most importantly represents Death. In only one instance, a scene where Stevie breaks off her engagement, does a reenactment further the plot. She describes her life in chronological order, but the events are anecdotal, otherwise insignificant details related according to their importance in her own mind. One gets the strong sense that it is autobiography, that the telling itself reveals the personality of the teller.

In Edna O'Brien's *Virginia* (1981), the narrative voice of Virginia Woolf serves to preserve material written by her, but more important, it allows the audience access into the inner workings of her mind. Even though the play roughly follows the chronology of her life, its real subject matter is interior: her struggle against insanity and the disintegration of rational order in her thought process. Her monologues become increasingly demented as she loses sanity. With a world war and Bloomsbury in the background, Virginia relates the story of her own mental breakdown. This degree of subjectivity occurs rarely in historical drama, even in biographical drama with a strong psychoanalytic orientation, perhaps because of some reluctance to relinquish the illusion of objectivity.

Narrator as Alienator. A major tenet of Brecht's epic-style was that a narrator can "alienate" an audience, disrupting any tendency to identify with the characters. In theory, Brecht proposed that all actors be seen as narrators to the degree of not allowing the persona of the actor/interpreter to dissolve into that of the character.[27] Each actor narrated rather than "became" the character, a "third-person" acting style. In Charles Wood's *'H'*, at one point the actor playing Col. James Neill, a Patton-type soldier, comes forward, as the stage direction makes clear, "to speak to the audience, as the actor playing NEILL" and to complain that the play should really be about him (62). The leave-taking scene between Jones Parry and his wife is played with some third-person acting: "She said, but dearest, I said, God only knows what" (55). We hear Havelock offstage addressing his troops, then "Enter HAVELOCK while his voice is heard still speaking off. HAVELOCK listens to himself." After a while, "HAVELOCK joins in with his voice off" (60). In the "Production Notes" for their Arthurian epic *The Island of the Mighty*, John Arden and Margaretta D'Arcy indicate their wish to use this acting style; they warn, "Particular descriptions of characters, involving details of dress and physical appearance, are liable to produce excessive attempts by some actors at 'involvement' with their roles in a way that inhibits a clear rendering of the stories of the plays."[28]

The audience presumably remains detached by this approach to acting because they realize that they watch theatre, not reality. This parallels Burke and Carrard's observation that the New Historians emphasize the presence of the narrator in order to remind the reader that the historian presents only a point of view, not some objective truth. A number of history plays have no particular storytelling function for narration but introduce a narrator none-theless for "alienation affect."

John Arden, often cited as one of the English playwrights most influenced by Brecht,[29] frequently inserts narration that serves principally to remind the audience of the theatricality of the production. His Christmas play, *The Business of Good Government* (1963), and *Armstrong's Last Goodnight* (1964) owe as much to medieval staging conventions as they do to Brecht's style. Arden's Herod is too politic to rage in the audience like his medieval counter-part, but he still talks to the audience, as do several other characters. These asides, given in character, explain a character's attitude rather than forwarding the action. The plot of *Armstrong's Last Goodnight* is less familiar to the audience; so Arden's characters occasionally explain what is happening. Most of the narration, however, consists of self-introductions by the characters that serve primarily to emphasize the artificiality of the style. Narration plays a somewhat more prominent part in *Left-Handed Liberty* (1965), where the protagonist King John and the papal legate Pandulph share narrative responsibilities and occasionally comment on the significance of the action. Although they speak in character during the narrative sections, they also have a prescient voice that addresses the modern audience. For example, Pandulph cautions the audience, "As for King John himself—that almost Oriental monster of your history books—do not forget that the records of his Household shew him to have been a tireless administrator."[30] Before the final scenes depicting his death, John begins a long address to the audience: "There comes a time in any stage play, when the stage itself, the persons in front of it, must justify their existence—and I think this is the time now: because on the 18th of October, I have to die."(8).

The style of the nineteenth-century nautical melodrama that Arden and his coauthor and wife, Margaretta D'Arcy, borrow for *The Hero Rises Up* (1968) uses almost as much narration as dramatization. In "A Necromantic Prologue," "an Academic Representative of the Author" presents a mock-scholarly debate on the issue of whether individuals make the historical moment or vice versa. He then "calls up" the play as a case study on the question. Nelson appears on stage to introduce himself and, speaking from the twentieth century, to reflect on events in his life. Nelson does not, however, control the narrative, because minor characters call up scenes to make specific points. For example, Captain Josiah Nisbet, Nelson's stepson, enters early in the play to complain of Nelson's version of events and to set into motion the first dramatic episode, which exposes Nelson's perfidy. Allen, Nelson's orderly, provides most of the commentary in the play, but the majority of the characters directly address the audience at one time or another, usually for comic effect. A multiviewpoint debate on the character of Nelson results with some characters depicting him as a hero, others as a self-serving opportunist. Arden challenges the myth but tries to avoid taking sides. As he has his prologuer say: "I want you all to observe them, what they do, and what they say: and to learn from it such lessons for your future as you may. *That* is the part of the proceedings in which I have no competence to guide you. If you are wise, you will benefit; if you are foolish, you will not."[31]

Charles Wood's play '*H*' (1969) uses narrative elements from nineteenth-century melodrama, including self-introductions, asides, soliloquies, and direct comments to the audience, all usually made in character. In a few instances, actors break character to explain a term, and once, Wood uses the Brechtian device of having an actor step out of his role to talk about the character he plays. Even though the narration allows the sepoy Bombardier to articulate the Indian view of events, the narrative elements serve more to reinforce the play's toy theatre style than to emphasize the extent to which our interpretation of events depends on the manner of their telling.

Narration also serves foremost to establish style in Peter Nichols's *Poppy* (1982), which draws on another native narrative tradition, the panto, whose characters regularly talk directly to the audience and comment on the action. The "boys and girls" tone of the traditional panto narrative emphasizes the artifice of the form. This limits the possibility of using the narrative elements for sincere commentary, but Nichols creates comic irony and dramatic tension by applying this style to a "serious" historical situation, the Chinese Opium Wars.

Narrative as Provider of Documentary Background. In plays growing out of agitprop theatre, narrators provide background information, statistics, and other forms of documentation. The persona of the narrator is of little consequence in these plays, and several characters may share narrative tasks, shifting from character to narrator as circumstances demand. Peter Cheeseman's Stoke-on-Trent documentaries, including *The Knotty* (1966); Plater's *Close the Coalhouse Door* (1968); the 7:84 history plays of John McGrath; Gooch's *Will Wat? If Not, What Will?* (1972); and Edgar's *Entertaining Strangers* (1985) divide narration among a number of characters. The sequencing of these voices in a play like *Entertaining Strangers* can at times approach the sound of a collective chorus, but for the purpose of providing background more than commentary. Peter Cheeseman even insists that the multiple voices, rather than reflecting a community of opinion, suggest multiple viewpoints, thus assuring a degree of objectivity and avoiding the weakness of a play "in which all of the characters really speak with the voice of the dramatist."[32] This New History strategy of using many narrators diminishes the importance of a single overriding narrative viewpoint.

Alan Plater makes particular inventive use of documentary narration in *Close the Coalhouse Door*. Although several actors provide utilitarian narration to set dates or historical context, a character designated as "Expert" furnishes most of the factual background. Expert also plays specific roles that always represent the oppressive and unsympathetic establishment. Plater often fuses Expert's narrative tasks with one of his establishment voices; so the "facts" appear as tools of the ruling powers to oppress the coal miners.

Narrator as Commentator. Rather than using a narrator to advance the story, some history plays use a narrative voice principally to comment on the action or characters. Brecht had advocated using a narrator to provide commentary on the action, and in various plays used both choruses and single characters who stepped out of the action to provide commentary that often carried the message of the play. T. S. Eliot had used a chorus effectively in his

1935 verse drama *Murder in the Cathedral*, and a few contemporary plays follow his example. Christopher Fry's *Curtmantle* (1961), another historical verse drama set at the same time, used two groups of characters, one identified as "The Bishops," the other as "The Talk," to serve as choruses. Both Caryl Churchill's *Vinegar Tom* (1976) and Steve Gooch's *The Women Pirates Ann Bonney and Mary Read* (1978) use a detached chorus of singers to provide lyrical commentary. The scenes in Churchill's play require no narrative introductions and the songs appear only between a third of the scenes. Although the actors serve in the chorus when not otherwise on stage, Churchill insists that they be out of character and out of costume. The modern perspective of the chorus keeps the contemporary relevance of the seventeenth-century action before the audience. Gooch's chorus also comments on the action but still provides a narrative introduction for each scene.

Tim Rice and Andrew Lloyd Webber's *Evita* (1976) is as close as mainstream theatre comes to using a Brechtian narrator. Rice and Webber created a history of Evita not only through the artifice of a musical without dialogue, but through the critical eyes of an alienated Che Guevara, who interacts with minor characters, but has no influence over the main action. Rice and Lloyd Webber invented his role to provide an alienated commentary on the main action.

The clearest use of narrative commentary to remind the audience of the role of the storyteller in recreating events occurs in Howard Brenton's *H.I.D.*, a play largely *about* the fabrication of history that contains layers of narration. The reporter, Larry Palmer, speaks directly to the audience, both to set the situation and to comment on it. He interviews Charity Luber, who has summoned him to investigate the circumstances of Rudolf Hess's death, and, in the process, using videotapes, interpretive dance, and spoken commentary, she presents her account of events, a version that Palmer, in a final analysis at the play's end, concludes that she has fabricated using her expertise as a TV producer. Within a flashback scene, which itself began as a tape presentation, we see yet another videotape made by Charity's husband, since dead, narrating his interpretation that the Hess in Spandau was an imposter. Brenton uses vestiges of earlier tapings and a variety of technical glitches to remind us that the tapes are contrived, suggesting the similar contrivance of the events shown on the tapes The play leaves us with the suspicion that political powers manipulate the narration of past events for their own purposes.

In all of these plays, narrators serve, to varying degrees, as an antirealistic device, denying the illusion that the events depicted on stage represent an objective recreation of history. A narrator in a play calls attention to history as a story related from a particular point of view, told to create a specific effect.

LANGUAGE

Both the writers of history and the playwrights of historical drama struggle with the issue of finding an appropriate language for contemporary historical writing. Historians before the late nineteenth century shared the assumption that historical writing demands literary skill, but the positivist historians called for more impersonal prose. The debate between the use of "scientific" language and history as literature has raged since. Technical or "academic historians" tended to use a less embellished style, and most writers of popular history paid more attention to literary matters.

The New Historians had particular difficulty determining the appropriate language for historical writing because the deconstructionists had revealed the extent to which language carries the predispositions of the dominant culture. This led to studies of language in its historical context to uncover the assumptions underlying any period but also to the discomforting realization that all language carries a set of embedded biases. It produced a greater effort to expunge the more overt use of vocabulary that reflected cultural dominance but also exposed the impossibility of a truly objective "scientific" language.

In his analysis of the "poetics" of New History, Phillipe Carrard notes that the New Historians called for what Bernadette Plot has described as "scientific, referential discourse," a mode that can best bring the audience into "direct contact" with the object under investigation.[33] Carrard, however, analyzed the style of the texts of the New Historians and discovered, "Figurative language has far from disappeared from the texts of the New History. It is, in fact, one of the most salient features of those texts, together with other 'poetic' devices that call attention to the message at the expense of the referent."[34]

The British historian John Tosh, in his analysis of the methods of New History, candidly asserts the inescapability of literary devices in modern historical writing: "The insights derived from the exercise of historical imagination cannot be shared at all without a good deal of literary flair—an eye for detail, the power to evoke a mood, temperament and ambience, and an illusion of suspense—qualities which are most fully developed in creative writing."[35]

Dramatists also differed widely regarding the use of language in history plays, ranging between writers of documentaries who tried to adhere rigidly to a verbatim replication of sources to writers who contended that the principal appeal of historical material was that it offered an escape from the mundaneness of contemporary speech.

Peter Cheeseman, at Stoke-on-Trent, was the most extreme advocate of adhering to sources:

Primary source material can be cut and edited into very small chunks, pieces from heterogeneous sources can be juxtaposed in a scene (providing we make it clear in the show that this is what we are doing) and however complex the process, each piece retains its original flavor and quality, and can exude this on stage. But the moment passages are totally dismantled, down to their constituent words, and reassembled, then the process becomes writing, and is no longer valid for us in a documentary.

For Cheeseman, the difference between this adherence to sources and rewriting material was the difference between "an imaginative penetration of the source material" and "a plain lie about a man or an event."[36]

When a writer borrows the words of a historical figure who made public pronouncements, the language is likely to be more elevated than when the documents are tidbits of statistical data, official reports, or items from the local newspaper. For Robert Bolt, the artificiality of his Renaissance source material in *A Man for All Seasons* provided an escape from fourth-wall realism. In the "Preface" he wrote: "As Brecht said, beauty and form of language are a primary alienation device. I was guaranteed some beauty and form by incorporating passages from Sir Thomas More himself. For the rest my concern was to match with these as best I could so that the theft should not be too obvious" (xvii). Writers who use period sources, often not intended for speech, must confront this stylistic challenge of fusing added dialogue. In a review of the 1988 revival of *Bloody Poetry*, Michael Billington wrote: "Do poets, I wondered, actually talk like their own letters and diaries? But my doubts are stilled by the muscularity of Mr. Brenton's language and by the totally non-naturalistic, dream-like structure that he has given the play."[37] Heightening the unfamiliarity of the period provides one solution for justifying the artificiality.

Even without incorporating primary source materials into the plays, many writers struggle with the problem of making the dialogue sound as if it were from an earlier period. In his introduction to *Leonardo's Last Supper* (1969), Peter Barnes discussed the difficulty of finding "a live theatrical language which had the feel of a historical period (Renaissance and A.D. 395), yet could be understood by a contemporary audience. This artificial vernacular had to have historical weight yet be flexible enough to incorporate modern songs and jokes."[38] The historical setting presumably allows for what Robert Bolt called a "bold and beautiful verbal architecture,"[39] but the language also helps to create the sense of period. The danger is that it merely sounds labored. Martin Hovie, reviewing the National Theatre production of David Edgar's *Entertaining Strangers*, complained, "Nothing can redeem the stilted, lifeless dialogue with which the author evidently intends to convey the period's formal speech, peppered with solecisms and jarring anachronisms."[40]

Kenneth Tynan used a review of a 1961 production of Henry de Montherlant's *Queen After Death* at the Oxford Playhouse as a basis for attacking and parodying language conventions used in some historical drama. He begins by citing an article by George Devine in *Twentieth Century*, claiming that although younger British playwrights began by writing what was close to them, they were now turning away from modern dress naturalism to explore a much wider territory. If a resurgence of historical drama is imminent, speculates Tynan, de Montherlant provides an object lesson in how not to do it:

For Montherlant, history is dignified, and dignity is sententious; every speech comes tripping across the footlights with a ball and chain of pseudo-profundity attached to its ankle. The characters, so many robed machines for the production of densely scrambled platitude, exchange lectures on the state of their souls, the danger of love, the nature of power, the claims of justice, the necessity of duty, and other topics calculated to exploit the full capacity of the French language for exquisite, lapidary emptiness.

Quite often the people on stage seem to be engaged in earnest discussion of a play that is not in fact taking place. They express formal opinions; they swap sentiments, anecdotes, and metaphors; but outside the printed text they have no existence at all. They are walking figures of speech, syntactical fictions. Stung by a crafty stroke of litotes, they may riposte with a shrewd oxymoron to the bread-basket; but it is all shadow-boxing, a sort of Tussaud tournament.[41]

The notion that historical drama uses a language more elevated than contemporary vernacular persists from earlier stage conventions. In the nineteenth century, the use of verse for historical drama continued long after prose had become commonplace even for tragedy. Matthew Wikander, in his study of early history plays, noted that Nicholas Rowe with *Jane Shore* "effectively institutionalized consciously archaistic blank verse as the language of the past."[42] Even though prose became the preferred medium for history plays after George Bernard Shaw's works appeared at the turn of the century, historical drama remained one of the last refuges for writers of verse drama even after 1956, and we have discussed a number of these in the consideration of biographical history plays. Plays using traditional metrics, particularly blank verse, remain largely outside the commercial theatre, but Charles Wood successfully used freer verse forms, and John Arden and Howard Barker employed verse selectively to emphasize specific moments in plays. Even without formal verse, the historical subject matter often provides a license for figurative language.

Peter Barnes, to create a historical language for his plays, by his own admission, "pillaged: everything, from Elizabeth [*sic*] argot to the Bible."[43]

Other playwrights also fabricated period language. John Arden describes the process he used for *Armstrong's Last Goodnight* (1964):

It would clearly be silly to reconstruct the exact Scots speech of the period. . . . But on the other hand, Scots was at this time a quite distinct dialect, if not a different language, and to write the play in 'English' would be to lose the flavor of the age. . . . In the end I have put together a sort of Babylonish dialect that will, I hope, prove practical on the stage and yet will suggest the sixteenth century. My model in this was Arthur Miller's adaptation of early American speech in *The Crucible*.[44]

For *Left-Handed Liberty* (1965) Arden noted that most of his characters would have conversed in Norman French, but he had "tried to write a kind of dialogue which has the straightforwardness of medieval speech—more florid for courtly scenes and more colloquial for other episodes." Arden acknowledged that the characters would have had regional dialects, but he saw them, in this case, as insignificant to his dramatic purposes.[45]

The few plays that deal with archaic Britain exacerbate even further the problem of finding appropriate stage language for a history play. By Howard Brenton's own account, when Peter Hall commissioned *The Romans in Britain* (1980) for the National Theatre, his first question was "How are they going to talk?" Brenton explained that he was able, without too much trouble, to develop an anachronistic prose for the Romans, who were "nearer to us," but for the Celts he invented a dialect based on his perception of their asymmetrical view of the world: "a triple-rhythmed speech, fiery, full of a kind of self-display and relish . . . and a language hopelessly ill-equipped to even describe the Romans."[46]

David Rudkin, who was trained as a linguist, uses invented dialects as well as a reconstructed form of a primitive Celtic tongue in *The Saxon Shore*, his dramatization of the clash of different cultures in fifth-century Britain, produced at the Almeida Theatre on February 27, 1986. Beyond the strangeness of the archaic setting, Rudkin adds a strong element of fable with a pack of Saxon werewolves and a Druid priestess who is the daughter of King Lear. In "A Note on Pronunciation and Sound" that followed the published play, Rudkin explained that in addition to occasional Latin phrases for the Roman rulers, he had used a "dense and packed" English for the "ur German" of the Saxons, and "more sinuous and melodic" English for the Celts. The protagonist, Athdark, a Roman Saxon, reverts to his werewolf state and kills a Celtic priestess who earlier had saved his life and fallen in love with him. Rudkin explains: "After the werewolves have finally alienated the Celts, and the separation between the two cultures is made unbridgeable, I give the Celts an entire scene in their own language. This is a reconstruction of my own, going much further than a real philologist would dare."[47]

Earlier, for *The Triumph of Death*, performed in Birmingham in 1981 but never staged professionally in London, Rudkin created archaisms by using a fractured syntax. One scene involves a group of Iron Age characters who speak in broken phrases: "Sun. This I make thee. For to stand in middle of this world, for thy great gladness; and our thanks, that thou be strong again, and come to us with lent and summer."[48] This is less a play about structured history than a blend of myth, history, and fantasy into a disorganized Artaudian ritual that uses historical referents—Jesus, Martin Luther, Joan of Arc, and Crusaders—to depict the destruction of a primitive, animistic world by an anal-centered established church: the destruction of intuition by casuistry.

In one respect, these imaginary "historical" dialects aim to create the impression of authenticity, equally conceding the illusion of realism and acknowledging the artificiality of any recreated history. In another way, these dialects emphasize the "otherness" of a period and how language influences perception and behavior. *The Romans in Britain*, *The Saxon Shore*, and Brian Friel's *Translations*, in part, dramatize the New History view that language differences reinforce cultural biases and lead to conflict.

STAGING

Does the new historical drama consistently use particular staging methods, and what influences shape the staging of these plays? Up until the 1960s, history plays blended the conventions of Shakespeare and romantic melodrama. Gordon Daviot in the thirties and James Forsyth in the fifties used similar methods, dramatizing the personal lives of public figures. Characters spoke in "elevated" prose or occasional blank verse. With multiple scenes, fairly large casts, and some pageantry, the plays still focused on short periods depicted with a degree of realism.

Realism powered the new wave of playwriting that began in Britain in 1956. The characterization "kitchen sink realism" described both a refocusing on social problems and a style of staging depicting a causally developed domestic action in a setting that faithfully reproduced the surroundings of the characters. A few history plays such as Simon Gray's *The Rear Column* (1978) or William Nicholson's *Shadowlands* (1989) are fundamentally realistic, and many others maintain a realistic core in spite of occasional narrative intrusions, but the majority of history plays eschew realism.

Although *Look Back in Anger* may have signaled the demise of drawing room drama, realism remained only one current in an eddy of models that included foreign influences such as the work of Brecht and Artaud as well as the continuation of forms of drama and popular entertainment traditional in Britain. Writers like John Osborne, Ann Jellicoe, and John Arden, who were among the early "Angries," broke out of the constraints of realistic drama. George Devine, who headed the Royal Court Theatre and had produced much of the New Drama, wrote, as early as 1961, of these new playwrights: "There's a movement away from modern dress naturalism. To begin with, they had to write what was close to them, from their own experience. Now they're starting to explore a much wider territory."[49]

Traditional Staging Conventions

Many contemporary plays continued to use the traditional conventions for staging historical drama. That Terence Rattigan's 1970 *Bequest to the Nation* follows the format of earlier plays is not surprising since Rattigan's first history play, *Adventure Story*, appeared in 1949. Rattigan had used a somewhat experimental form in 1960 for *Ross* but returned to a more traditional approach for the later play. Other plays, like John Whiting's *The Devils* (1961), Michael Dyne's *The Right Honorable Gentleman* (1964), or Robert Bolt's *Vivat! Vivat Regina!* (1970) largely follow earlier staging traditions. Even *A Man for All Seasons* (1960), which Bolt himself associates with a Brechtian style of staging,[50] would resemble earlier history plays if stripped of its narrator, a deletion that would deprive it of much charm but not hurt the flow of the central plot.

The impact of *Look Back in Anger* was not that it opened a new age of realism, but that it marked the beginning of an era of experimentation, a climate also charged by the appearance in London of Beckett's *Waiting for Godot* at the Arts Theatre in 1955 and of the Berliner Ensemble in 1956. Experimental staging soon appeared in all kinds of plays, including historical drama. In the process, British playwrights innovatively borrowed staging practices from their own earlier theatre, from forms of popular entertainment, and from foreign models.

Without the constraint of a realistic depiction of history, writers intentionally resurrected period conventions. John Arden drew on medieval theatre for *The Business of Good Government* (1960) and *Armstrong's Last Goodnight* (1964), using simultaneous staging for the latter, a convention whereby widely spaced locales are shown on stage at once. Without explicitly using medieval staging conventions, Arden also evokes a medieval ambience for *Left-Handed Liberty* (1965) as the scenery for each locale is painted in the style of medieval manuscripts. Timberlake Wertenbaker has male and female choruses in her faux Greek tragedy *The Love of the Nightingale* (1988) but otherwise ignores the conventions of classical Greek drama.

In *The Bewitched* (1974) and *Laughter*, which premiered at the Royal Court Theatre on January 25, 1978, Peter Barnes emulated the Jacobean theatre that he so greatly admires, largely through his brilliant use of violent or scatological metaphors and pageantry that forwards the action and bridges scenes. The first half of *Laughter*, set between 1572 and 1581, uses Ivan the Terrible's murder of his son ironically to establish a philosophical justification for the cruelty and violence demonstrated in the second half, where we see the same actors playing parallel roles, but in Auschwitz in 1942. Ivan's victory in a hand-to-hand combat with Death could occur in a medieval play, but Barnes's depiction of the modern death camp owes more to the Jacobeans John Webster and Cyril Tourneur, as well as a bit to Antonin Artaud's Theatre of Cruelty. To the sound of a gas-chamber door being opened, the office of the death camp bureaucrats

splits and its two parts slide Up Stage Left, and Up Stage Right to reveal Up Stage Centre, a vast mound of filthy, wet straw dummies; vapour, the remains of the gas, still hangs about them. They spill forward to show all are painted light blue, have no faces, and numbers tattooed on their left arms. . . . Two monstrous figures appear out of the vapor, dressed in black rubber suits, thigh-length waders and gas-masks. Each has a large iron hook, knife, pincers and a small sack hanging from his belt. As they clump forward, they hit the dummies with thick wooden clubs. Each time they do so there is the splintering sound of a skull being smashed.[51]

The symbolic pageantry in Peter Shaffer's *Royal Hunt of the Sun* (1963) and *Amadeus* (1974) derives from similar influences.

Edward Bond's *Restoration* (1981) and Timberlake Wertenbaker's *The Grace of Mary Traverse* are less history plays than plays written in the style of period drama, Restoration and eighteenth-century, respectively. Bond's *Narrow Road to the Deep North* (1968) uses Gilbert and Sullivan to satirize British intervention into the affairs of seventeenth-century Japan, but the play owes as much to Brecht and to conventions of traditional Japanese theatre. John Arden and Margaretta D'Arcy's *The Hero Rises Up* (1968), Charles Wood's '*H*' (1969), Steve Gooch's *The Women Pirates* (1978), Peter Nichols's *Poppy* (1982), and Shirley Gee's *Warrior* (1989) draw on the conventions of popular nineteenth-century theatre: nautical melodrama, toy theatre, and pantomime.

Popular theatre, particularly the music hall, provided another important native influence on contemporary history plays. One of the best known examples was Joan Littlewood's satiric debunking of World War I myths in *Oh What a Lovely War* (1963). Plays using music hall conventions to develop historical themes include Charles Wood's *Dingo* (1967), Alan Bennett's *Forty*

Years On (1968), Peter Barnes's *Leonardo's Last Supper* (1969), Adrian Mitchell's *Tyger* (1971), Caryl Churchill's *Softcops* (1984), and Howard Brenton's *Moscow Gold* (1990). Community-based political drama such as Peter Cheeseman's "Documentaries" at Stoke-on-Trent and the plays of John McGrath, Red Ladder, and Steve Gooch also drew from music hall staging: self-contained songs, dances, and comic routines; a master of ceremonies; direct address to the audience; pierrot shows; cross dressing; tableaux; and ventriloquists' dummies.

Foreign Staging Influences

These staging conventions of the music hall were shared by popular theatre throughout Europe and North America and also found their way into agitprop and epic theatre, which with Artaud's Theatre of Cruelty constituted the principal foreign influences on the British history play.

Agitprop. Agitation/propaganda (agitprop) theatre grew largely out of the Marxist and labor movement and amateur workers' theatre. Originating in Russia after World War I and spreading through Germany to labor movements in the rest of Europe and the United States, agitprop used two-dimensional characters, often treated allegorically, in short sketches, with songs and narration to demonstrate an overt social message. These plays had a historical perspective only to the extent that they usually set out to expose an existing social injustice. Of the plays that we have discussed, Steve Gooch's *The Motor Show* most overtly imitates agitprop.

Agitprop also influenced Erwin Piscator, Brecht, and the American Living Newspaper produced by the Federal Theatre Project in the 1930s. Piscator worked with Brecht in the 1920s and introduced many of the epic devices later associated with Brecht. He became the director of the Freie Volksbühne in Berlin in 1962, where he produced "documentaries," plays that drew on newspaper articles, official reports, film clips, and transcripts of trials. In 1963 Piscator produced Rolf Hochhuth's *Der Stellvertreter*, which exposed the nonintervention of Pope Pius XII in the extermination of the Jews. The Royal Shakespeare Company subsequently produced the play in London as *The Representative*. Other documentary-based histories originally produced by Piscator include Heinar Kipphardt's *In the Matter of J. Robert Oppenheimer* (1964) and Peter Weiss's *The Investigation* (1965), which dramatizes the 1964 Frankfurt war crimes trial. Kipphardt's play was staged in London in 1966 and Peter Brook gave a rehearsed reading of *The Investigation* the same year. Piscator's productions stimulated interest in documentaries in Britain, and Joan Littlewood's heavy use of projected slide images to provide background visual commentary in *Oh What a Lovely War* (1963) certainly owes much to

Piscator's staging methods. However, documentaries in Britain were popular mostly with community-based productions such as those of Peter Cheeseman and John McGrath and used the simpler staging conventions of street theatre.

Brecht's Epic Theatre. The degree of influence of Bertolt Brecht on British theatre has been hotly debated. The extent to which Brecht himself borrowed from period British staging conventions creates difficulty in isolating his influence. Brecht's adaptations of Marlowe's *Edward II* and Shakespeare's *Coriolanus* show that he found the staging methods of the early English history play compatible with his own.

Writing in 1966, Martin Esslin cited productions of Brecht in England but denied any substantive impact on British playwrights.[52] Howard Brenton, who adapted Brecht's *Galileo* for the National Theatre in 1980, disavowed, in the preface to a 1986 collection of plays, Brecht's influence: "Even Brecht's theories are really a series of running-battles he fought with casts or with the theatrical 'norms' of his day—or they are blatant puffs for the show he had on hand!—and can be understood in the context of what he was actually doing in the theatre at the particular time he wrote. They were useful to him, but are useless to us."[53] Janelle Reinelt disputes this in *After Brecht: British Epic Theatre*, including Brenton among the six playwrights whom she discusses as carrying on the Brechtian legacy. Significantly, all six wrote history plays: Howard Brenton, Edward Bond, Caryl Churchill, David Hare, Trevor Griffiths, and John McGrath. Equally significantly, all six are socialist or Marxist playwrights and might be expected to share the view of history that Reinelt takes to be the defining feature of Brecht's influence:

In a sense all epic plays are history plays; it's just that some deal with the contemporary historical moment and others with the past. To "historicize the incidents of the narrative" as Brecht would have playwrights do is probably the single most important aspect of epic writing, because it involves situating events within a context that both explains them and yet is not necessary (i.e., it could have been otherwise).[54]

This process of historicizing consisted largely of emphasizing the unique social circumstances surrounding any event. Esslin discounted the Brechtian influence on plays like *A Man for All Seasons*, *Luther*, and *A Patriot for Me* precisely because he thought that they demonstrated no such consciousness of the social and political background of the periods they depicted. The English playwrights, however, *thought* that they were imitating Brecht. Bolt, Osborne, and Arden, along with the six later writers discussed by Reinelt, all credited Brecht's influence. Esslin argued that the English translation of Brecht's theoretical work was not widely available until 1964; so that earlier writers had an imprecise idea of his production approach.

With respect to staging, Esslin conceded Brecht's influence:

Indeed, as far as design is concerned, one can safely say that practically *all* British stage design, outside the area of the most old-fashioned drawing-room comedy, today derives from the work of the main Brechtian designers, Neher, Otto, and von Appen. The principal lessons learned concerned the lightness of construction of Brecht's sets, their flexibility and mobility . . . and above all their marvelous use of the texture of the materials employed.[55]

To this list could be added other Brechtian staging devices: minimalist staging, white lights, projected scene titles, and emblematic devices hanging over the stage. Favorite nonscenic conventions include mimed business with a narrative commentary, direct address to the audience, songs whose lyrics comment on the action, and short scenes that illustrate a thematic point rather than acts that build to a dramatic peak. Jocelyn Herbert, who was the principal designer at the Royal Court, was one of the major British scene designers using Brechtian devices, exemplified in her staging of Arden's *Serjeant Musgrave's Dance*, Osborne's *Luther*, and Storey's *Cromwell* at the Royal Court Theatre (RCT).

We can see the impact of Brecht on the staging of a play like John Arden's Magna Carta play *Left-Handed Liberty* (1965). The minimalist scenery uses "emblems" such as a chart, a parchment, a map of England, and projections on a screen above with locations drawn in the style of a thirteenth-century manuscript. Arden scatters occasional sections of loosely rhyming verse throughout the dialogue. A narrator bridges the episodic scenes and near the play's end, the thirteenth-century King John addresses the modern audience.

The path of Brecht's influence extends largely through William Gaskill and John Dexter, who were the original assistants to George Devine at the RCT and the principal directors using Brechtian techniques. Gaskill's early Brecht productions included *The Caucasian Chalk Circle* for RSC in 1962, *Baal* in the West End in 1963, and *Mother Courage* at the National in 1965. He conducted workshops on Brechtian improvisations with Edward Bond, Ann Jellicoe, and John Arden among others.[56] Among the British history dramas that he directed were Arden's *Armstrong's Last Goodnight* (with John Dexter); Charles Wood's *Dingo*; Edward Bond's *Early Morning, Narrow Road to the Deep North*, and *Lear*; and Stephen Lowe's *Touched*. Gaskill also directed for RSC and was associate director for the National Theatre. His interest in Brechtian staging spread further when he cofounded the Joint Stock Theatre Group with David Hare and Max Stafford-Clark; their first production was Hare's *Fanshen*. Stafford-Clark had directed Brenton's *Hitler Dances* and later Hastings's *Tom and Viv* and Churchill's *Light Shining in Buckinghamshire, Cloud Nine*, and *Top*

Girls. John Dexter directed Shaffer's *The Royal Hunt of the Sun, Tyger* by Adrian Mitchell, and Trevor Griffiths's *The Party.*

When the artistic staff was first appointed for the new National Theatre, one of the first things that Laurence Olivier, John Dexter, Kenneth Tynan and Gaskill did was to visit the Berliner Ensemble to view the workings of an existing state-supported national theatre.[57] History plays were a regular part of the Berliner Ensemble repertory, made possible, in part, by a large resident company. Brecht plays showed the social consequences of action on groups of people and therefore tended to require large casts.

Because of the availability of subsidized companies at RSC and the National Theatre, many contemporary history plays could revert to the pre-twentieth-century practice of using large casts to depict the scope of major events, a luxury not readily accessible to the regular West End theatres. All of the history plays done by the National Theatre during its early years had casts of between twenty-five and thirty: *The Royal Hunt of the Sun, Armstrong's Last Goodnight, 'H', Tyger, State of Revolution, Lark Rise, The Woman, Candleford, Amadeus,* and *The Romans in Britain.* Much was the same at RSC, which before 1978 had produced *The Devils, The Island of the Mighty, The Bewitched, Queen Christina, Captain Swing,* and *The Women Pirates Ann Bonney and Mary Read.* Even the Royal Court with its more modest resources had done plays like *Serjeant Musgrave's Dance, Luther,* and *A Patriot for Me,* but these casts were still about half the size of those of plays done by the ensemble companies. The more typical history play at the Court had a cast of around ten and therefore tended to avoid sweeping approaches to history. The West End theatres, which did fewer history plays in the first place, might occasionally do a play like Bolt's *Vivat! Vivat Regina!,* which requires a cast of thirty, but the play had first been produced at the nonprofit Chichester Festival. More common in West End theatres were biographical histories with very small casts like *Stevie, Virginia,* and *Breaking the Code.*

One device utilized by Brecht to maintain audience detachment was a play-within-a-play structure, also frequently used in contemporary British history plays. For Brecht, the framing of an inner play reminded the audience that it was watching a constructed story, subject to other interpretations. Saunders's *Next Time I'll Sing to You* (1962), Bennett's *Forty Years On* (1968), Brenton's *The Churchill Play* (1974) and *H.I.D.* (1989), Bowen's *Florence Nightingale* (1975), and Wertenbaker's *Our Country's Good* (1988) all use this device. In all, except in Wertenbaker's, the inner play contains historical material commented upon in some way by the characters in the outer play, an approach consistent with the New Historians' desire to make obvious the interpretive aspect of any historical construct.

Artaud's Theatre of Cruelty. The influence of Antonin Artaud's staging ideas on British history plays appears largely in the metaphorical use of ritualized stage business, often with shocking content, to evoke emotion and communicate larger ideas. He proposed "to create a metaphysics of speech, gesture, and expression, in order to rescue [theatre] from its servitude to psychology and 'human interest.' "[58] These "theatrical hieroglyphics" would affect an audience directly without the intervention of verbal language. Though no British playwright practiced "Theatre of Cruelty" to the extreme advocated by Artaud, his ideas probably influenced history plays written by Peter Shaffer, Howard Brenton, Peter Barnes, David Rudkin, and Howard Barker. Artaud's ideas spread in England principally through the agency of Peter Brook and Charles Marowitz. Brook began directing at the Shakespeare Memorial Theatre in Stratford in 1946 and was codirector of the Royal Shakespeare Company at its founding in 1961. He directed several of Shakespeare's history plays, but his direction of contemporary history plays was limited to his 1964 production of Peter Weiss's *Marat/Sade*, a 1966 production about American involvement in Vietnam called *US*, and *The Ik* in 1975. In 1963 Brook joined Charles Marowitz, another Artaud enthusiast, to form an ensemble group of actors associated with the RSC to experiment with some of Artaud's ideas. This collaboration resulted in a five-week Theatre of Cruelty season at the London Academy of Music and Dramatic Art (LAMDA) Theatre Club in 1964, the highlight of which was *Marat Sade*. Marowitz also directed Peter Barnes's one-act plays *Leonardo's Last Supper* and *Noonday Demons* at the Open Space Theatre in 1969, and *Laughter* at the Royal Court in 1978.

The plot for Shaffer's *Royal Hunt of the Sun* resembles a plot concerning Cortez's conquest of Mexico proposed by Artaud in *The Theatre and Its Double*,[59] but more significantly, Shaffer used elaborate stage metaphors to forward the action and make a thematic statement. For example, during the first part of the play, the Inca god-king Atahuallpa looms over the stage standing in a giant golden sun, which after his capture, the Spaniards demand that he fill with gold:

They begin to explore the sun itself, leaning out of the chamber and prodding at the petals with their halberds. Suddenly DIEGO gives a cry of triumph, drives his halberd into a slot in one of the rays, and pulls out the gold inlay. The SUN gives a deep groan, like the sound of a great animal being wounded. With greedy yelps, all the SOLDIERS below rush at the sun and start pulling it to bits; they tear out the gold inlays and fling them to the ground, while terrible groans fill the air.[60]

This destruction vividly represents cultural pillage. Although Shaffer did not fully embrace Artaud's vision of a world with an underlying element of cruelty, the principal images in *The Royal Hunt of the Sun* are of invasion and plunder.

Of Howard Brenton's history plays, *Hitler Dances* (1972) most clearly reflects Artaud's *Weltanschauung*. Brenton described the central "Resurrection Sequence," in which a group of children enact the revivification of a dead German soldier as "a horror holy theatre piece."[61] In Brenton's other plays, the influence of Artaud appears in occasional but striking theatrical metaphors: a danced reenactment of Rudolf Hess's death in *H.I.D.*, the entrance of a modern army with supporting helicopters into the first century B.C. setting at the end of the first act of *The Romans in Britain*, or the pageants that introduce the acts in *Moscow Gold*.

Peter Barnes moves a step further toward dramatizing a world of cruelty, but more than an exposé, his plays show a struggle to find solutions. Barnes's affinity for Jacobean drama makes it difficult to isolate the influence of Artaud, but also demonstrates the similar use of spectacular stage effects in the earlier English theatre. Barnes has a talent for discovering striking pieces of stage business to provide transitions between individual scenes in his history plays. These theatrical symbols forward the action or convey a situation very economically and vividly. For example, in *Bewitched* (1974), the members of the Spanish court follow a grotesquely deformed King Carlos in a dance: "With their MAJESTIES in the lead, they wobble, lurch, do the splits, skid and spin with poker-faced dignity. Only ANTONIO tries to do the stately 'Pavan' but as they reverse and dance back Up Stage, he succumbs and joins the OTHERS in their grotesque cavortings."[62] Barnes thus shows succinctly how the court reflects the king's degenerating condition.

David Rudkin shares Barnes's sense of the grotesque. *The Triumph of Death* (1981), which even contains a character named Artaud, uses vivid images of defecation, blood, and violence to create an emblematic history. Papatrix, a pope figure sitting in a jakes, a nun, and debating monks frame a vague plot involving a Paleolithic tribe destroyed by monk soldiers. The opening stage direction conveys something of the play's indebtedness to Artaud:

Within the throbbing vibrance, stroke impending, of a massive bell. Human whisperings gather like flocks of birds. Gibbering choral fragments; harsh organ-chords. Bell-vibrance loudening, painful on the ear. Human babel towering to a shrieking ecstasy of need: cries of "Papa! Papa! Pater Sanctus! Pastor Nobis! Father!" Vast bell-stroke crushes all. From filthy golden gloom, a dark form, monstrous, slowly materializes to the sight: PAPATRIX, throned. Face a farded skull of cancerous death.[63]

The transformation ritual of a pack of werewolves begins *The Saxon Shore* (1986) and recurs to emphasize the violent underpinnings that British culture struggles to overcome.

Howard Barker's plays reflect even more Artaud's sense of pervasive violence and rely less on coherent plots than the enactment of extended metaphors. The building of a castle becomes the focus for gender warfare in *The Castle*, produced by the RSC in 1985. In *Bite of the Night* (1988), the eleven Troys of antiquity mark stages in a journey of discovery, revealing the powers and limitations of eroticism. *The Europeans* (1990) uses the aftermath of the Turkish siege of Vienna in 1683 as a vehicle for exploring the relationship between cruelty and sexual power. In addition to images like the decayed body of a man whom she has mutilated and murdered tied to the man-hating witch in *The Castle* or Helen's gradual loss of limbs in the Trojan War parable, Barker's dialogue reflects the style advocated by Artaud. Although not reducing speech strictly to the level of evocative sound that Artaud suggested, Barker's dialogue frequently breaks into a series of self-contained proclamations. The audience can often explicate speeches only by reference to meanings that lie apart from any realistic development of the dramatic situation. Leopold, the emperor of Austria, wanders through *The Europeans*, declaming, "I laugh," nine times in the first minute of the play, and repeatedly throughout the rest of the play. Barker's dialogue approximates Artaud's idea of "giving words approximately the importance they have in dreams," of treating language as a form of incantation with the power to shock.[64]

A play like David Pinner's *The Drums of Snow* (1968) illustrates the fusion of staging techniques influenced by Brecht and Artaud. Pinner depicts larger actions with emblematic staging devices. For example, the first scene shows Charles II hanging the corpses of Cromwell and John Bradshaw, the judge at Charles I's trial, but both corpses begin talking. In a scene with simultaneous action, Charles I and Queen Henrietta dance while members of Commons plot the overthrow of the monarchy. The black star of the Star Chamber is lowered and members of Parliament tear it to pieces. A boar hunt becomes a ritual hunt after a Puritan dressed as a boar. A scene where two Scotsmen strip Bishop Laud to his underwear is followed by Lilburne's comment "This, of course, only happened in the Scots' over-fertile imaginations—but they did declare war!"[65] Eight actors stage the battle between Scots and English armies: "Stylistically the Scots slash the English Army to death. Comically if possible" (357). In the somewhat chaotic second act, battles are shown as ritualized cock fights or depicted using banners. Later, after Charles I is beheaded, Cromwell tries to sew the head back on the body. Other Brechtian devices include "semi-modern costumes to which historical finery was added" (13), songs interspersed throughout, and actors referring in the dialogue to the fact that they have earlier played other characters.

The wide range of staging conventions used for contemporary history plays generally reflects a tendency to reject any pretense of a naively realistic depiction of history. Brecht's methods of staging grew explicitly out of his version of Marxist history, and other proactive attitudes accounted for the more overtly didactic methods used in left-wing and feminist history plays. Although new approaches to history may not have directly impelled other staging innovations that grew largely out of theatrical influences, the social mood of the fifties and sixties encouraged the rejection of traditional methodology in both history and theatre practice. The political turbulence created by the rise and fall of Labour governments, the resistance to the Vietnamese War, the demise of censorship in 1968, and the rise of state-supported theatres not totally dependent on the marketplace all contributed to a climate that made possible challenges to conventional history as well as to established methods of staging history plays.

NOTES

1. G. M. Trevelyan, *Clio, a Muse* (London: Longman's, Green & Co., 1913), p. 148.
2. Ibid., p. 160.
3. Philippe Carrard, *Poetics of the New History* (Baltimore: Johns Hopkins University, 1992), p. 30, cites Lucien Febvre, *Combats pour l'histoire* (Paris: Armand Colin, 1965), pp. 22 and 268.
4. John Tosh, *The Pursuit of History* [1984], 2d ed. (London: Longman's, 1991), p. 118. Tosh attributes the phrase "silent changes" to R. W. Southern, *The Making of the Middle Ages* (London: Hutchinson, 1953), pp. 14–15.
5. Tosh, *The Pursuit of History*, p. 62. See Lawrence Stone, "The Revival of Narrative: Reflections on a New Old History," *Past and Present* 85 (1979): 3–24.
6. Carrard, *Poetics*, p. 35.
7. Jean-François Lyotard, *The Postmodern Condition: A Report on Knowledge* [1979], trans. Geoff Bennington and Brian Massumi (Manchester: Manchester University, 1984), p. xxiv.
8. Natalie Z. Davis, J. C. Carrière, and D. Vigne, *Le Retour de Martin Guerre* (Paris: R. Laffont, 1982).
9. R. H. Tawney, *History and Society* (London: Routledge & Kegan Paul, 1978), p. 54.
10. Tosh, *The Pursuit of History*, p. 117.
11. Peter Burke, "History of Events and the Revival of Narrative," in *New Perspectives on Historical Writing*, ed. Peter Burke (University Park: Pennsylvania State University, 1992), p. 245.
12. Ibid., p. 246.

13. Charles Wood, '*H*' (London: Methuen, 1970), p. 181.

14. Shirley Gee, *Warrior* (London: Samuel French, 1989), p. xii.

15. Howard Brenton, *The Romans in Britain*, in *Plays: Two* (London: Methuen, 1989), p. 56.

16. Howard Brenton, *H.I.D. (Hess is Dead)* (London: Nick Hern, 1989), p. 34.

17. Caryl Churchill, *Cloud Nine*, in *Plays: One* (London: Methuen, 1985), p. 320.

18. Howard Barker, *The Bite of the Night* (London: John Calder, 1988), pp. 3–4.

19. Howard Barker, "The Triumph in Defeat," *Guardian*, Aug. 22, 1988.

20. Barbara A. Hanawalt's, *The Ties That Bound: Peasant Families in Medieval England* (Oxford: Oxford University, 1986).

21. Carrard, *Poetics*, p. 47.

22. Ibid., p. 239.

23. Ibid., pp. 87–104.

24. Ibid., p. 104.

25. Paul Thompson, *The Edwardians* (Bloomington: Indiana University, 1975).

26. Milton Shulman, "Wit and Sympathy," *Evening Standard*, May 7, 1965.

27. See "A Short Organum for the Theatre" [1948], par. 48–50 in *Playwrights on Playwriting*, ed. Toby Cole (New York: Hill & Wang, 1960), pp. 90–91.

28. John Arden and Margaretta D'Arcy, *The Island of the Mighty* (London: Eyre Methuen, 1974), p. 24.

29. Cf. Philip Barnes, *A Companion to Post-War British Theatre* (Totowa, NJ: Barnes & Noble, 1986), p. 16.

30. John Arden, *Left-Handed Liberty* (New York: Grove, 1965), p. 57.

31. John Arden and Margaretta D'Arcy, *The Hero Rises Up* (London: Methuen, 1969), p. 15.

32. Peter Cheeseman, *The Knotty* (London: Methuen, 1997), p. xiv.

33. Bernadette Plot, *Écrire une thèse ou un mémoire en sciences humaines* (Paris: Champion, 1986), p. 19, quoted in Carrard, *Poetics*, pp. 198–99.

34. Carrard, *Poetics*, p. 199.

35. Tosh, *The Pursuit of History*, p. 128.

36. "Introduction" in *The Knotty* (London: Methuen, 1970), pp. xv–xvi.

37. *Guardian*, Apr. 14, 1988.

38. In *Collected Plays* (Portsmouth, NH: Heinemann, 1981), p. 122.

39. "Preface," in *A Man for All Seasons* (New York: Random House, 1962), p. xix.

40. *Financial Times*, Oct. 17, 1987.

41. A 1961 review reprinted in Kenneth Tynan, *A View of the English Stage, 1944–63* (London: Davis-Poynter, 1975), pp. 324–25. The Devine citation is from "The Right to Fail," *Twentieth Century*, 169, no. 1003 (Feb. 1961): 132.

42. Matthew Wikander, *The Play of Truth & State: Historical Drama from Shakespeare to Brecht* (Baltimore: Johns Hopkins University, 1986), p. 88.

43. *Collected Plays*, p. 122.

44. *Plays: One*, p. 239.

45. "Author's Notes," in *Left-Handed Liberty*, p. xiii.

46. *Plays: Two*, p. ix.

47. David Rudkin, *The Saxon Shore* (London: Methuen, 1986), p. 51.

48. David Rudkin, *The Triumph of Death* (London: Eyre Methuen, 1981), p. 10.

49. "The Right to Fail," p. 132.

50. "Preface" in *A Man for All Seasons*, p. xviii.

51. Peter Barnes, *Laughter* [1978], in *Collected Plays*, pp. 404–5.

52. Martin Esslin, "Brecht and the English Theatre," in *Reflections* (Garden City, NY: Doubleday, 1969), pp. 75–86. First appeared in *The Tulane Drama Review*, 11, no. 2 (Winter 1966): 63–70.

53. Brenton, *Plays: One*, p. xii.

54. Janelle Reinelt, *After Brecht: British Epic Theatre* (Ann Arbor: University of Michigan, 1994).

55. Esslin, *Brecht*, p. 78.

56. Reinelt, *After Brecht*, p. 51.

57. William Gaskill, *A Sense of Direction* (London: Faber & Faber, 1988), p. 55.

58. Antonin Artaud, *The Theatre and Its Double*, trans. Mary Caroline Richards (New York: Grove, 1958), p. 90.

59. Ibid., pp. 126–32.

60. Peter Shaffer, *The Royal Hunt of the Sun* (London: Samuel French, 1964), pp. 72–73.

61. Howard Brenton, *Hitler Dances* (London: Methuen, 1982), p. 17.

62. Peter Barnes, *The Bewitched* [1974], in *Collected Plays*, p. 216.

63. Rudkin, *The Triumph of Death*, p. 1.

64. Artaud, *The Theatre and Its Double*, pp. 94, 46.

65. David Pinner, *The Drums of Snow*, rev. version, in *Plays of the Year*, vol. 42 (New York: Frederick Ungar, 1972), p. 352.

Performance Dates of Contemporary British History Plays

1959

Arden, John. *Serjeant Musgrave's Dance*

1960

Arden, John. *The Business of Good Government*
Bolt, Robert. *A Man for All Seasons*
Kemp, Robert. *Master John Knox*
Rattigan, Terence. *Ross*

1961

Duncan, Ronald. *Abelard & Héloïse*
Fry, Christopher. *Curtmantle*
Osborne, John. *Luther*
Whiting, John *The Devils*

1962

Saunders, James. *Next Time I'll Sing to You*

1963

[Littlewood, Joan]. *Oh What a Lovely War*

1964

Arden, John. *Armstrong's Last Goodnight*

Dyne, Michael. *The Right Honorable Gentleman*

Shaffer, Peter. *The Royal Hunt of the Sun*

1965

Arden, John. *Ironhand*, adapt. Goethe's *Goetz von Berlichingen*

————— . *Left-Handed Liberty*

Francis, William. *Portrait of a Queen*

Jellicoe, Ann. *Shelley, or the Idealist*

Osborne, John. *A Patriot for Me*

1966

Cheeseman, Peter. *The Knotty*

Hastings, Michael. *Lee Harvey Oswald*

1967

Wood, Charles. *Dingo*

1968

Arden, John, and Margaretta D'Arcy. *The Hero Rises Up*

Bennett, Alan. *Forty Years On*

Bond, Edward. *Early Morning*

————— . *Narrow Road to the Deep North*

Cowan, Maurice. *The Six Wives of Henry VIII*

Pinner, David. *The Drums of Snow*

Plater, Alan. *Close the Coalhouse Door*

1969

Barnes, Peter. *Leonardo's Last Supper*

————— . *Noonday Demons*

Brenton, Howard. *Christy in Love*

Spurling, John. *MacRune's Guevera as Realised by Edward Hotel*

Wood, Charles. *'H'; being Monologues at Front of Burning Cities*

1970

Bolt, Robert. *Vivat! Vivat Regina!*

Brenton, Howard. *Wesley*

Gittings, Robert. *Conflict at Canterbury*

Griffiths, Trevor. *Occupations*

Millar, Ronald. *Abelard and Heloise*

Rattigan, Terence. *A Bequest to the Nation*

Taylor, Don. *The Roses of Eyam*

Terson, Peter. *The 1861 Whitby Lifeboat Disaster*

1971

Bond, Edward. *Lear*

Brenton, Howard. *Scott of the Antarctic or What God Didn't See*

Mitchell, Adrian. *Tyger*

1972

Brenton, Howard. *Hitler Dances*

Gooch, Steve. *Will Wat? If Not, What Will?*

Oulton. Brian. *Mr Sydney Smith Coming Upstairs*

1973

Arden, John and Margaretta D'Arcy. *The Island of the Mighty*

Bond, Edward. *Bingo: Scenes of Money and Death*

————— . *The Sea*

Gooch, Steve, *Female Transport*

McGrath, John. *The Cheviot, the Stag, and the Black, Black Oil*

Stoppard, Tom. *Travesties*

Storey, David. *Cromwell*

1974

Barnes, Peter. *The Bewitched*

Brenton, Howard. *The Churchill Play*

McGrath, John. *The Game's a Bogey*

Wilson, Snoo. *The Beast*

1975

Bond, Edward. *The Fool*

Bowen, John. *Florence Nightingale*

Gooch, Steve. *The Motor Show*

Hare, David. *Fanshen*

1976

Brenton, Howard. *Weapons of Happiness*

Churchill, Caryl. *Light Shining in Buckinghamshire*

———— . *Vinegar Tom*

Higgins, Colin, and Denis Cannan, adapters. *The Ik*

Rice, Tim, and Andrew Lloyd Webber. *Evita*

1977

Bolt, Robert. *State of Revolution*

Gems, Pam. *Queen Christina*

Hastings, Michael. *For the West*

Lowe, Stephen. *Touched*

Whitemore, Hugh. *Stevie*

1978

Barnes, Peter. *Laughter*

Bond, Edward. *The Woman*

Dewhurst, Keith. *Lark Rise*

———— . *The World Turned Upside Down*

Gems, Pam. *Piaf*

Gooch, Steve. *The Women Pirates Ann Bonney and Mary Read*

Gray, Simon. *The Rear Column*

Red Ladder Theatre. *Taking Our Time*

Whelan, Peter. *Captain Swing*

1979

Churchill, Caryl. *Cloud Nine*

Dewhurst, Keith. *Candleford*

McGrath, John. *Joe's Drum*

Shaffer, Peter. *Amadeus*

1980

Brenton, Howard. *The Romans in Britain*

Friel, Brian. *Translations*

O'Brien, Edna. *Virginia*

Spurling, John. *The British Empire, Part One*

1981

Bond, Edward. *Restoration*

Lochhead, Liz. *Blood and Ice*

Mitchell, Julian. *Another Country*

Rudkin, David. *The Triumph of Death*

Wertenbaker, Timberlake. *New Anatomies*

1982

Churchill, Caryl. *Top Girls*

Nichols, Peter. *Poppy*

1983

Barker, Howard. *Victory*

Edgar, David. *Maydays*

Mitchell, Julian. *Francis*

1984

Brenton, Howard. *Bloody Poetry*

Churchill, Caryl. *Softcops*

Hastings, Michael. *Tom and Viv*

1985

Barnes, Peter. *Red Noses*

Brenton, Howard. *The Castle*

Edgar, David. *Entertaining Strangers*

Keeffe, Barry. *Better Times*

Wertenbaker, Timberlake. *The Grace of Mary Traverse*

1986

Mitchell, Julian. *After Aida*

Rudkin, David. *The Saxon Shore*

Whitemore, Hugh. *Breaking the Code*

1988

Barker, Howard. *The Bite of the Night*

Bennett, Alan. *Single Spies*

Friel, Brian. *Making History*

Wertenbaker, Timberlake. *Our Country's Good*

Wright, Nicholas. *Mrs Klein*

1989

Brenton, Howard. *H.I.D. (Hess is Dead)*

Gee, Shirley. *Warrior*

Nicholson, William. *Shadowlands*

Wertenbaker, Timberlake. *The Love of the Nightingale*

1990

Ali, Tariq, and Howard Brenton. *Moscow Gold*

Barker, Howard. *The Europeans*

Jeffreys, Stephen. *The Clink*

1991

Bennett, Alan. *The Madness of George III*

Tomalin, Claire. *The Winter Wife*

1992

Whelan, Peter. *The School of Night*

1993

Samuels, Dianne. *Kindertransport*

Stoppard, Tom. *Arcadia*

1995

Stoppard, Tom. *Indian Ink*

1996

Boubil, Alain, Hert Kretzmer, and Claude-Michel Schönberg. *Martin Guerre*
Gems, Pam. *Stanley*
Whelan, Peter. *The Herbal Bed*

1997

Churchett, Stephen. *Tom and Clem*
Gems, Pam. *Marlene*
Stoppard, Tom. *Invention of Love*
Whitemore, Hugh. *A Letter of Resignation*
Wilson, Snoo. *H.R.H.*

Performance Locales of Contemporary British History Plays

NATIONAL THEATRE

Arden, John. *Armstrong's Last Goodnight*, Oct. 12, 1965
Bennett, Alan. *The Madness of George III*, Nov. 28, 1991
———. *Single Spies*, Dec. 1, 1988
Bolt, Robert. *State of Revolution*, May 18, 1977
Bond, Edward. *The Woman*, Aug. 10, 1978
Brenton, Howard. *The Romans in Britain*, Oct. 16, 1980
———. *Weapons of Happiness*, July 14, 1976
Dewhurst, Keith. *Candleford*, Nov. 14, 1978
———. *Lark Rise*, March 29, 1978
———. *The World Turned Upside Down*, Nov. 2, 1978
Edgar, David. *Entertaining Strangers*, Oct. 15, 1987 (rev.)
Friel, Brian. *Translations*, Aug. 6, 1981
Gems, Pam. *Stanley*, Feb. 1, 1996
Mitchell, Adrian. *Tyger*, July 20, 1971
Shaffer, Peter. *Amadeus*, Nov. 2, 1979
———. *Royal Hunt of the Sun*, Aug. 12, 1964
Stoppard, Tom. *Arcadia*, Apr. 13, 1993
———. *Invention of Love*, Oct. 1, 1997
Wood, Charles. *'H,'* Feb. 13, 1969
Wright, Nicholas. *Mrs Klein*, Aug. 5, 1988

ROYAL SHAKESPEARE COMPANY

Ali, Tariq, and Howard Brenton. *Moscow Gold*, Barbican, Sept. 20, 1990

Arden, John, and Margaretta D'Arcy. *The Island of the Mighty*, Aldwych Theatre, 1973
Barker, Howard. *The Bite of the Night*. Barbican Pit, August 31, 1988
———— . *The Castle*, Barbican Pit, Oct. 16, 1985
Barnes Peter. *The Bewitched*, Aldwych Theatre, London, May 1974
———— . *Red Noses*, Barbican, July 2, 1985
Brenton, Howard. *The Churchill Play*, Other Place, Aug. 8, 1978.
———— . *H.I.D. (Hess is Dead)*, Almedia Theatre, Sept. 26, 1989
Churchill, Caryl. *Softcops*, Barbican Pit, Jan. 23, 1984
Edgar, David. *Maydays*, Barbican, Oct. 13, 1983
Gems, Pam. *Queen Christina*, Other Place, Oct. 1977
Gooch, Steve. *The Women Pirates Ann Bonney and Mary Read*, Aldwych Theatre, July 31, 1978
Nichols, Peter. *Poppy*, Barbican, Oct. 5, 1982
Stoppard, Tom. *Travesties*, Aldwych Theatre, London, June 10, 1974
Wertenbaker, Timberlake. *The Love of the Nightingale*, Other Place, Oct. 28, 1988
Whelan, Peter. *Captain Swing*, Other Place, June 26, 1978
———— . *The Herbal Bed*, Other Place, May 23, 1996
———— . *The School of Night*, Other Place, Nov. 4, 1992
Whiting, John. *The Devils*, Aldwych Theatre, Feb. 20, 1961

ROYAL COURT

Arden. John. *Serjeant Musgrave's Dance*, Oct. 22, 1959, 1965
Barker, Howard. *Victory*, Mar. 25, 1983
Barnes, Peter. *Laughter*, Jan. 25, 1978
Bond, Edward. *Early Morning*, Mar. 31, 1968, restaged in 1969
———— . *The Fool*, Nov. 18, 1975
———— . *Lear*, Sept. 29, 1971
———— . *Restoration*, July 21, 1981
———— . *The Sea*, May 22, 1973
Brenton, Howard. *Bloody Poetry*, 1988
Churchill, Caryl. *Cloud Nine*, Mar. 29, 1979 (Joint Stock)
———— . *Light Shining in Buckinghamshire*, Sept. 27, 1976
———— . *Top Girls*, Aug. 28, 1982
Hastings, Michael. *Tom and Viv*, Feb. 3, 1984
Jeffreys, Stephen. *The Libertine*, Dec. 6, 1994
Jellicoe, Ann. *Shelley, or The Idealist*, Oct. 18, 1965
Lowe, Stephen. *Touched*, Jan. 20, 1981 (revival)
Osborne, John. *Luther*, July 27, 1961
———— . *A Patriot for Me*, June 30, 1965
Storey, David. *Cromwell*, Aug. 15, 1973
Wertenbaker, Timberlake. *The Grace of Mary Traverse*, Oct. 17, 1985
———— . *Our Country's Good*, Sept. 10, 1988

Wood, Charles. *Dingo*, Nov. 15, 1967
————. *Veterans*, Mar. 9, 1972

AMATEUR OR FRINGE PERFORMANCES IN LONDON

Arden, John, and Margaretta D'Arcy. *The Hero Rises Up*, Institute of Contemporary
    Arts, Chalk Farm, Nov. 6, 1968
Barnes, Peter. *Leonardo's Last Supper* and *Noonday Demons*, Open Space, Nov. 25,
    1969
Brenton, Howard. *Christy in Love*. Portable Theatre, Nov. 23, 1969
Churchill, Caryl. *Vinegar Tom*, Monstrous Regiment, Humberside Theatre, Hull,
    Oct. 12, 1976, then ICA and Half Moon Theatre, London
Gooch, Steve. *Female Transport*, Half Moon Theatre, London, Nov. 1973
————. *Will Wat? If Not, What Will?*, Half Moon Theatre, May 27, 1972
Hastings, Michael. *Lee Harvey Oswald: A Far Mean Streak of Independence Brought on
    by Negleck*, Hampstead Theatre Club, London, Nov. 22, 1966
Keeffe, Barrie. *Better Times*, Theatre Royal, Stratford East, Jan. 31, 1985
[Littlewood, Joan]. *Oh What a Lovely War*, Theatre Royal, Stratford, Mar. 19, 1963
Rudkin, David. *The Saxon Shore*, Almeida Theatre, Feb. 27, 1986
Samuels, Diane. *Kindertransport*, Soho Theatre Company at Cockpit Theatre, April
    13, 1993
Wertenbaker, Timberlake. *New Anatomies*, ICA, 1981

OTHER LONDON THEATRES (WEST END)

Aldwych Theatre—Churchett, Stephen. *Tom and Clem*, Apr. 15, 1997
    —Stoppard, Tom. *Indian Ink*, Feb. 27, 1995
Apollo Theatre—Bennett, Alan. *Forty Years On*, Oct. 31, 1968
Globe Theatre—Bolt, Robert. *A Man for All Seasons*, July 1960
Lyric Theatre—Gems, Pam. *Marlene*, Apr. 4, 1997
    —Gray, Simon. *The Rear Column*, Feb. 22, 1978
Mermaid Theatre—Arden, John. *Left-Handed Liberty*, June 1965
New Arts Theatre—Saunders, James. *Next Time I'll Sing to You*, Jan. 23, 1963 (later
    at Criterion)
Picadilly—Bolt, Robert. *Vivat! Vivat Regina!*, Oct. 8, 1970
Prince Edward—Boubil, Alain, Herbert Kretzmer, and Claude-Michel Schönberg.
    Martin Guerre, July 10, 1996
Theatre Royal Haymarket—Rattigan, Terence. *A Bequest to the Nation*, Sept. 23,
    1970; *Ross*, May 12, 1960
    —O'Brien, Edna. *Virginia*, Jan. 29, 1981
    —Whitemore, Hugh. *Breaking the Code*, Oct. 21, 1986
Vaudeville Theatre—Francis, William. *Portrait of a Queen*, May 6, 1965
    —Whitemore, Hugh. *Stevie*, March 1977

REGIONAL PROFESSIONAL THEATRE

Bond, Edward. *Narrow Road to the Deep North*, Belgrade Theatre, Coventry, June 24, 1968

Bowen, John. *Florence Nightingale*, Marlowe Theatre, Canterbury, Nov. 1975

Brenton, Howard. *The Churchill Play*, Nottingham Playhouse, May 8, 1974

———. *Hitler Dances*, Traverse Theatre Club, Edinburgh, January 1972

Cheeseman, Peter. *The Knotty*, Victoria Theatre, Stoke-on-Trent, July 12, 1966

Churchill, Caryl. *Light Shining in Buckinghamshire*, Traverse Theatre, Edinburgh, Sept. 1976

Francis, William. *Portrait of a Queen*, Bristol Old Vic, Mar. 2, 1965

Friel, Brian. *Making History*, Field Day Theatre Company in the Guildhall, Derry, 1988

———. *Translations*, Field Day Theatre Company in the Guildhall, Derry, 1980

Gee, Shirley. *Warrior*. Chichester Festival Theatre, Minerva Studio, June 23, 1989

Jeffreys, Stephen. *The Clink*, Plymouth Theatre Royal, Sept. 20, 1990

Lochhead, Liz. *Blood and Ice*, Traverse Theatre, Edinburgh, August 1982

Lowe, Stephen. *Touched*, Nottingham Playhouse, June 9, 1977

McGrath, John. *The Cheviot, the Stag, and the Black, Black Oil*, Scottish 7:84, Mar. 31, 1973

Oulton, Brian. *Mr Sydney Smith Coming Upstairs*, Harrogate Theatre, Oct 12, 1972

Rudkin, David. *The Triumph of Death*, Birmingham Repertory Studio Theatre, Mar. 9, 1981

Saunders, James. *Next Time I'll Sing to You*, Questors Theatre, Ealing, 1962

Spurling, John. *The British Empire, Part One*, Birmingham Repertory Studio Theatre, Feb. 14, 1980

Taylor, Don. *The Roses of Eyam*, Northcott Theatre, Exeter, Sept. 23, 1970

Terson, Peter. *The 1861 Whitby Lifeboat Disaster*, Victoria Theatre, Stoke-on-Trent, May 5, 1970

Tomalin, Claire. *The Winter Wife*, Nuffield Theatre, Southampton, Feb. 12, 1991

Wood, Charles. *Dingo*, Bristol Arts Centre, April 28, 1967

REGIONAL AMATEUR THEATRE

Arden, John. *The Business of Good Government*, Brent Knoll, Somerset, Christmas season, 1960

Bond, Edward. *Bingo: Scenes of Money and Death*, Northcott Theatre, Devon, Nov. 14, 1973

Edgar, David. *Entertaining Strangers*, St. Mary's Church, Dorchester, Nov. 18, 1985

Gooch, Steve. *The Motor Show*, Dagenham, Essex, 1974; Half Moon Theatre, 1975

Plater, Alan. *Close the Coalhouse Door*, Newcastle Playhouse, April 9, 1968

Red Ladder Theatre. *Taking Our Time*, East Hunslet Labour Club, Leeds, Jan. 17, 1978

Bibliography

CONTEMPORARY BRITISH HISTORY PLAYS

Ali, Tariq, and Howard Brenton. *Moscow Gold.* London: Nick Hern, 1990.

Arden, John. *Armstrong's Last Goodnight* in *Plays: One.* New York: Grove Press, 1978.

———. *Ironhand.* London: Methuen, 1965.

———. *Left-Handed Liberty.* New York: Grove, 1965.

———. *Serjeant Musgrave's Dance: An Un-Historical Parable* in *Plays: One.* New York: Grove, 1978.

Arden, John, and Margaretta D'Arcy. *The Business of Good Government.* New York: Grove, 1963.

———. *The Hero Rises Up.* London: Methuen, 1969.

———. *The Island of the Mighty.* London: Eyre Methuen, 1974.

Barker, Howard. *The Bite of the Night.* London: John Calder, 1988.

———. *The Castle* with *Scenes from an Execution.* London: John Calder, 1985.

———. *The Europeans* in *The Europeans and Judith.* London: John Calder, 1990.

———. *Pity in History* with *Women Beware Women.* London: John Calder, 1986.

———. *Victory.* London: John Calder, 1983.

Barnes, Peter. *The Bewitched* [1974] in *Collected Plays.* Portsmouth, NH: Heinemann, 1981.

———. *Laughter* [1978] in *Collected Plays.* Portsmouth, NH: Heinemann, 1981.

———. *Leonardo's Last Supper* [1969] in *Collected Plays.* Portsmouth, NH: Heinemann, 1981.

———. *Noonday Demons* [1969] in *Collected Plays.* Portsmouth, NH: Heinemann, 1981.

———. *Red Noses.* London: Faber & Faber, 1985.

————— . *Revolutionary Witness* in *Revolutionary Witness and Nobody Here but Us Chickens*. London: Methuen, 1989.

Bennett, Alan. *An Englishman Abroad* in *Single Spies and Talking Heads*. New York: Summit, [1988] 1990.

————— . *Forty Years On* [1969] in *Forty Years On, Getting On, Habeas Corpus and Enjoy*. London: Faber & Faber, l992.

————— . *The Madness of George III*. London: Faber & Faber, l992.

Bolt, Robert. *A Man for All Seasons* [1960]. New York: Vintage, 1990.

————— . *State of Revolution*. London: Heinemann, 1977.

————— . *Vivat! Vivat Regina!*. London: Heinemann, 1971.

Bond, Edward. *Bingo: Scenes of Money and Death*. London: Eyre Methuen, 1974.

————— . *Early Morning* [1968] in *Plays: One*. London: Methuen, 1977.

————— . *The Fool* [1975] in *Plays: Three*. London: Methuen, 1987.

————— . *Lear* [1971] in *Plays: Two*. London: Methuen, 1978.

————— . *Narrow Road to the Deep North* [1968] in *Plays: Two*. London: Methuen, 1978.

————— . *Restoration* in *Plays: Four*. London: Methuen, 1992.

————— . *The Sea* [1973] in *Plays: Two*. London: Methuen, 1978.

————— . *The Woman* [1978] in *Plays: Three*. London: Methuen, 1987.

Bowen, John. *Florence Nightingale*. London: Samuel French, 1976.

Brenton, Howard. *Bloody Poetry* [1985] in *Plays: Two*. London: Methuen, 1989.

————— . *Christie in Love* [1970] in *Plays: One*. London: Methuen, 1986.

————— . *The Churchill Play* [1974, 1978] in *Plays: One*. London: Methuen, 1986.

————— . *H.I.D. (Hess is Dead)*. London: Nick Hern, 1989.

————— . *Hitler Dances*. London: Methuen, 1982.

————— . *The Romans in Britain* [1980] in *Plays: Two*. London: Methuen, 1989.

————— . *Scott of the Antarctic or What God Didn't See* in *Plays for Public Places*. London: Eyre Methuen, 1972.

————— . *Weapons of Happiness*. London: Eyre Methuen, 1976.

————— . *Wesley* in *Plays for Public Places*. London: Eyre Methuen, 1972.

Cheeseman, Peter. *The Knotty*. London: Methuen, 1970.

Churchill, Caryl. *Cloud Nine*, rev. American ed. New York: Methuen, 1984.

————— . *Light Shining in Buckinghamshire*. London: Pluto, 1978.

————— . *Softcops* [1984] in *Plays: Two*. London: Methuen, 1990.

————— . *Top Girls* [1982] in *Plays: Two*. London: Methuen, 1990.

————— . *Vinegar Tom* in *Plays: One*. London: Methuen, 1985.

Cowan, Maurice. *The Six Wives of Henry VIII*. London: Leslie Frewin, 1968.

De, Olexander. *Stalin: Persona Non Grata*. London: Mitre, 1969.

Dewhurst, Keith. *Lark Rise to Candleford*. London: Hutchinson, 1980.

Duncan, Ronald. *Abelard & Héloïse: A Correspondence for the Stage in Two Acts*. London: Faber & Faber, 1961.

Dyne, Michael. *The Right Honorable Gentleman*. New York: Random House, 1966.

Edgar, David. *Entertaining Strangers*. London: Methuen, 1986.

————. *Maydays*. London: Methuen, 1983, 1984.

England, Barry. *Conduct Unbecoming*. London: Heinemann, 1971.

Francis, William. *Portrait of a Queen*. London: Samuel French, 1963.

Friel, Brian. *Making History*. London: Samuel French, 1989.

————. *Translations* in *Collected Plays*. Washington, D.C.: Catholic University of America, 1986.

Fry, Christopher. *Curtmantle*. London: Oxford University, 1961.

Gee, Shirley. *Warrior*. London: Samuel French, 1991.

Gems, Pam. *Piaf* in *Three Plays*. Harmondsworth: Penguin, 1985.

————. *Queen Christina*. London: St. Luke's, 1982.

————. *Stanley*. London: Nick Hern, 1996.

Gittings, Robert. *Conflict at Canterbury*. London: Heinemann, 1970.

Gooch, Steve. *Female Transport*. New York: Samuel French, 1974.

————. *Will Wat? If Not, What Will?*. London: Pluto, 1972.

————. *The Women Pirates Ann Bonney and Mary Read*. London: Pluto, 1978.

Gooch, Steve, and Paul Thompson. *The Motor Show*. London: Pluto, 1975.

Gray, Simon. *The Rear Column* in *Plays: One*. London: Methuen, 1986.

Griffiths, Trevor. *Occupations*, rev. ed. London: Faber & Faber, 1980. [First published London: Calder and Boyars, 1972.]

Hare, David. *Fanshen*. London: Faber & Faber, 1976.

Hastings, Michael. *For the West* in *Three Plays*. London: Penguin, 1980.

————. *Lee Harvey Oswald: A Far Mean Streak of Independence Brought on by Negleck*. Harmondsworth: Penguin, 1966.

————. *Tom and Viv*. Harmondsworth: Penguin, 1985.

Higgins, Colin, and Denis Cannan, adapters. *The Ik*. New York: Dramatic, 1984.

Jeffreys, Stephen. *The Clink*. London: Nick Hern, 1990.

————. *The Libertine*. London: Nick Hern, 1994.

Jellicoe, Ann. *Shelley, or the Idealist*. New York: Grove, 1966.

Keeffe, Barrie. *Better Times*. London: Methuen, 1985.

Kemp, Robert. *Master John Knox*. Edinburgh: St Andrew, 1960.

Kilty, Jerome. *Dear Liar*. New York: Dodd, Mead, 1960.

————. *The Ides of March*. New York: Samuel French, 1971.

Lochhead, Liz. *Blood and Ice* in *Plays by Women*, vol. 4. Ed. Michelene Wandor. London: Methuen, 1985.

Lowe, Stephen. *Touched*, rev. ed. London: Methuen, 1981.

McGrath, John. *The Cheviot, the Stag, and the Black, Black Oil*. London: Eyre Methuen, 1981.

————. *The Game's a Bogey*. Edinburgh: Edinburgh University Student Publications, 1975.

————. *Joe's Drum*. Aberdeen, Scotland: People's, 1979.

Millar, Ronald. *Abelard and Heloise*. London: Samuel French, 1970.

Mitchell, Adrian. *Tyger: A Celebration Based on the Life and Work of William Blake*. London: Jonathan Cape, 1971.

Mitchell, Julian. *Another Country*. New York: Samuel French, 1982.

————. *Francis*. London: Amber Lane, 1984.

Nichols, Peter. *Poppy* [1982] in *Plays: Two*. London: Methuen, 1991.

Nicholson, William. *Shadowlands*. London: Samuel French, 1989.

O'Brien, Conor Cruise. *Murderous Angels*. Boston: Little, Brown, 1968.

O'Brien, Edna. *Virginia*. London: Hogarth, 1981.

Osborne, John. *Luther* [1961]. New York: New American Library, 1963.

————. *A Patriot for Me*. London: Faber & Faber, 1966.

Oulton, Brian. *Mr Sydney Smith Coming Upstairs* in *Plays of the Year*, vol. 42. New York: Frederick Ungar, 1972.

Pearce, Brian Louis. *The Eagle and the Swan*. London: Mitre, 1966.

Pinner, David. *The Drums of Snow* in *Plays of the Year*, vol. 42. New York: Frederick Ungar, 1972. Also published in *New English Dramatists 13*. London: Penguin, 1968.

Plater, Alan. *Close the Coalhouse Door*. London: Methuen, 1969.

Rattigan, Terence. *Adventure Story*. London: Samuel French, 1950.

————. *A Bequest to the Nation*. London: Hamish Hamilton, 1970.

————. *Ross* [1960] in *Collected Plays*, vol. 3. London: Hamish Hamilton, 1964.

Red Ladder Theatre. *Taking Our Time*. London: Pluto, 1979.

Rice, Tim, and Andrew Lloyd Webber. *Evita*. New York: Music Theatre International, 1978.

Rudkin, David. *The Saxon Shore*. London: Methuen, 1986.

————. *The Triumph of Death*. London: Eyre Methuen, 1981.

Samuels, Diane. *Kindertransport*. London: Penguin, 1995.

Saunders, James. *Next Time I'll Sing to You* [1963]. London: Heinemann Educational, 1965.

Shaffer, Peter. *Amadeus*. New York: Harper & Row, 1980.

————. *The Royal Hunt of the Sun*. London: Samuel French, 1964.

Spurling, John. *The British Empire, Part One*. London: Marion Boyars, 1982.

————. *MacRune's Guevera as Realised by Edward Hotel*. London: Caldar and Boyars, 1969.

Stoppard, Tom. *Arcadia*. London: Faber & Faber, 1993.

————. *Travesties*. London: Faber & Faber, 1975.

Storey, David. *Cromwell*. London: Jonathan Cape, 1973.

Taylor, Don. *The Roses of Eyam*. London: Samuel French, 1976.

Terson, Peter. *The 1861 Whitby Lifeboat Disaster*. Todmorden: Woodhouse, 1979.

Theatre Workshop, Charles Chilton, and members of the original cast. *Oh What a Lovely War*. London: Methuen, 1965.

Tomalin, Claire. *The Winter Wife*. New York: Samuel French, 1991.

Waine, Harry. *The Lord Protector*. Gateshead on Tyne: Northumberland, 1963.

————. *Oliver Cromwell*. Bristol: Linden, 1958.

Wertenbaker, Timberlake. *The Grace of Mary Traverse* in *The Love of the Nightingale and The Grace of Mary Traverse*. London: Faber & Faber, 1989.

————. *The Love of the Nightingale* in *The Love of the Nightingale and The Grace of Mary Traverse*. London: Faber & Faber, 1989.

————. *New Anatomies*. Woodstock, IL: Dramatic, 1984.

————. *Our Country's Good*. London: Methuen, 1988.

West, Morris. *The Heretic*. London: Heinemann, 1970.

Whelan, Peter. *Captain Swing*. London: Rex Collins, 1979.

————. *The School of Night*. London: Warner Chappell, 1992.

Whitemore, Hugh. *Breaking the Code*. New York: Samuel French, 1987, 1988.

————. *Stevie*. London: Samuel French, 1977.

Whiting, John. *The Devils*. New York: Hill & Wang, 1961.

Wilson, Snoo. *The Number of the Beast*. London: John Calder, 1983.

Wood, Charles. *Dingo* [1967]. New York: Grove, 1969.

————. *'H.'* London: Methuen, 1970.

Wright, Nicholas. *Mrs Klein*. London: Nick Hern, 1988.

SECONDARY SOURCES

Books on History and Historical Writing

Appleby, Joyce, Lynn Hunt, and Margaret Jacob. *Telling the Truth About History*. New York: W. W. Norton, 1994.

Barker, Francis, Peter Hulme, Margaret Iversen, eds. *Uses of History: Marxism, Postmodernism and the Renaissance*. Manchester: Manchester University, 1991.

Breisach, Ernst. *Historiography: Ancient, Medieval and Modern*, 2d ed. Chicago: University of Chicago, 1994.

Burke, Peter, ed. *New Perspectives on Historical Writing*. University Park: Pennsylvania State University, 1993.

Butterfield, Herbert. *The Whig Interpretation of History* [1931]. New York: W. W. Norton, 1965.

Carr, E. Hallett. *What Is History?* New York: Alfred A. Knopf, 1962.

Carrard, Philippe. *Poetics of the New History: French Historical Discourse from Braudel to Chartier*. Baltimore: Johns Hopkins University, 1992.

Collingwood, R. G. *The Idea of History*, rev. ed. Oxford: Clarendon, 1993.

Esposito, Joseph L. *The Transcendence of History*. Athens: Ohio University, 1984.

Higdon, David Leon. *Shadows of the Past in Contemporary British Fiction*. Athens: University of Georgia, 1985.

Himmelfarb, Gertrude. *The New History and the Old*. Cambridge, MA: Harvard University, 1987.

Hutton, Patrick H. *History as an Art of Memory*. Hanover, NH: University Press of New England, 1993.

Kaye, Harvey J. *British Marxist Historians*, new ed. New York: St. Martin's, 1995.

Lerner, Gerda. *The Majority Finds Its Past: Placing Women in History*. Oxford: Oxford University, 1979.

Lukács, George. *The Historical Novel* [1962], trans. Hannah Mitchell and Stanley Mitchell. Lincoln: University of Nebraska, [1962] 1983.

Lyotard, Jean François, *The Postmodern Condition: A Report on Knowledge,* Trans. Geoff Bennington and Brian Massumi. Manchester: Manchester University, 1984.

Parker, Christopher. *The English Historical Tradition Since 1850.* Edinburgh: John Donald, 1990.

Plumb, J. H. *The Death of the Past.* Boston: Houghton Mifflin, 1970.

Scanlan, Margaret. *Traces of Another Time: History and Politics in Postwar British Fiction.* Princeton, NJ: Princeton University, 1990.

Tosh, John. *The Pursuit of History,* 2d ed. London: Longman, 1991.

Veeser, H. Aram, ed. *The New Historicism.* New York: Routledge, 1989.

Weinstein, Fred. *History and Theory.* Chicago: University of Chicago, 1990.

White, Hayden. *Tropics of Discourse.* Baltimore: Johns Hopkins University, 1978.

White, Morton. *Foundations of Historical Knowledge.* New York: Harper & Row, 1965.

Zinsser, Judith P. *History and Feminism: A Glass Half Full.* New York: Twayne, 1993.

BOOKS ON THEATRE

Barnes, Philip. *A Companion to Post-War British Theatre.* Totowa, NJ: Barnes & Noble, 1986.

Beauman, Sally. *The Royal Shakespeare Company.* Oxford: Oxford University, 1982.

Berney, K. A. *Contemporary Dramatists,* 5th ed. London: St. James, 1993.

Bull, John. *New British Political Dramatists.* New York: Grove, 1984.

Campbell, Lily Bess. *Shakespeare's "Histories": Mirrors of Elizabethan Policy.* San Marino, CA: Huntington Library, 1947.

Cave, Richard Allen. *New British Drama in Performance on the London Stage: 1970 to 1985.* New York: St. Martin's, 1988.

Cohn, Ruby. *Retreats from Realism in Recent English Drama.* Cambridge: Cambridge University, 1991.

Craig, Sandy, ed. *Dreams and Deconstructions: Alternative Theatre in Britain.* Ambergate: Amber Lane, 1980.

Findlater, Richard. *At the Royal Court: 25 Years of the English Stage Company.* New York: Grove, 1981.

Garstenauer, Maria. *A Selective Study of English History Plays in the Period between 1960 and 1977.* Salzburg: Institut fur Anglistik und Amerikanistik, 1985.

Gaskill, William, *A Sense of Direction.* New York: Limelight, 1990.

Gooch, Steve. *All Together Now: An Alternative View of Theatre and Community.* London: Methuen, 1984.

Goodwin, Tim. *Britain's Royal National Theatre; The First 25 Years.* London: Nick Hern, 1988.

Harbage, Alfred B. *As They Liked It.* New York: Macmillan, 1947.

Harben, Niloufer. *Twentieth-Century English History Plays from Shaw to Bond.* Totowa, NJ: Barnes & Noble, 1988.

Hayman, Ronald. *John Osborne,* 2d ed. London: Heinemann Educational, 1970.

Jellicoe, Ann. *Community Plays: How to Put Them On.* London: Methuen, 1987.

Lindenberger, Herbert. *Historical Drama: The Relation of Literature and Reality.* Chicago: University of Chicago, 1975.

MacLennan, Elizabeth. *The Moon Belongs to Everyone: Making Theatre with 7:84.* London: Methuen, 1990.

McGrath, John. *A Good Night Out: Popular Theatre—Audience, Class and Form.* London: Methuen, 1981.

Peacock, D. Keith. *Radical Stages: Alternative History in Modern British Drama.* Westport, CT: Greenwood, 1991.

Reinelt, Janelle. *After Brecht: British Epic Theatre.* Ann Arbor: University of Michigan, 1994.

Ribner, Irving. *The English History Play in the Age of Shakespeare,* rev. ed. New York: Barnes & Noble, 1965.

Ritchie, Rob, ed. *The Joint Stock Book: The Making of a Theatre Collective.* London: Methuen, 1987.

Tillyard, E.M.W. *Shakespeare's History Plays.* New York: Macmillan, 1946.

Wandor, Michelene. *Understudies: Theatre and Sexual Politics.* London: Methuen, 1981.

Wikander, Matthew H., *The Play of Truth & State: Historical Drama from Shakespeare to Brecht.* Baltimore: Johns Hopkins University, 1986.

Wilmut, Roger. *From Fringe to Flying Circus.* London: Eyre Methuen, 1980.

COLLECTIONS OF THEATRICAL REVIEWS

Elsom, John. *Post-War British Theatrical Criticism.* London: Routledge & Kegan Paul, 1981.

Fenton, James. *You Were Marvellous: Theatre Reviews from the Sunday Times.* London: Jonathan Cape, 1983.

Lloyd-Evans, Gareth, and Lloyd-Evans, Barbara, eds. *Plays in Review, 1956–1980: British Drama and the Critics.* New York: Methuen, 1985.

London Theatre Record [serial]. Middlesex, 1981– .

Marowitz, Charles. *Confessions of a Counterfeit Critic: A London Theatre Notebook 1958–71.* London: Eyre Methuen, 1973.

Morgan, Geoffrey, ed. *Contemporary Theatre: A Selection of Reviews, 1966/67.* London: London Magazine, 1968.

Morley, Sheridan. *Our Theatre in the Eighties.* London: Hodder and Stoughton, 1990.

———. *Shooting Stars: Plays and Players, 1975–1983.* London: Quartet, 1983.

Plays and Players [serial]. London, 1953– .

Roberts, Peter ed. *The Best of Plays and Players,* vol. 1, 1953–1968; vol. 2, 1969–1983. London: Methuen, 1988.

Turner, Barry, and Mary Fulton. *The Playgoer's Companion.* London: Virgin, 1983.

Tynan, Kenneth. *A View of the English Stage, 1944–63.* London: Davis-Poynter, 1975.

Young, B. A. *The Mirror Up to Nature: A Review of the Theatre, 1964–1982.* London: William Kimber, 1982.

Index

About the Author

RICHARD H. PALMER is Professor of Theatre at the College of William and Mary, where he balances an interest in theatre history and literature with practical work as a stage director and designer. His specialty in theatre aesthetics encompasses topics ranging from stage lighting to dramatic theory. His previous books include *The Lightening Art* (1994), *Tragedy and Tragic Theory* (Greenwood, 1992), and *The Critics' Canon* (Greenwood, 1988).

ISBN 0-313-30497-1

90000>

EAN

9 780313 304972

HARDCOVER BAR CODE